Virginia Erhardt, PhD

Head Over Heels
Wives Who Stay with Cross-Dressers and Transsexuals

Pre-publication REVIEWS, COMMENTARIES, EVALUATIONS . . .

"**N**ot every woman will find her own story here, but reading these women's stories might liberate her to write her own down, to compare theirs to her own, to find new ways of looking at how she has dealt or not dealt with her own situation. Better still is that therapists will have a much larger range of experiences and may come to understand the huge variation. The most important thing this book accomplishes, however, is to put us on the map. To have a therapist other than Arlene Istar Lev discuss us, in print, is a very important historical moment: we partners have arrived. I can't imagine any wife or girlfriend of a trans person not having a copy of *Head Over Heels* on their bookshelf—one that will no doubt be warped from numerous readings. I strongly suggest that MTF cross-dressers or transsexuals who want to tell their wives, or their future girlfriends, read this book very carefully. For gender therapists and couples' counselors, moderators of online support groups for trans couples or partners, for those who give workshops at the various conferences on these topics, and for those who plan those conferences, this is essential reading."

Helen Boyd
Author,
My Husband Betty

"**A** long-awaited and essential contribution to the literature on transgender people and their families. Erhardt has provided us with detailed and engaging narratives of the wives of cross-dressers and transsexuals. This book will provide essential insight for clinicians on gender transgression in families and the power of committed loving partnerships. The myth that marriages to transgender people are doomed to failure has been put to rest. Erhardt's book will hopefully guide clinical theory to better serve families struggling with the lifecycle upheaval of transgender emergence."

Arlene Istar Lev, LCSW, CASAC
Author, *Transgender Emergence: Therapeutic Guidelines for Working with Gender-Variant People and Their Families*

Head Over Heels
*Wives Who Stay
with Cross-Dressers
and Transsexuals*

Human Sexuality
Eli Coleman, PhD
Editor

Head Over Heels
Wives Who Stay with Cross-Dressers and Transsexuals

Virginia Erhardt, PhD

Routledge
Taylor & Francis Group
New York   London

Routledge is an imprint of the
Taylor & Francis Group, an informa business

For more information on this book or to order, visit
http://www.haworthpress.com/store/product.asp?sku=5737

or call 1-800-HAWORTH (800-429-6784) in the United States and Canada
or (607) 722-5857 outside the United States and Canada

or contact orders@HaworthPress.com

Published by

The Haworth Press, Inc., 10 Alice Street, Binghamton, NY 13904-1580.

PUBLISHER'S NOTE
The development, preparation, and publication of this work has been undertaken with great care. However, the Publisher, employees, editors, and agents of The Haworth Press are not responsible for any errors contained herein or for consequences that may ensue from use of materials or information contained in this work. The Haworth Press is committed to the dissemination of ideas and information according to the highest standards of intellectual freedom and the free exchange of ideas. Statements made and opinions expressed in this publication do not necessarily reflect the views of the Publisher, Directors, management, or staff of The Haworth Press, Inc., or an endorsement by them.

Some identities and circumstances of individuals discussed in this book have been changed to protect confidentialiy.

Cover design by Jennifer M. Gaska.

Library of Congress Cataloging-in-Publication Data

Erhardt, Virginia.
    Head over heels : wives who stay with cross-dressers and transsexuals / Virginia Erhardt.
        p. cm.
    Includes bibliographical references and index.
    ISBN-13: 978-0-7890-3094-8 (case : alk. paper)
    ISBN-10: 0-7890-3094-2 (case : alk. paper)
    ISBN-13: 978-0-7890-3095-5 (soft : alk. paper)
    ISBN-10: 0-7890-3095-0 (soft : alk. paper)
    1. Wives. 2. Sexual minorities—Family relationships. 3. Marriage. I. Title.

HQ759.E723 2006
306.872'3—dc22

                                                                    2006022966

This book is dedicated to

The women who shared their stories and all partners of gender-variant people, who risk so much for love.

My gender-variant clients and their partners
who have allowed me the privilege
of accompanying them in their explorations.

ABOUT THE AUTHOR

Virginia Erhardt, PhD, is a clinical psychologist and gender specialist in private practice. She is a member of the Georgia Psychological Association, the American Association of Sex Educators, Counselors and Therapists (AASECT), and the Harry Benjamin International Gender Dysphoria Association. She has offered presentations and facilitated seminars internationally on topics related to transgender, partners of gender-variant individuals, and intersex conditions. She appeared in 2003 on a *Dateline NBC* segment about married couples who stay together when one spouse is transitioning from male to female. Dr. Erhardt is co-author of *Journey Toward Intimacy: A Handbook for Lesbian Couples.* She has been published in *Transgender Tapestry* magazine and *Transgender Community News,* and was a columnist for the *Southern Voice* newspaper for three years.

CONTENTS

Foreword

The book that you are about to read is a significant contribution to the desperately needed literature about women who are partnered with natal males who identify somewhere on the spectrum of transgender identity and expression (male-to-female). In fact, this publication is a pioneering contribution to current transgender literature. This publication is the first to include the contributed life stories of spouses and partners collected by a gender therapist who offers these stories and meticulously provides helpful commentary about the life experiences of each contributor. Of particular note is the unique way the manuscript is presented. Dr. Erhardt has gathered the stories of women in transgender relationships, each sharing in their own style the details of their unique journeys from discovery to the present. However, this is not a "show and tell" book by any means. The wide variety of stories, representing a wide spectrum of life experiences with cross-dressers; transgenderists; transsexuals who are nonsurgeried, presurgery, and postsurgery; families without children; families with children in the home; and families with children who have left the home opens our eyes and awareness to the tremendous diversity of expression and personal lives of those who have contributed to this publication.

Dr. Erhardt carefully reflects on the evolution of each story, adding helpful insights and identifying the complexities within the events as reported by the contributor. She offers wisdom of clinical experience and perspective, helpful suggestions about challenges experienced, and she provides validation and acknowledgment of the positive contributions the spouse had made in her personal journey while clearly indicating possibilities where counseling and therapy could have been or might be of great assistance to the couple. This innovative style offers broad and helpful education and information to spouses

Head Over Heels: Wives Who Stay with Cross-Dressers and Transsexuals
Published by The Haworth Press, Inc., 2007. All rights reserved.
doi:10.1300/5737_a

and partners seeking to know about others similar to themselves as well as to transgender individuals of all identities who are in relationships.

Most important, mental health professionals and gender specialists will be informed more fully about the individual journey of the female partner, and of the simultaneous journey of the transgender couple. Dr. Erhardt's perspective and suggestions indicate important markers for the therapist to recognize when helping a partner or couple as they journey together in the transgender experience. As you read, it cannot be overemphasized that certain components must be assessed in order to work effectively with the spouse or couple, specifically, *how* the natal female partner learns, whether from partner, others, or through discovery; *when* she learns, whether before the relationship begins, or, if after, when; whether children are present, and if so, what their ages and stage of development are; and other essential information about *her own sexual history and experiences.*

The book is presented in a readable and personal style, and provides comprehensive resources for further reading. Although *Head Over Heels* is focused on content specific to the partner's journey, it will take its place alongside contemporary books recently published about counseling and therapy for transgender persons and their families (Lev, 2004) and of peer-driven perspectives of the relationships of cross-dressing men and their partners (Boyd, 2003).

At this time in our culture I am struck with the plethora of information, activities, and learning opportunities available to the entire transgender community, and with the inarguable energy present as this community reaches to achieve its broad goals of equality, respect, and compassion. This effort is not complete in any respect, but I recall how little information was available to the community just a few years ago. A huge information implosion has occurred since the 1980s, reshaping this extensive community and creating legislation, accommodations, policies, social justice progress, information, improved services, and expansive communication to all, so much so that transgender life before the 1980s seems so distant and unrecognizable, and much of that history is lost to those who have more recently come into the transgender community.

Toward this end, some of the stories in *Head Over Heels* will provide a critical historic reference that illuminates the impact of isolation and separation commonly experienced by those whose journeys occurred before recent progress. I hope that the messages gleaned from this publication will move to honor and respect the journeys of the individual narrators and increase compassion from those whose lives are not touched by such challenges in this more knowledgeable time in our culture.

In 1983 I was invited to attend a local meeting of cross-dressers and transsexuals to be introduced to various individuals who wanted me to know their stories. None of them had "come out" to their families or communities, only two or three had told their spouses, and none of them had ever talked about their personal gender issues with a mental health professional. Yet they all had a keen desire, if not urgency, to reach out, ask questions, and to help me learn about their personal and varied journeys. The group met very privately, once a month. They used alternative "femme" names and were diligent about keeping their meeting places and true identities extremely private or secret.

I accepted the kind invitation and attended. As is the story of most professionals, including sexologists, information or training in the subject of gender identity was not available. How curious this subject omission was to me during the years of my training. From 1968 to 1983 I had the opportunity to meet, listen to, and talk with only three or four gender unique people, always in informal settings. Academe offered little or no learned information to share with sexuality educators, counselors, or therapists in the field of sexual health. Nothing was routinely offered in curriculum, and during those early years most activities of the transgender community were kept private and hidden, except in closed transgender circles.

Language describing such life experiences and the spectrum of gender identities was not well developed. A few surgeons did "sex change" surgeries for male-to-female transsexual persons, and any information available to society seemed sensationalized by the media and press. In the 1950s, society learned to recognize the name and story of Christine Jorgensen and the "scandal" of her transition and transsexual surgery, which all the tabloids dutifully and elaborately described nationally and internationally. Personal human interest stories, information about the families of persons who identified as cross-dressers or transsexuals, research studies, basic health care needs, and mental health recommendations for caregiving were not known or understood very well, if at all, and therefore were not available or provided to those of us in the helping professions.

Needless to say I was honored to have been invited and was privileged to have been trusted to attend this meeting and to have personal discussions with cross-dressers and transsexuals that evening. The experience profoundly influenced my professional interests as a sexologist, sex educator in the medical professions, and as a sex counselor. The experience challenged my professional goals.

From that evening to the present I have focused on and devoted a major part of my professional work to the lives and concerns of persons who identify as gender questioning across the entire spectrum of gender identity, including a specific focus on their spouses and partners and families.

During that initial evening meeting in 1983 I can identify one specific incident that impressed me and entirely consumed my awareness and attention. About fifteen "gals" (male-to-female cross-dressers and transsexuals) attended the meeting, all dressed fashionably and fancifully, with large curly wigs, lots of jewelry, perfume, high heels, pretty suits and dresses, red nails, meticulously applied makeup, some of which was quite theatrical. All were dressed in their very best, obviously feeling quite beautiful, enjoying the wonderful opportunity to express their feminine feelings and their perceptions of feminine attributes. The conversation was greatly animated as the "gals" talked with me and one another about their desires, fears, euphoria, and the utter necessity they felt to "dress," despite the perceived societal danger in doing so.

During the midmeeting break, followed by a brief business meeting of the club, I noticed two individuals sitting in the back of the room, somewhat in the shadows, continually smoking cigarettes. I walked back toward their table to introduce myself, anticipating that they were two cross-dressers not quite comfortable sitting up front with the others.

As I reached the table I recognized that they were two natal women, casually dressed in slacks and blouses, just sitting there, smoking. Introducing myself I learned that they were the wives of two of the club members. I asked why they weren't up front and participating. They looked surprised and said that they always just sat in the back, waiting for the meeting to be over.

I was stunned. I realized that this apparent exclusion was customary, since the meetings focused exclusively on the "gals." I will always remember the feelings I had upon recognizing the disenfranchisement that spouses and partners must experience along with the probable inherent feelings of separation.

What followed was an enlightening conversation with these women who had much to say to me about their feelings, their marriages, their partners' femme persona, their isolation, fears, shame, and concerns of stigma, their anger, their benign acceptance of being left out, and their distinct desire to be a part of the group. They described not being recognized or respected for their presence let alone their role in their husbands' or partners' journeys. They explained that the organizers of the club didn't build anything for partners into these meetings. The wives would like to have had opportunities to meet other wives, talk with other "gals," and learn more, but to them it seemed as if no one was interested in their lives, their stories, or their participation.

They found the meetings boring, exclusive, and insensitive to their presence. They didn't feel they could comment on the overdramatization of femininity by some of the members and how uncomfortable it made them feel. They commented that they had no desire to put on their best clothes to come to a meeting, and therefore dressed inconspicuously in casual clothes in neutral colors. I realized that each was there because of her cross-dressing husband whom she loved, and that each was fearful of harm coming to her husband every time "she" went out of the house, so these wives went along "just in case."

I learned many important things from these women that evening, in addition to the stories, information, and explanations so generously offered to me by those who invited me to the meeting. I decided then and there that I would do whatever was possible to reach out to find wives and partners, to learn and to share, and to encourage their presence in all aspects of the transgender experience.

I volunteered my time and skills at national gender conferences, conducting as many wives' discussion groups as I could be assigned. After a few years I also began conducting discussion groups for couples, but mostly, in the beginning, I focused exclusively on wives and other partners. I specifically selected the regional and national conferences to conduct my groups because they were highly attended in those years by one or two hundred people, with perhaps ten to fifteen wives accompanying their husbands. (Over these two decades the numbers of conferences and numbers of attendees have swelled greatly, with several hundred people attending each.)

These specially focused discussion groups were usually the only offerings for spouses to really meet, tell their stories, and personally share with one another their concerns, challenges, and fears. I tried to provide discussion groups every day of each conference so that a continuum of sharing and honest discussion could evolve. Most of the women attending these conferences were older and had been socialized in an earlier era in which the role of women in the marriage, home, and workplace was very different from the cultural standards of today. Girls socialized in the 1940s, 1950s, and 1960s were taught to be the "good wife": accommodating, quiet, nice, to "not make waves," essentially to not confront or have an open "voice" in the family. Yet at the same time they were supposed to raise the children, manage the home, contribute to the community, and, if necessary, be employed. To me, it is patently understandable that wives and partners of transgender individuals, emerging from such female socialization as young girls, could feel completely overwhelmed by the intrusion of transgender issues and adrift in such imposed chaos in their personal lives and families.

Until recently, very little discussion included any happiness or joy in the transgender presence in their relationships. However, the more these spouses had opportunities to meet and share in a safe, respectful, and caring environment of carefully facilitated group discussion, the stronger their self-confidence, self-esteem, and personal strength emerged. Eventually, by finding other wives or emerging groups or conferences where they could gather together, collectively they were able to begin to address the strengths, emotional attachment, love, and positive qualities of their partners and relationships while permitting themselves to talk about the truths of their feelings, struggles, fears, guilt, and shame. I learned how strong and self-reliant these women are, and how their inner strength and integrity prevailed for them as they proceeded in their individual journeys, virtually alone, without much support from anyone.

Once able to connect and gather together, wives and partners of transgender individuals reached out to support and help one another. The humanity, love, and respect shown to one another was powerful for all to experience, holding on to one another, and going forward with greater self-respect, validation, and stronger confidence.

It was, and remains, an honor to offer and conduct these meaningful sessions for spouses, and soon their presence was being acknowledged and respected in the large conferences across the country. Today in most of the big conferences entire session tracks are set aside for wives and partners to attend and present workshops, participate in discussion groups, panel discussions, and much more.

It is important to remember that years ago, before the computer and Internet arrived in individual homes, networking and association with others was limited to local or regional conferences and occasional national annual conferences scattered around the country. It was very expensive to pay for travel, hotel, food, and attendance at the conferences, in addition to the cost of clothing desired to wear by the attendees for these special events. More than occasionally, such expense dictated whether the couple could accommodate the costs of attendance of a willing partner. Such limitations naturally put strains on spouse participation as well as cause resentment about again being left out. Of course, many spouses did not even know about their husbands' transgender identity, and many spouses chose not to be involved at all, particularly those who were shamed, repulsed, and angry. Often, wives, upon discovery of their spouses' transgender uniqueness, chose to leave the marriage or relationship and, in addition, some chose to publicly expose their partners, even in the courts, causing further calamity and damage to the relationship and family, creating loss of employment, divorce, custody fights/losses, and community opinion and shunning.

Occasionally in some of the private newsletters that existed then in the transgender community one could read about other wives' experiences, and sometimes the local wives would try to get together to discuss their lives with one another. However, they were limited to their own experiences with transgender partners or to the stories of very few other wives. Many received some peer support, and many received useful, as well as not so useful, recommendations from others. Still, very little, if any, gender-experienced professional help was available. Little or no organized effort existed to establish any wider range of communication with other women in other parts of the country. Very few articles appeared in transgender-related magazines or in books that related to the experiences of spouses, nor were private opportunities available for women to have their own collective meetings or conferences until recent years.

No resource materials were readily available for partners and families to learn about transgender and gender identity. Nor were many, if any, education or clinical guidelines available for helping professionals to provide transgender services. And most important, the limited numbers and therefore extreme scarcity of experienced and knowledgeable mental health specialists who effectively could reach out to transgender individuals and their families during these stressful personal journeys further isolated people from seeking help. The few professionals who were providing services focused mostly, if not exclusively, on the transgender individual. Over the years in my discussion groups scores of wives and partners have expressed anger or frustration at not being invited into the therapy experience, or, when invited, not really feeling that their voices were heard with any compassion or understanding. Some will report feeling the expectation that they were supposed to just "join up" and be supportive of their spouses' transgender journey. Many report having fled therapy for those reasons.

Eventually, computer technology progressed with wide availability, and by the 1980s the World Wide Web was introduced into domestic homes. This presence offered opportunities for women to find and meet other spouses and enter into private communication with one another, sometimes anonymously, from the safety of their own homes. Suddenly, the emergence of transgender groups imploded in our culture: organizations, virtual discussion groups, bulletin boards, stories, publications, chat rooms, notices of events, personal Web sites, and more recently, blogs.

In the past ten to fifteen years it has become possible to search the Internet and find vast amounts of information, contacts, and people with whom to have discussions. This has been particularly helpful to spouses and partners, enabling them to find one another and to find their "community" in the same way that their transgender spouses have done.

Head Over Heels will fill the void of learning about the lives and precious stories of the journeys experienced by these extraordinary women. Some have struggled; some have found joy, peace, comfort, inner strength and self-esteem, humor, fun, erotic pleasure, and sexual satisfaction; and some have discovered new and positive aspects about themselves and the priorities in life that make relationships truly rich and bountiful.

Emily Dickinson once advised us all to "believe in possibility . . ."

Sandra S. Cole, PhD
Professor
University of Michigan Medical School
Ann Arbor, Michigan

Preface

THE FOCUS OF THIS BOOK

In this book, you will hear the voices of women who have found that their spouses are cross-dressers and male-to-female transsexual persons. These women have chosen to stay in a relationship with their gender-variant partners. This book was not written to provide information about the relationships of drag queens, gender benders, intersex people, or female-to-male (**FTM**) transgendered people. It is about the partners of male-to-female cross-dressers and transsexuals.

The women you will get to know in these pages did not know that their partners were gender-variant when they first met. Some found out early on; others learned of their husbands' gender variance only after decades of marriage. Some of the women were told by the people they thought were "just regular guys"; others found out on their own, sometimes in shocking ways. For some of the women, the shock caused a tectonic shift in their psyches, whereas other women describe a much less earth-shattering reaction.

Many of the women in this collection talk about their battles with traditional notions of gender and their need to explore, redefine, and create novel ways of looking at relationships. They share with us their desire for intimacy, social acceptance, dignity, and respect. They grapple with the juxtaposition of their own and their partners' bodies and their ways of loving. Some reject traditional notions of femininity and masculinity, the dichotomy our culture worships and urges us to emulate. Their heartfelt stories reveal their vision and experience of gender, family, love, and desire.

Women who remain with their gender-variant partners may call upon themselves—many without articulating it—to enact a kind of gender subversion. Empowering themselves within their nontraditional relationships they find themselves coloring outside culturally acceptable lines, struggling to deal with unusual relational dynamics,

Head Over Heels: Wives Who Stay with Cross-Dressers and Transsexuals
Published by The Haworth Press, Inc., 2007. All rights reserved.
doi:10.1300/5737_b

and looking for ways to make their relationships work. They may explore vulnerable parts of themselves and push beyond their comfort boundaries. Their stories, related here, are full of pain, courage, curiosity, and joy. Those who realize that they are primarily in love with and drawn to their spouses' hearts and souls seem to be more able to explore with what Sandra Cole (personal communication, April 25, 2004) calls open, yet somewhat cautious hearts, this new facet of personality, this change in social presentation or even physiological reconfiguration.

These are not just "happily ever after" stories. I wanted to include the voices of women who are having a difficult time, who are trying but are uncertain whether they will be able to stay in relationships with their gender-variant partners. It was my desire that this book offer the women who responded to my questions an opportunity to explore and share their ongoing journeys, and to make their revelations available to others as a supportive resource.

THE NATAL FEMALE PARTNERS

I made contact with the women who responded to my questions at conferences at which I presented, online through announcements posted to the Gender Advocacy Internet News and Web sites for partners of transgendered people, and via notices placed in *Transgender Tapestry* journal and the *Transgender Community News* (see Resource section and Bibliography). The stories I have chosen to include offer a wide range of reactions among the wives, and considerable diversity of presentation among the transgendered partners.

I asked the women to address certain topics. They tell us how they found out about their partners' gender issues and what their initial reactions were to this information. They discuss issues that arose for them related to their own self-esteem, sexual orientation, and identity as a person. They talk about how they handled secrecy, jealousy, resentment, and financial issues. The women disclose how they relate sexually to their partners with the gender issues having come to light as well as any concerns they have about their partners' feelings toward them.

The natal female partners describe situations that have arisen and how they have coped in terms of the relationship between them and extended family, children, friends, and their spiritual and secular communities. They also discuss negotiation of decisions with their partners, particularly decisions related to boundaries and timing about acting on the desire to cross-dress or to transition. They tell us how the relationship has changed over time, what has impacted or challenged them the most, what they have learned, and what they have gained.

I am sure that readers will feel privileged, as have I, to be welcomed into the private lives of these partners through the very personal information they have contributed. Many of the women expressed appreciation of the opportunity to have their experience heard and honored.

For most of the contributors, anonymity is very important, so names have been changed and certain demographic information has been left out. The couples live all over the United States, in Canada, England, and Australia. The natal women are, for instance, homemakers and mothers, teachers and businesswomen, a sign language interpreter, a scientist, and a convenience store clerk. The gender-variant partners are even more vocationally diverse. They are truck drivers and salesmen, business executives and professors, a doctor, a police officer, a firefighter, retired and active duty military personnel, and even a former CIA agent. A few of the women who tell their stories here do not require anonymity. This is either because they have chosen to be visible in their roles as community educators, or because they already have been involuntarily "outed."

All stories are voluntary and reflect a broad spectrum of life experiences since the material offered in response to my questions required extensive reorganization and, in some cases, condensation, the narratives are not presented verbatim, and therefore do not follow national standards for oral history. Instead I chose a model that uses a consistent writing style while retaining the integrity and accuracy of the content, and, I hope, the personality of each participant.

ORGANIZATION

Dr. Sandra Cole has written a foreword that sheds light on the historical neglect of the needs of significant others of gender-variant people and her contributions in filling those needs. This offers a context for my work and the work of other current gender specialists.

Chapter 1 is an introduction to partners' experiences of learning the secret and processing their emotional reactions. I also discuss whether gender variance is a choice, why transgendered people keep this part of their nature a secret, and the increasing understanding of gender variance and visibility of transgendered people in the world.

In Chapter 2 I offer introductory material on transgender persons, describing aspects of sexual identity and the transgender spectrum. I hope this will be helpful to people who would like to increase their knowledge of basic issues, and particularly to partners of gender-variant individuals who, like most people, have never been exposed to this information.

Next are the contributors' stories. I have commented at the end of each narrative, highlighting individual and relational dynamics. I offer a therapist's voice, moderating and qualifying the stories, offering other clinicians the opportunity to gain a professional perspective about the issues faced by women in relationship with gender-variant individuals. I amplify the stories and generalize from them, talking about aspects of each story that resonate with many or most such relationships, based on my clinical experience with this population. I mention common threads in an effort to point out the feelings and reactions that are often common to wives who walk this path. I have also identified some responses that seem unusual in my experience.

My analyses are suppositions, offering possible lines of inquiry for professionals working with clients presenting similar narratives. Clearly, in a therapeutic setting one would have the contextually richer material offered by face-to-face contact, nonverbal cues, and interaction, etc. I comment much more on some stories than others in order to avoid repetition.

To reflect the nonbinary, fluid nature of the transgender spectrum, I've arranged the stories loosely according to the intensity of the spouses' gender issues, moving from milder to more intense. The stories of women in relationship with people who identify as cross-dressers are placed earlier, and the stories of women in relationship with people who strongly intend to transition or have already done so are placed later.

After the narratives I offer some concluding comments. Finally, at the end of the book, I have placed a resource section, a glossary, and a bibliography. It might be helpful for some people to read the glossary prior to reading the stories. This way the reader who is less well-versed in the language of gender variance will gain a basic familiarity before reading the stories, and will be less likely to have to flip back and forth.

MY HOPES FOR THIS BOOK

My foremost wish is that this book will be a resource for women who have recently found out that their partners are gender-variant—that it will offer them the support that comes with knowing that they are not alone. If you are in this position, perhaps in these pages you will find other women with whom you can identify, hear voices that echo your feelings, and glean ideas about how to get information, understand new concepts, forgive, accept, and go on with your life, maybe feeling more confident, respected, and valued. The narratives may offer you hope that it is possible for you and your partner to stay together, in whatever form your relationship evolves.

I hope that this book will also be valuable for gender-variant people themselves. It might offer insight into wives' concerns, thus increasing the likelihood that a transperson will disclose well, better understand the feelings of a woman in this situation, and offer effective support.

If you are a helping professional I hope that this book offers you a tool, a window into the lives of a population you may rarely or never have encountered. It is certainly not a comprehensive primer, but it might offer new understanding of transgender relationships. My commentaries after each story are designed to offer you additional clinical information, insight, and suggestions.

I will also be pleased by the interest of readers who are unrelated or only peripherally related to the transgender community. The very existence of transgendered people and their partners stimulates curiosity as it questions and challenges society's norms about sex and gender. I believe that someone who is intrigued by this phenomenon and wants to learn more about it will find the contributors' stories fascinating. I hope this book offers much needed consciousness raising for any members of the general public who are drawn to learning more about this topic. For readers who are unfamiliar with the world of gender-variant people and their relationships, I hope the introductory material will offer some sense of its geography. For your benefit I have included a glossary at the end of the book. Words contained in the glossary appear in bold in the text at first mention.

It is very important to me that the road transgendered people and their partners travel be as free as possible of impediments such as scorn and marginalization, and that society grows in understanding and acceptance of them as worthwhile members of the ever diverse human tapestry.

Acknowledgments

I would like to thank the following individuals for input about this manuscript and support during its development:

Sandra S. Cole, PhD, has shared her time and expertise, mentoring me since we first met at the Southern Comfort Conference in 1997. She has been unstinting in the generosity of her advisory and editorial contributions to this work, particularly the introductory sections concerning partners' experience. Dr. Cole is past president of the American Association for Sex Educators, Counselors, and Therapists (AASECT) and an elected Fellow of the Society for the Scientific Study of Sexuality. She is a sexologist and professor at the University of Michigan Medical School and founder and director (retired) of the University of Michigan Health System Comprehensive Gender Services Program. She is professional services director of Gender Education and Advocacy (GEA) and has been an integral part of the trans community for more than twenty years and a strong activist and advocate for transgender social justice policy and legislation.

Ms. Dallas Denny, MA, who is secretary of the board of GEA, director of the transgender conference Fantasia Fair, and editor of *Transgender Tapestry* magazine, has written many books and articles on gender identity. Dallas founded AEGIS (American Education Gender Information Service), the precursor of GEA, and the National Transgender Archive, the world's largest cataloged collection of material aboug gender identity. She was the founder and publisher of *Chrysalis Quarterly.* Over the years Dallas has become a treasured friend and was my first mentor on trans issues. She has unstintingly shared her enormous, encyclopedic wealth of knowledge, and has schlepped numerous books to convenient locations to lend me.

I am grateful to Reverend Erin Swenson, PhD, the Atlanta-based marriage and family therapist who successfully fought to retain her ordination as a Presbyterian minister after transitioning from male to

Head Over Heels: Wives Who Stay with Cross-Dressers and Transsexuals
Published by The Haworth Press, Inc., 2007. All rights reserved.
doi:10.1300/5737_c

female. Our therapeutic, presenting, and writing collaborations have been as invaluable as our friendship has been enriching.

Many other wise and caring friends and colleagues have encouraged and supported me. I appreciate them all. I particularly want to acknowledge the ever-creative Dr. Jay Beard, who suggested the title.

My dear companion, Judy Dorman, has loved, challenged, and nurtured me since 1979, through times happy, peaceful, and turbulent, with steadfast devotion. Her generosity of spirit never ceases to amaze and inspire me. Thank you, Judy, for your support, particularly during my work on this project. I'm grateful for all the lessons I have learned from you and for the time you have spent reading, commenting, and editing.

Chapter 1

Introduction

THE PARTNERS' EXPERIENCES

Partners' Reactions to Learning the Secret

This book contains stories, told in the voices of women who have chosen to continue in relationships with **cross-dressers** and male-to-female **transsexual** persons. Some found out early in the relationship; others learned of this aspect of their husbands' lives after having been together for many years. Women's reactions vary significantly, depending on a number of factors. Obviously, her own temperament, personality, and life experience come into play (S. S. Cole, personal communication, February 6, 2004). The emotional intensity of a woman's reaction is related to some extent to how she finds out, and how long the secret has been held. Voluntary disclosure, especially early in a relationship, tends to yield a less negative response than a shocking discovery (Cole, 1998; Cole et al., 2000).

If a woman enters a relationship knowing that her partner is **gender-variant,** a stronger possibility of the relationship enduring exists. It is also more likely that the **transgender** piece will be sustained, although the relationship has the same dangers as any others (Cole, 1998; Cole et al., 2000). A **natal woman**'s receptivity to the gender variance will be colored by her past history. Many women have experienced some form of violation: child sexual abuse, rape (including date rape), and affairs, as well as physical and emotional abuse in childhood or in adult relationships. Unexpected discovery of a gender-variant spouse's secret can trigger old trauma in a woman who has a past history of violation. The unconscious retains the imprint of emotional trauma from such experiences forever, and betrayal can be

Head Over Heels: Wives Who Stay with Cross-Dressers and Transsexuals
Published by The Haworth Press, Inc., 2007. All rights reserved.
doi:10.1300/5737_01

a posttraumatic stress experience (S. S. Cole, personal communication, February 6, 2004; Cole et al., 2000). Men in our culture often have no inkling of the impact of their transgressions. They rarely realize that when a partner discovers that they are transgendered, the impact can parallel that of an affair. Lack of remorse further compounds the effect on the natal woman.

Lev (2004) posits a four-stage developmental process for the family members of transgendered and transsexual people. These stages include discovery and disclosure, turmoil, negotiation, and finding balance. Common initial reactions of partners who are not told about gender variance early in the relationship can include shock, disbelief, a sense of betrayal at the deception, revulsion, fear, and shame (Cole et al., 2000; Lev, 2004). Once the initial shock wears off, hurt, rage, fear, anxiety, and shame may prevail (Cole et al., 2000).

In my private practice, I have witnessed countless questions arising: Is he having an affair? Is he gay? Why does he want to do it? Is it because I'm not enough of a woman? Will the cross-dressing ever be taken out in public? Will anyone else find out? Will he actually want to go further and actually become a woman? If the spouse acknowledges being transsexual, the questions may be: How will this affect our children? Will our families turn their backs on us? Will we lose our friends? As **transition** progresses, what will people think? Will I be seen as a lesbian? *Am* I a lesbian? The thought of other people finding out is painful, but so is the loneliness of being isolated with the secret, alone and **closeted** with no one to talk with (Cole et al., 2000).

Frequently so much focus is placed upon the gender-variant person that the natal female partner has no opportunity to explore her own journey. She may feel partially or totally left out, and she may not feel respected. She brings her own knowledge, life experiences, and sexual history into the relationship, and she too requires attention, yet natal female partners are so groomed to pay attention to their husbands' needs in this situation that translates to their husbands' gender journeys, that they often lose their own voices (S. S. Cole, personal communication, April 8, 2004).

At one time in such cases divorce seemed inevitable, particularly if transition to full-time in the nonnatal gender role was indicated for the **transperson.** In fact, in the past, most sex reassignment surgeons would insist that a couple divorce before performing the surgery on one of the marital partners. This is no longer the case. In fact, it is illegal to require anyone to divorce unless the couple desires it themselves (S. S. Cole, personal communication, February 6, 2004).

Processing the Confusion and the Emotional Reactions

I find it hard to imagine that anyone would, at the beginning of a relationship, believe that they already know all there is to know about their beloved. Most of us expect and hope that we will come to know our partners in greater depth over the years. But what woman, in her wildest dreams, would ever anticipate being confronted by the notion of her man wanting to dress like, or to *be,* a woman?

As is the case for the rest of society, knowledge about transgender issues has not been an integral part of the social learning experience for wives of gender-variant people. For the most part, transgender experience has been a hidden entity in our population until recently, that is until the late 1980s, when the gender-variant population began to make its collective voice apparent in the culture (S. S. Cole, personal communication, February 6, 2004).

After the secret is known, partners often struggle with confusion over myriad issues. Among other things, these issues involve self-esteem; perplexity about their own sexual orientation, insecurity about their attractiveness, mistrust of their intuition about people, and their perception that their husbands are usurping their role in the relationship. The wife of a cross-dresser is likely to express jealousy about the sense that she's losing her husband to "the other woman," who is the focus of what she sees as his preening, primping attention. The financial drain of acquisition of wardrobe and accouterments and the **binge/purge** cycle may concern, furstrate, or anger the nontransgender person. Wives who stay with spouses who are actually transitioning from male-to-female find themselves living with another woman instead of the "guy" they married. Even wives who try hard to be accepting may at times cry, "I want my husband back!" Their own lack of information, fear, vulnerability, and sense of isolation may influence their responses and accommodations.

Some wives understand that they are the only reason why their husbands do not transition. The natal female partner's acceptance of the gender-variant identity but reluctance to endorse transition may cause the transgendered partner to vacillate between resentment and appreciation. As Helen Boyd (personal communication, February 20, 2004), author of *My Husband Betty* (2003) has said, we are the love and the stability that allows them to explore their gender identity, but some days it feels like being loving and supportive is bound to bite you in the ass one way or the other: either by your partner finding the confidence to transition, or not doing so, and making you feel like the only "gatekeeper" worth her salt.

Greater complications are likely to occur if the couple has a public persona, i.e., established roles in the community—including involvement in a religious community—especially if public exposure belies these roles (Cole, 1998). If the natal woman's quality of life, friendships, guidance, and spirituality are wrapped up in any form of fundamentalism, she may not find comfort where she would ordinarily seek it. In fact, she may be at extreme risk of being shunned (S. S. Cole, personal communication, April 8, 2004).

If children are involved, the situation, and the wife's responses, are likely to be more extreme. Some women claim that although others are aware of their partners' transgender issues, the children do not and will not ever know; however, children generally know that something is going on. The children's ages are significant, and Cole et al. (2000, p. 182) point out that

> in general, adolescents and pubescent youth are considered to be more vulnerable to negative emotional responses than either younger or older children, as they themselves are personally experiencing enormous physical, hormonal, and emotional changes and challenges to their bodies, feelings, gender identity, and sexual orientation.

Younger children seem to have less difficulty coping with the transition of a parent (Lev, 2004).

It is important to understand the family's dynamics, support system, and subculture before deciding what to tell the children. Instead of automatically assuming that it is necessary to protect the children from information about a family member's gender variance for fear that they will be damaged, it is useful to look at how the family operates, and what kind of coping skills the children have. Lev (2004) points out that although they will have issues to face, no evidence proves that being raised by a gender-variant parent puts children at greater risk of developing sexual or gender identity issues than children raised by gender-conforming parents. Ettner and White (2000) said that other parental and family dynamics have a much greater impact upon how the children are affected by a transition than the transition itself.

I included the voices of women who are having a difficult time, who are trying, but uncertain whether they will be able to stay in relationships with their gender-variant partners. Helen Boyd (personal communication, June 7, 2006), from her perspective as the partner of a transperson, made an excellent point when she said,

> I don't always think staying together is the most positive outcome for a couple. Some **SO**s are much happier when they leave, and it's right for them to do so. Often the transperson is happier too, especially vis-à-vis transition, but this can also be the case for cross-dressers, especially those who had wives who denigrated them for the corss-dressing for a long time. There's a huge potential for (mostly verbal) abuse of transpeople by partners that no one is really talking about much yet.

Some of the women who have told their stories seem to experience and deal with more pain and rage than others. Often this is related to how they found out about their partners' gender variance. Voluntary disclosure, especially early in a relationship, tends to yield a less negative response than does a shocking discovery. A number of other variables are crucial: Did the partner find out before the beginning of a relationship? Did she learn after its inception? Did she not know until after marriage? Had the couple been together for many years when the secret came out? Did the couple already have children when she found out? What were the ages of the children when she learned? These and other factors mediate the existence and intensity of the partner's reaction (Cole, 1998; Cole et al., 2000).

THE GENDER-VARIANT INDIVIDUAL

Is Gender Variance a Choice?

I think it is important for everyone, and particularly those in relationships with gender-variant people, to remember that being transgendered is not a lifestyle, not a choice at all, in fact. A person doesn't wake up one morning and decide to adopt feelings and needs that will cost an enormous price. That price for a cross-dresser, prior to achieving understanding and acceptance of his identity, might include fear, self-loathing, shame, and depression.

One certainly would not choose to be a transsexual person, voluntarily suffering all the emotional pain initially experienced by a cross-dresser, and much, much more. Transsexual women (male-to-female transsexual persons) often endure many years of debilitating gender confusion and **gender dysphoria,** i.e., emotional discomfort, sadness, and depression. Then, if transition is possible, they may undergo hundreds of hours of painful, expensive electrolysis on their faces (with needles penetrating tender skin, then shooting electric currents); the treatment protocol during transition usually involves expensive hormones that potentially can damage the liver and produce blood clots that can cause heart attacks and strokes, shrivel the testicles, and make one impotent and sterile; those who do not present a convincingly feminine appearance may risk ridicule and threats to physical safety; most risk the loss of everyone and everything precious to them while beginning to live full-time as women; they may endure the pain of expensive surgery to make the face more feminine and the genitals resemble those of a natal woman. A choice? Who would choose this path?

When she is engaged in her decision about whether to stay in the relationship, it is extremely important for a woman to remember that being a person of transgender experience is involuntary. I have heard women who leave insist on believing that their partner was frivolously choosing a "transgender lifestyle." Of course the distinction exists between "being" transgendered and what one does about it. The intensity of the transgender feelings, i.e., the degree of discordance between one's anatomy and mental gender identity informs the possibilities.

Keeping the Secret

Although many transgendered individuals know that they are somehow "different" at an early age, they usually make valiant attempts to fit in, and they sometimes manage to convince themselves that they can be "just like other people." Society projects a stigma onto people who are "different." This is particularly true if the difference involves any aspect of sexual identity.

As a clinician I have a problem with the diagnosis of **gender identity disorder** as a mental illness. Medical intervention will always be desirable and necessary for some transpeople. I am certain, however, that without having to cope with the pressures to which cultural ignorance subjects them, gender-variant people would have significantly greater ease of self-acceptance and a much lower incidence of the anxiety and depression that is natural for them given the prejudice, stigmatization, marginalization, ridicule, and physical endangerment that at times are outrageous realities for them in our culture. Given this societal bias, it should be no surprise that many transgendered people try their best to live what society might consider "normal" lives. They often guard this secret until they are discovered unintentionally or realize that the secret is destroying their mental health. Numerous cross-dressers and some transsexual women have reported to me that they have engaged in super macho professions and hobbies. They often say that this is an attempt to overcome or mask from detection their internally experienced femininity or femaleness.

Many gender-variant people report great difficulty with **coming out.** My clinical experience suggests that it is especially so if they intuitively know that it is not safe, if they are not able to come out when they are young, or if they were caught and shamed for cross-dressing during childhood or adolescence. Why don't otherwise honest transgendered people tell their partners about this vitally important part of their identities prior to getting seriously involved? Some do, but it's true that more don't. I have extrapolated a number of reasons for withholding this information from disclosures made by my clients.

Numerous gender-variant people have told me that they kept the secret from their partners out of a hope that the right relationship would heal this aspect of their personalities. This belief that love will "cure" them of their transgender feelings and identities is not uncommon. So, when a gender-variant person meets the girl of her/his dreams, she/he may fervently cling to the belief that the gender variance will resolve, becoming involved in a relationship without mentioning the gender variance.

We don't have statistics about how many women would be willing to become involved with or stay in relationship with a gender-variant person. However, anecdotal evidence from my own practice and those of colleagues suggests that it is not unreasonable for a transgendered person to be fearful that the woman with whom he or she has fallen in love might reject him or her if she knew "the secret." Societal stigmatization can create deep shame. Shame and fear of rejection and loss of the relationship keep some transgendered people silent.

Another reason why usually honest gender-variant people may not tell a spouse is the defense mechanism of denial. They may find it difficult to admit to themselves that gender variance could really be an integral part of them. This is an aspect of human experience about which it can be very difficult to be honest with oneself. If you don't want to know something about yourself, and you are skilled at denial, you can keep yourself in the dark for a long time.

The possibility exists as well that the transgendered person lacks understanding of the nature of the condition. I have heard gender-variant people say so many times, "I knew I was different, but for such a long time I didn't know how to identify my experience." This still happens, although less frequently than it did years ago, when few informational resources were available on the topic. Even in the age of the Internet and occasional media coverage, it is possible for gender-variant people to fail to identify, or to misidentify until later in life. Sometimes earlier self-misunderstanding is modified by collaboration with a knowledgeable therapist who offers new information.

These are some of the reasons why otherwise honest people may keep this secret from people they love. Many transgendered people struggle mightily with the issue of disclosure. It is important that significant others realize that this secrecy is rarely motivated by lack of caring or general deceptiveness.

Greater Visibility and Understanding of Transgendered People

Even though society is slow to accept diversity in any aspect of sexual identity, change *is* happening. Cross-dressers are coming out of the closet and declaring their right to live without shame. Miqqi (Dr. Michael) Gilbert, a professor of philosophy at York University in Toronto, occasionally goes to class cross-dressed (Gilbert, 2002a,b). The person once known as Jim Boylan was warmly welcomed when she returned to Colby College in Maine as Jennifer Finney Boylan, a transsexual woman. Professor Boylan wrote a memoir of her life and transition (2003), and appeared on *Oprah* and the *Today* show. Her memoir describes the reaction of her wife and children. As of those television appearances, she, her wife, and their children were still living together.

Trans people are beginning to come out in academia and beyond. Corporate management is demonstrating support for employees in gender transition and adding nondiscrimination policies for gender identity. Margaret Stumpp, PhD, a senior managing director at Prudential Investment Management, was in the news when she began to live and work as a woman. Dr. Judy Lively, physician-in-chief for more than 350,000 Kaiser Permanente patients, 500 doctors, and 6,000 staff in the San Francisco Bay area was until recently known as Dr. Judson Lively (DeFao, 2005). Companies such as IBM, CNN, Sears, Home Depot, and major airlines are setting policy to accommodate people who are in transition from one gender role to another. This is vital, given the international medical standards that require transsexuals to live full-time in the target gender role for a year prior to having sex reassignment surgery.

Respectable media attention is raising public awareness about transgendered people and their partners. The Associated Press, United Press International, *The New York Times,* the Discovery Channel and The Learning Channel, and the major broadcast networks are beginning to report transgender issues in a balanced, informed, and respectful manner.

In September of 2002, Dawn Fratangelo, a *Dateline NBC* correspondent, interviewed me for what turned out to be a one-hour segment titled "Scenes from a Marriage," which aired on February 27, 2004. The piece had been conceived by producer Julie Cohen, who thought that the viewing public would find it intriguing to see couples go all the way through the process of gender transition together. Julie recruited couples who were willing to be followed through transition by *Dateline NBC* cameras.

Since Julie Cohen and I first spoke, the issue of the impact of transsexual transition on families has become even more prominent in the media. For example, in 2003 HBO presented the film *Normal,* starring Tom Wilkinson and Jessica Lange, whose performances offer a representation of a realistic life story. The film, a Sundance Film Festival selection and Emmy nominee, portrays a couple's family life that is intensely impacted by the husband's announcement, in a pastoral counseling session, after twenty years of marriage, that he had always felt that he was a woman. Felicity Huffman was nominated for an Academy Award for her portrayal of a transitioning transsexual in the 2005 film *Transamerica,* and in June 2006, Oscar, Tony, and Golden Globe award-winner Mercedes Ruehl starred as the mother in *A Girl Like Me: The Gwen Araujo Story,* an inspiring and consciousness-raising made-for-TV movie based on the true story of a murdered transgender teen and her mother's determination to see her killers brought to justice.

THE IMPETUS FOR THIS BOOK

My First Transgendered Client

"Can you help me to stop cross-dressing? I feel terrible about it, but every time I go away on business I feel compelled to cross-dress in my hotel room. My wife doesn't know. Nobody knows. I feel so ashamed! It's not just a sexual thing any more; I feel so peaceful. It's the most relaxing thing I know to do. But if anyone found out they'd just think I'm some kind of pervert, my wife might leave me, my parents might disown me, I might lose my job, and my friends might turn their backs on me."

I felt so ignorant when, in 1994, this anguished cross-dresser came to me for help. My clinical course work in graduate school included no information whatsoever about gender identity or diversity of gender expression. My postdoctoral psychology training included some discussion of the treatment of fetishistic behavior, which suggested that to whatever degree this client's cross-dressing was erotic, it was unlikely that anything but intensely aversive behavioral therapy (not a modality I care to practice) would be effective in squelching his desire or need even temporarily.

However, the way he presented the description of his behavior and feelings seemed incompatible with what I knew about paraphilia or fetishes. My recommendation was that he look for a way to disclose this part of himself to his wife, and hope that she loved him enough and was open-minded enough to learn more and, perhaps, eventually, accept his cross-dressing. He worked up the courage to talk with his wife, and she was much more understanding than he had expected.

Following that experience this couple chose to pursue their continued journey independently without counsel.

Soon thereafter another transgendered person found her way to my office. At first this client presented as a cross-dresser. Later she admitted that if it weren't for the effect it would have on her children and her career she would investigate the possibility of living full-time as a woman. I knew that if I were going to be able to help people effectively with these issues I needed to educate myself further.

Educate myself I did. At a local meeting of Quad S (Society for the Scientific Study of Sexuality), I inquired about resources and was referred to AEGIS (American Educational Gender Information Service). I contacted the founder and director, Ms. Dallas Denny, MA, who suggested readings and made herself available for consultation.

In addition to my reading, I began attending the Southern Comfort Conference (SCC), a major conference for transgendered people, their significant others, and allied professionals. I learned a great deal from the presentations and from talking with gender-variant people and other professionals at my first SCC. Most helpful in my work with partners and in conceptualizing this book have been my extensive conversations with Sandra Cole, whose generosity of spirit has benefited so many.

I made contact with a group of local professionals and we consulted with one another, when needed, about complex cases. Eventually at SCC we presented the first continuing education training for counseling professionals ever to be offered at a transgender conference. In addition to presenting annually at SCC, I have also presented at the **SPICE** conference, at the IFGE (International Foundation for Gender Education) conference, and at the Harry Benjamin International Gender Dysphoria Association (**HBIGDA**) Symposium (see Resource section) in Bologna, Italy.

The more I learned, the more I wanted to know. Working with people all across the gender variance spectrum became a passion for me. At this point in my life my work as a gender specialist is anywhere from 40 to 60 percent of my practice. I find it incredibly meaningful to facilitate people's exploration of their gender identity. I enjoy helping them, their partners, and their families to achieve comfort. It is my privilege, where relevant and helpful, to accompany some through transition to the desired gender, which may include surgery. In addition I help my transgender clients and their partners to acquire valuable skills that enable them to respond well to the reactions of people in their lives to the gender variance.

Although I often witness people's pain, fear, and shame, I also witness joy and laughter. I remember receiving a postcard from Scottsdale, Arizona, from a client who was recovering from her genital reconstruction surgery. The postcard simply said, "It's a girl!" and was signed "Lucy."

A twenty-two-year-old male-to-female transsexual client shared her mother's initial reaction to her disclosure. First her mom said, "Thank God! The jewelry will stay in the family!" Immediately following that exclamation came the question, "Where on earth will you buy shoes?"

A cross-dresser's wife told me a story about the transgender support group she and her husband attend. The wives in the group were getting tired of seeing the "crown jewels" of cross-dressers who wore short skirts to meetings and sat with their legs open, exposing the shape of their genitals, which were not camouflaged with a **gaffe** under their pantyhose. These wives talked to the group's leaders, who kept reminding the cross-dressers that they needed to cross or keep their legs together when seated. The cross-dressers either couldn't remember or didn't seem to think that this was a big deal. One wife came up with a solution, which she shared with the others. They could secretly take pictures of the cross-dressers with their legs open. Then they could play a game called "Name That Crotch." They would show the cropped pictures to each cross-dresser and ask if they could identify the crotch in the picture and name the cross-dresser to whom it belonged.

They never actually took the pictures (it was a joke), nor did they plan to mention the idea to the cross-dressers, but when they had erupted in hysterical laughter often enough one of the husbands demanded to know, despite the wives having consistently refused to disclose the joke. His wife gave in: This husband found the idea very funny, and told the other cross-dressers. Everyone had a good laugh. Clearly though, it hit home with the offending cross-dressers. After that everyone tried to remember to sit more modestly.

Although humorous, this story is also an example of the husbands' lack of social awareness and experience with dressing and modesty, a topic diligently monitored by most women. As Sandra Cole has pointed out (personal communication, February 6, 2004), older MtF transpeople missed rehearsal of the psychosocial sexual aspect of their gender.

On the other hand, young people, such as the twenty-two-year-old I mentioned, are coming out while having more societal permission to explore their psychological development. Since the mid-1990s the population of people claiming gender variance is much younger, even decades younger than most of the couples in this book. The average age of gender-variant people "out" and seeking assistance used to be significantly more advanced. Many were in long-term relationships, or had been in serial marriages (S. S. Cole, personal communication, April 8, 2004).

The life experience of older transgendered people is vastly different from those identifying younger. Most of my participants' spouses explored their gender issues in deep **stealth.** Once they do come out, gender-variant people and their partners deal with public presentation in the context of their life experience.

The "Name That Crotch" story also illustrates what women tend to do if they don't have power. They tease and ridicule. The covert nature of women's humor is another way to experience some control in their lives. Challenging disturbing behavior or dealing with conflict by gently using humor is a classic management skill (S. S. Cole, personal communication, April 8, 2004).

The Need for This Book

It has been my experience in the past few years that increasingly, wives are recovering from the initial shock of discovery or disclosure and staying in relationships with cross-dressers and transsexuals. If you are one of these women, I would guess that you will find these accounts helpful, particularly if you found out not long ago that your spouse is gender-variant.

Recently, many more women have accompanied their gender-variant spouses into counseling with me. I have been moved by the courage and compassion of the wives with whom I have worked therapeutically and by the women who have shared their stories with me for this project. Those who consider staying in the relationship have the courage to defy societal imperatives and risk the hostility of family, friends, and community, standing by and supporting their gender-variant partners.

They often find themselves taking a backseat to their spouses' gender issues, thus having little or no opportunity to explore their own journey, struggling to find their own voices (Cole, 1998). They tend to demonstrate a willingness to examine themselves and their relationships and to work toward healing in situations rarely of their choosing. These clinical findings are congruent with what Sandra Cole, in her pioneering work with partners at gender conferences, has discovered. Dr. Cole (personal communication, February 25, 2005) points out that

> the natal woman's real journey starts the minute she inherits the information about her partner's gender variance. Prior to this point, she has been experiencing various degrees of angst and pain while trying to figure out what's going on in her life.

In the service of their healing, there are a few books (see Bibliography), Internet support lists and online groups (see Resources), and a few in-person support groups to which I can refer wives. Many of those with whom I have worked have expressed a desire to hear "unsugarcoated" stories of other women with whom they might identify. SOs have a plethora of questions: How have other people felt in this situation? How have they dealt with their feelings? How have they found ways to accept and stay with their partners? How have such relationships evolved? Have they told children, extended family, and friends? If so, how? This book answers those questions, in the voices of wives themselves. If you are the wife of a gender-variant individual, I hope you will find it helpful to read about how other people in your situation have coped. My wish is that as you read these stories, you will feel less alone.

Chapter 2

Transgender 101

For readers who are not well versed in gender issues I'm providing a primer, a bare-bones overview of some of the significant concepts that contribute to an understanding of transgender phenomena. I have included, for instance, sections outlining my view of aspects of sexual identity, the transgender spectrum, and a glossary (located at the end of the book). Without an understanding of the basics of gender identity issues it is impossible to understand the dynamics of relationships between gender-variant people and their natal female (non-gender-variant) partners.

ASPECTS OF SEXUAL IDENTITY

One of the most significant aspects of humanness is sexual identity. My experience as a clinician suggests that many partners, as well as gender-variant people themselves, struggle with confusion about their own and each others' sexual identities. Several elements comprise sexual identity. One schema for describing the components of sexual identity includes biological sex, sexual orientation, erotic orientation, gender role presentation, and gender identity. Society is much more comfortable seeing these components as binary, that is either/or, one or the other, such as male or female; gay or straight (Ochs, 1996). Most people are squeamish about gray areas, particularly when it comes to sex and gender, but they exist. Inhabitants of the gray areas include Intersexed people (who in the past were more often called hermaphrodites), people who are androgynous in presentation rather than more clearly recognizable as men or women, and bisexual people. Comfort increases when we put people into nice,

Head Over Heels: Wives Who Stay with Cross-Dressers and Transsexuals
Published by The Haworth Press, Inc., 2007. All rights reserved.
doi:10.1300/5737_02

neat, either/or, binary categories, but that's not really the way nature works.

Biological sex is what your body looks like, inside and out. This aspect of sexual identity is comprised of genetic factors, endocrine function, gonads (ovaries or testes), internal and external genitals, and secondary sexual characteristics, such as facial and body hair, breasts, and fat distribution (Crooks & Baur, 1996). Even biological sex, which one might see as the most clear-cut factor in sexual identity is not binary (Chase, 1997). Numerous intersex conditions exist, in which not all the indicators of biological sex are in concordance (Dreger, 1998b, 1999). Genital ambiguity, an extreme manifestation of intersexuality, naturally occurs in as many as one in 1,500 births (Dreger, 1998a).

Sexual orientation is the aspect of sexual identity concerning the sex to which you're attracted (Bohan, 1996; Crooks & Baur, 1996). The possibilities are not binary: gay or straight (Bohan, 1996; Ellis & Mitchell, 2000); nor is sexual orientation predicted by your biological sex or your gender identity (Bentler & Prince, 1969; Blanchard, 1987, 1989; Blanchard, Clemmensen, & Steiner, 1987; Cole et al., 2000; Denny & Green, 1996; Gooren & Cohen-Kettenis, 1991; Pauly, 1990, 1992; Prince, 1957; Prince & Bentler, 1972). People can be heterosexual, homosexual, bisexual, asexual, omnisexual (capable of attraction to males, females, intersexuals, and transgendered individuals), or particularly attracted to gender-variant people.

The sexual orientation of gender-variant people "mirrors the range of sexual attractions in the large society" (Denny & Green, 1996, p. 161). Philosopher Michel Foucault (1980) suggests that prior to the twentieth century people performed various sex acts with various partners, but were not categorized or defined according to the people they had sex with. It might have been said that a person had engaged in eroticism with someone of the same sex, but the person wouldn't have been called "a homosexual." Likewise, the category heterosexual was unheard of.

Erotic orientation is what kind of sexual fantasy or activity one finds arousing. A person may prefer sex to be wild or tame, gentle or rough, "vanilla" or "kinky." Some transgendered people report that they are aroused by certain aspects of their gender variance itself, for instance, wearing clothing associated with their nonnatal sex, or physical modifications (Blanchard, 1989; Lawrence, 2000; Money, 1986).

Most of my gender-variant clients report that when they were adolescent they found cross-dressing in fantasy or reality erotic. For some, thoughts of physical transformation were sexually stimulating. Many suggest that these aspects of their transgender experience and journey became less erotic over time. Often, the experience of gender variance evolves, and identity, comfort, and congruence become central (Docter, 1988; Erhardt, 2001; Prince, 1957). In addition, living with the internal feelings can become agonizing. When this occurs, external expression often feels necessary.

Gender role is "a set of expectations that one will look, dress, and behave as a man or woman" (Denny & Green, 1996, p. 86). Gender role differs from one culture to another, and may change across time within the same culture. Anthropologists Anne Bolin and Patricia Whelehan (1999) describe gender role as "the internalization of culturally recognized attitudes, behaviors, beliefs and values that compliment one's gender identity" (p. 282).

Gender role presentation is the way you behave: public demonstrations via what you say, do, and wear that indicate various degrees of masculinity, femininity, or androgyny. This aspect of sexual identity can be an accurate representation, or a carefully constructed façade that hides true gender identity. For instance, many of my gender-variant natal males have reported that, in part to disguise their internally experienced femininity or femaleness, they have engaged in "super macho" vocational or recreational pursuits.

Gender identity is a person's private, internal mental and emotional experience of being a boy or a girl, a man or a woman (Hoenig, 1985; Nangeroni, 2003). It used to be thought that gender identity developed within the first three years of life, but according to geneticist Dr. Anne Moir (with Jessel, 1991), the once tentative theory that gender identity develops in utero as a result of the timing and intensity of a hormonal surge is now accepted by virtually every neuroscientist. "A male foetus may have enough male hormones to trigger the development of male sex organs, but these organs may not be able to produce the additional male hormones to push the brain into the male pattern" (p. 24).

Theoretically, mental gender identity forms in a similar manner but at a different time during pregnancy from sexual orientation (Moir &

Jessel, 1991). However, it is important to remember that while for some people gender variance may be inborn, for others, some form of gender variance is chosen, and such people do not consider themselves to have been born gender-variant (Xavier, 2003).

Many people confuse gender identity with sexual orientation, but they are two separate aspects of sexual identity; one does not predict the other (Bentler & Prince, 1969; Blanchard, 1987, 1989; Blanchard, Clemmensen, & Steiner, 1987; Cole et al., 2000; Denny & Green, 1996; Gooren & Cohen-Kettenis, 1991; Pauly, 1990, 1992; Prince, 1957; Prince & Bentler, 1972; Xavier, 2003). Cross-dressers are often equated with drag queens and seen as gay, which is simply erroneous. In fact, the vast majority of cross-dressers are heterosexual (Bentler & Prince, 1969; Blanchard, 1987; Green & Money, 1969). Uninformed people mistakenly assume that transsexuals are homosexual, perhaps because the term "transsexual" seems to refer to the person's sex life, but male-to-female transsexuals are as likely to be attracted to women as to men (Blanchard, 1987, 1989; Green & Money, 1969; Pauly, 1990).

THE TRANSGENDER SPECTRUM

Although the stories in this collection are limited to women who are in relationship with cross-dressers and male-to-female transsexuals, a great deal of variation exists in the identities of people on the transgender spectrum. Describing the diversity of the spectrum may help to place the people on whom we will focus in context. I will go into no detail about female-to-male individuals, since their issues are beyond the scope of this project.

- *Transgendered* (e.g., in TG people, transpeople) is an umbrella term that includes any individual who transgresses gender norms.
- *Drag kings and drag queens* are people who present exaggerated, larger-than-life, stereotypical images of men and women. They may do this for the purpose of entertaining others, for attention, or simply for their own pleasure.
- *Angrogynes, gender benders, or gender blenders* integrate masculinity and femininity in various ways, sometimes extreme, and sometimes more subtle.

- *Cross-dressers* (probably about 5 percent of the population, according to **Tri-Ess** [see Glossary and Resource sections], the international support and social organization for heterosexual cross-dressers and their families) identify primarily as their natal sex and yet need to express their inner femininity beyond fantasy. The desire to cross-dress is often primarily associated with eroticism at first (particularly during puberty), but for many the focus tends to evolve to include or exclusively focus on comfort, relaxation, relief from masculine demands, and the experience and expression of a softer, more feminine part of the personality.
- *Transgenderists* are people for whom cross-dressing does not satisfy. They often lack the need or desire to alter their bodies in extreme ways that transsexuals wish to do. Although they may take hormones and have treatments such as facial electrolysis or breast augmentation surgery, they usually address their desire to present as the opposite sex without genital surgery. Some cross-live full-time, perhaps permanently. Some, who can't or do not wish to live full-time in their desired gender-role, may cultivate a more androgynous mode or go back and forth. Others, who may identify with androgyny, express a "third gender" mode (Boswell, 1991, 2001), coloring outside the lines—or in the middle—of the binary male-female model.
- *Transsexuals* have a mental and emotional gender identity that is distinctly different from their biological sex. That is, their internal sense of being a man or a woman does not match their anatomy. They often seek medical treatment in order to modify their anatomy so that it becomes as congruent as possible with their mental gender identity. This is the strategy of choice, since it tends not to be fully or permanently successful to treat this condition in the reverse, i.e., changing the mental sense of being a man or a woman to match the body (Cole et al., 2000). Male-to-female individuals' preparation for transition or for beginning to live full-time as women may include hormones, facial electrolysis and/or laser treatment, and various surgeries, including tracheal shave to reduce the visibility of the Adam's apple, breast augmentation, and facial feminization. The final step is genital sex reassignment (Green & Money, 1969). Psychotherapy and/or a real-life experience in the target gender role are required under the Harry Benjamin International Gender Dysphoria Stan-

dards of Care (SOC) (Levine et al., 1998) for genital surgery. According to the diagnostic manual of the American Psychiatric Association (American Psychiatric Association, 1994), only .003 percent of the population is transsexual, but this is very old conjecture. Although other people have different perspectives, the APA's statement has never been challenged with accurate scientific data.

Is it Really a Spectrum?

Some people question how discrete these descriptions of trans-gendered people are in reality. It is, of course, more comfortable for society to fit people into nice neat categories. Even more than society in general, many cross-dressers' significant others seem to be invested in their husbands fitting into a categorical box with high walls, out of which they won't in some way relocate into the box next door in which these women believe transsexuals reside. I have observed this intense desire both in my clinical practice and in collecting material for this book.

This is understandable. It makes intuitive sense, and it is my clinical observation that the lives of women whose partners intend to transition from one gender role to another tend to be much more challenging than the lives of women whose partners are willing to limit expression of gender variance to cross-dressing, particularly if the gender-variant behavior is unlikely to be observed by anyone known to the couple. When transition is involved, not only do partners have to cope with their feelings about personal aspects of the relationship, they also have to deal with disclosure to the world, the possibility of rejection by friends and family, and issues related to employment that may put a family at financial risk.

By the end of 2005 I had worked with more than 300 trans-gendered people and a number of their partners. My observations suggest that transgender identity seems to fall on a spectrum. As people tell me their stories and enlist my assistance with sorting out how they can live with gender-variant feelings, and how they can integrate the disowned, incongruent parts of themselves, I'm struck with how many transpeople are ambivalent about what to do. The ambivalence is not just about consequences, either. Many of my clients have offered extremely ambiguous self-descriptions—making it impossible to see them as fitting into any nice, neat category. They often describe struggles to determine whether they are transsexual or "just" cross-dressers. My impression of these self-reported dilemmas is that gender identity, rather than forming discrete categories, falls on a continuum, as do so many other aspects of the human experience. As you will see in the narratives that follow, the lack of stable, concrete transgender categories exacerbates the concerns of partners of gender-variant people.

PARTNERS' STORIES AND COMMENTARIES

Let me not to marriage of true minds
Admit impediments. Love is not love
Which alters when it alteration finds . . .

William Shakespeare, "Sonnet 116"

Chapter 3

Kate and Joe

Kate was shocked when, while he was out of town, Joe told her about his cross-dressing during a phone call. She went into an emotional spiral, but decided to seek individual and couples counseling, avoiding an impulsive decision about the fate of her marriage. She set strict limits, refusing to see or participate in Joe's cross-dressing. This is Kate's story.

I found out about my partner's gender issues a little over five years ago right after our fourteenth wedding anniversary. We come from healthy, well-functioning, wonderful, churchgoing, middle/upper-middle class families. After each having happy childhoods, we met in college. I am an elementary school teacher; my husband is a successful salesman. We had a home, two children, and a dog—a regular white-picket-fence life.

I had never even heard of heterosexual cross-dressers. I had virtually no clues about his "feminine side": no Halloween outfits, nothing missing from my closet. He did travel a lot for his job, and sometimes I joked with my friends, saying, "There's something I can't put my finger on—I bet I'll be one of those made-for-TV movies someday. With Joe gone so much, he must have another wife and kids in another city." He seemed to have a lower sex drive than I did, but I wrote that off to his being overweight, being tired from traveling, and drinking too much. He seemed very reserved and conservative.

In retrospect, the only thing that *should* have tipped me off was that one time, while we were still dating, Joe shaved his legs because, he said, he wanted to see what they would feel like next to mine. I freaked out and told him that I didn't want to see what that would feel like. Then, many, many years later, there was something else. Just a few months before he told me about his cross-dressing he made up a story about how a pharmacist told him to remove all his body hair be-

Head Over Heels: Wives Who Stay with Cross-Dressers and Transsexuals
Published by The Haworth Press, Inc., 2007. All rights reserved.
doi:10.1300/5737_03

cause of some bedbugs like lice he had encountered at a hotel. I told him that didn't sound right to me. "If there is something more here that you want to talk with me about," I said, "please do. Our love is deep and strong and we can handle anything together."

I wouldn't have sex with Joe until the hair grew back! I didn't put two and two together at that time, or maybe I should say one and one—I didn't even remember the earlier dating/leg shaving incident. But what I said about our love being strong must have really made an impression on him, because a few months later I got a call that changed my life.

Joe was on a business trip and called me long distance. "I have something to tell you that I don't think you are going to like," he said. When he told me he liked to wear women's clothes I remember initially thinking I could tell this was a huge painful secret for him to share and I wanted to be respectful of his feelings. I told him, "I love you." He said that his mother had found him wearing women's clothes as a teen and had screamed at him to stop it. She accused him of being gay, and told him this would kill his father. *How can a parent do this to their own child?* I thought. I didn't want to see Joe hurting.

He assured me he was not gay and he was not bi and he did not want to change his sex. Then he proceeded to tell me that a girlfriend in college had found his "stash" of clothing and called him "f***ing weird" in the middle of a campus hallway. It was obvious to me that his previous experiences had been extremely negative, even traumatic, and that he felt a lot of shame and confusion. We talked for a long time on the phone. Joe explained that he thought he would be able to quit when we got married. But the feelings never went away. He was afraid that if he ever told me, I'd leave him. So he kept it a secret.

I couldn't sleep that night. I called Joe in the middle of the night and asked him if he wanted to get out of our marriage. I wondered if that was the reason he had finally told me. He assured me that he wanted to stay married to me. I also asked him if he wore makeup and nail polish and jewelry and wigs. I asked him if he would go to see a counselor with me. I had so many questions.

The next morning I called a counselor and made an emergency appointment for that very day, finding a playdate for our five-year-old and a babysitter for our one-year-old. I was in shock! I could barely breathe in and out. It was as if the man I knew had never been. As the day went on I decided to make plans to take my own life. It seemed like the only logical alternative at the time. In twenty-four short hours I'd gone from being extremely content to severely depressed and panicky. I knew I did not want to be married to someone who was both male and female. Plus, I knew I would keep his secret. So if I divorced Joe our families and friends would never know the truth or understand. I would look like such a bad guy.

They all thought I was so fortunate to be married to Joe. After all, he is a loving, positive, generous, warm, romantic, sensitive, giving, and considerate husband, father, and son. He is successful professionally and a terrific provider, well-educated, and interesting. He is tall, dark, and handsome. They would think I was crazy to leave him. What a trap!

So when my husband called to check in that day I told him I planned to lock the garage door and turn on the car. He chose to come home from his business trip, 1,200 miles away, for twenty-four hours because I was scaring him. When Joe came home it was as if a stranger was in my home. He had gone to a beauty salon the day before and had all his body hair waxed off. My whole life seemed to be full of painful deception. I had given up everything for this man. I had allowed us to be transferred to two different states. I was far from my family and childhood home. The father of our children and my best friend had betrayed me, and I felt as though I had lost everything and had nowhere to turn.

Somehow, that same day, I pulled myself together enough to make a decision not to do anything for a whole year. I didn't want to be mentally planning for divorce, although that seemed inevitable. I pushed those thoughts from my mind. I decided to be proactive, working through it, and simply allowing myself to feel my feelings and to wait and see if we had a future together. I got on the Internet and within hours I had located more information on cross-dressing than my husband had found in years. We ordered books online. We contacted a nearby chapter of Tri-Ess. We arranged for weekly babysitting, we went for long walks, we saw a therapist. I cried a lot.

My own identity as a woman was in question. I couldn't relate to my husband sexually with all of his body hair gone. My self-esteem took a nosedive. I felt as if a significant part of my reality had been taken away. It was as if I was standing on a rug and someone just came and yanked the rug out from under me. I looked at everything differently. Boys dressed in blue and girls in pink in my world—everything in our society was that way.

I began to think that my husband had been living through me. I questioned every gift he had ever bought me, and worried about what other secrets he had kept. How could Joe keep this from me? I had told *him* everything. Our relationship had been a big lie! He had broken my trust. I could barely get dressed in the morning. I had no interest in clothes or makeup. I had a panic attack at the mall in the lingerie department one day.

I resented the times Joe had been away on business with his clothes. It was like he had a fantasy woman I couldn't compete with. He was having an affair with his clothes, and he would choose to be with "her" rather than me. What did he need me for? Some days I was so depressed I couldn't get out of bed. I told him it would have been easier if he had had an actual affair. That could end, but this was forever.

I didn't want this lifestyle. It was as if Joe had stepped out of the closet and put me in one. I had never felt so alone in all my life. I couldn't relate to my friends' relationships. Having to keep this secret distanced me from my friends and family. I stopped all my activities and cried some more. My emotional difficulties caused my husband to get depressed.

We went to weekly counseling for eight months. Except for the counselor (and Joe) I had no one to talk to. She asked us to read Harville Hendrix's books, and during counseling we had to practice active listening and communicating with each other. Our counselor rarely talked. We did the work; she facilitated. During this period I did the basics at home, the bare minimum to take care of my family and get through each day. Looking back, I'm surprised the counselor didn't put me on antidepressants.

Joe probably dresses up about six times a year. I have seen him dressed a few times. We are both uncomfortable when he does this, and he doesn't want to tell our young children, so he usually takes his clothes out of town if he feels the urge to dress. This is how we cope. It allows him privacy. My husband is a very private person about his "softer side" as we like to call it. Often, he just **underdresses,** wearing panties and hose under his guy clothes for a few days at a time. Not only is this relaxing for him, but it's erotic. He has fantasies and masturbates when dressed.

I think I have done way more work to come to grips with this than Joe has. He still doesn't feel good about it. I think he overcompensates in other areas of his life in order to see himself as "perfect."

At the end of that one-year commitment, although still extremely hurt, I decided that I was going to try to make our relationship work. I had invested a lot of time and energy into our marriage, plus we had children to think of. So, I forged on, feeling fortunate to find an e-group made up of significant others of cross-dressers. I spent hours at my keyboard, writing and writing. I found it very therapeutic. With my husband's permission I also told two out-of-state girlfriends, so then I didn't feel so isolated. Except for these two friends and some online friends who are in the same boat, we still keep it our little secret so it hasn't outwardly affected any other relationships.

Finally, I asked myself a tough question: Would I stay married to Joe if I didn't know? The answer was of course yes. Once I came to that conclusion the healing and forgiveness began. My bitterness and resentment slowly receded. I don't embrace his cross-dressing, but I don't forbid it either. It may be difficult for some people to understand, but I make every effort to accept this side of him. Since I am a Christian, I take my wedding vows and marital relationship very seriously.

Through struggling with this issue, I have gained compassion for others and I am less judgmental. I'm so glad to be able to share my story; this topic is very important to me. I hope this book reaches and educates other women so that no one ever has to be as shocked and alone as I was. The phrases "you never know what someone's life is like unless you walk in their shoes" and "you can't judge a book by its cover" have taken on new meaning for me.

I have some ground rules: no more lying, no more body hair removal, no taking hormones, no dressing in our bedroom, no full-time dressing. That is what I can live with. Those are my boundaries. Trust continues to be an issue for me. I only trust Joe about 98 percent. This is improving as time goes on, but for me, this betrayal has been a tough wound to heal. Sometimes it's easy to blame other things on cross-dressing, and I try not to do that.

Joe still doesn't like to talk about cross-dressing at all. Sometimes I bring it up, trying to joke lightly/lovingly about it. We notice it when we see the topic in a book or a joke or the media. I have given him a couple of silk unisex nightshirts. I buy him satin or silk men's underwear. There are times when cross-dressing is still a difficult subject, but I'm sure every marriage has something to deal with. Sometimes it seems like an obsessive-compulsive issue to me. When Joe gets self-centered and removes himself from dealing with reality, using cross-dressing as an escape, I do think of it as immature.

We try our best to negotiate, making sure that he has money to spend on himself/herself, freedom to dress when needed, a place to keep the clothes, etc. I am fortunate that it is very part-time for my husband, but the truth is that some days I wish he were able to quit forever. On a positive note, I think his cross-dressing will help him to be open and understanding of our children in their teen years. It should make it easier for him to look deeper than their clothing style choices, which often really bothers parents.

I never in my wildest dreams imagined that I would be dealing with this. I don't know what the future will bring, but then no one does. This is the only life I have. It's not, as they say, a dress rehearsal. Joe and I now take better care of ourselves and each other. We exercise regularly, eat better, drink less, communicate more, and don't take anything for granted. We even decided to add to our family and now have another baby. Our lives are rich and full and interesting. My husband is never boring! We treasure each other each day. We are happy and committed to making our unusual situation work. I believe that our relationship has a bright future. Marcia Brady never dealt with this one!

Kate had lived a rather sheltered life, and although she joked that it was too good to be true, she truly may have expected her "Brady Bunch" life to last forever. When Joe confessed that he cross-dressed, Kate went into shock. In that state she was extremely concerned about Joe's feelings. The next day, when Kate came out of shock she was panicky, depressed, and suicidal, yet she realized that she wanted to suspend making any decision about her marriage for a year.

Kate's response to Joe's disclosure of his cross-dressing is suggestive of a posttraumatic stress reaction. She reports having lived a sheltered life, yet this may be triggering past betrayals she has experienced. Even if no major past traumas occurred, some women feel intensely traumatized by such a disclosure. Had Kate discovered a stash of clothing or otherwise found out without Joe revealing his secret Kate would have been even more deeply wounded, and the marriage might have ended immediately.

Wisely, Kate made an appointment with a counselor immediately after Joe's disclosure. Anyone having such a strong emotional reaction needs support, and, initially, Kate intended to keep the secret from everyone. Many wives choose to isolate themselves with the secret of a partner's gender variance with no support, no one with whom they can confide their feelings. I have, however, in my clinical experience, observed, albeit rarely, wives who tell their husbands' family, friends, even employers in retaliation.

Kate began to wonder whether Joe had been living "through her." She considered the possibility that when he bought her gifts he was imagining someone buying such a gift for him. Wives often have such suspicions. After the disclosure, when her husband buys her some pretty thing, she may wonder if he is imagining himself wearing it. The woman may feel objectified, used, and insignificant to her spouse. This is a sensitive issue, worth taking time to discuss, ideally in the presence of and with the assistance of an objective facilitator.

Kate continued to feel betrayed. It was as if she had lost everything and had nowhere to turn. It is not uncommon for wives, upon finding out that information of this nature has been withheld from them, to feel very much alone. Often the woman has no one with whom she can discuss the situation. It is vital, rather than remaining isolated with her pain, that she find others who have experienced similar dynamics, with whom she can identify and share mutual support.

Kate educated herself, spent time with Joe, and went to couples therapy with him. She set limits, one of which was that Joe only cross-dress while away on business. Unlike some wives, she did not want to see or in any way participate in Joe's cross-dressing. It was helpful to Kate to participate in an online group for significant others of cross-dressers and to tell two girlfriends who lived out of town. Having done so, she ceased to feel so isolated. The couple also contacted Tri-Ess.

Similar to many partners, Kate has probably worked harder to come to grips with Joe's gender variance and to make the relationship work than he has. Although she is aware of this, she seems to accept it. After many months of struggle, and despite divorce having seemed inevitable early on, Kate decided to stay in her marriage. She is working to rebuild trust and has become more compassionate and more accepting. She and Joe are negotiating issues related to the cross-dressing, and Kate seems to have regained her sense of humor. When Kate started to forgive Joe, her healing began in earnest. She has developed a sufficiently positive attitude about the relationship and its future that she and Joe have had another child.

Chapter 4

Sally and Mike

Unlike Kate's story, more of the focus of Sally's narrative is her own erotic responses to her spouse. Initially, when Sally learned about Mike's cross-dressing, she thought that something must be wrong with her if she could still be attracted to Mike. She did have a difficult time relating to him sexually at first, feeling disgusted by seeing or feeling signs of his feminine side, such as shaved legs and body.

My current husband and I had been married for five years when, in October 2000, I spent a week visiting my daughter. When I arrived home, I unpacked the car and went to check the computer for e-mail. On the computer desk was a small yellow sheet of paper with the words "my husband wears my clothes." My initial thought was that Mike had been watching *Oprah* or some other talk show and was responding to their Internet site. I really didn't think much about it. I called him to let him know I was home safely and mentioned the note that I had found. There was silence. It was only a few seconds, but seemed like eternity to me. He asked if we could talk about this when he came home from work. I could tell by the tone of his voice that something was wrong.

While putting my clothes away I found a sales receipt on the bureau from K-Mart for shoes, a bra, and stockings! My immediate thought was that my husband had a girlfriend. I checked the Internet history on the computer to see what sites had been viewed while I was away. When I saw all the sites that he had checked out, I wanted to vomit. There were pictures of men dressed as women and sites for buying items to make a man look like a female. *Oh my God, he's gay! How could I not have known that?* I thought.

The time from our telephone conversation until Mike arrived home from work seemed endless. I imagined all sorts of things. Mike ap-

Head Over Heels: Wives Who Stay with Cross-Dressers and Transsexuals
Published by The Haworth Press, Inc., 2007. All rights reserved.
doi:10.1300/5737_04

peared visibly upset when he came in. He proceeded to confess that
he had been dressing up in my clothes ever since we'd been married.
I'd had no clue. He also told me that while I had been away he had
spent time on the Internet doing research, trying to learn more about
himself and his feelings about wearing women's clothes. The note I'd
found, he said, was the title of a book by Peggy Rudd (1999) that he
wanted to purchase so that he could tell me about all this. I honestly
felt as though our marriage had been a joke, that it had all been based
on dishonesty.

Initially, I believed that if I chose to remain in the relationship, and
if I could still be sexually attracted to my husband, even when he was
en homme, something must be wrong with me. I thought that any
normal woman would leave him. I also felt less attractive as a woman,
and cared less about my physical appearance. Fortunately, I was still
in intense personal therapy at the time of "discovery." This enabled
me to work through all the issues that arose and helped me to regain
the level of self-esteem I had developed through my therapy.

From the time we met until shortly after I found out about the
cross-dressing, I had never seen my husband without a beard or mustache. I was and still am attracted to that feature. Soon after "the revelation" he shaved off his beard. He also began shaving his body so
that when he dressed he would look more like a woman.

In the beginning, seeing or feeling signs of the female side of Mike
grossed me out. I was completely turned off by the shaven legs and
chest. I had a difficult time relating to him sexually at first, because
even though he was in male mode (not dressed up or made up or in a
wig) when we made love, I could see and feel the female side of him. I
used to separate the two like a split personality. One side was my husband, the other his female side. That was before I had integrated the
two sides of his personality in my mind.

I have felt resentment about not having been told about the cross-
dressing prior to our marriage, but I'm now certain that if I *had*
known and I had researched the issue, read all the books I could find
on the subject, and had been in therapy and worked through the issues, knowing what a wonderful person he is, I still would have married him.

He is aware that I am attracted to him and turned on when he has a
beard so he does let it grow back in from time to time. But now that
some time has passed, neither the lack of facial hair nor the shaven

body seems to matter to me. It doesn't interfere with my sexual attraction to him either. He's still my husband. Unless he is **en femme,** I no longer even *see* the female.

Sometimes, though, when I notice him looking at me as if he's aroused by me I suspect that what is actually turning him on is thinking of himself as a woman. I wonder whether when he looks at me while I'm getting dressed, for instance, he's wishing that *he* had breasts.

I felt threatened when I considered the possibility that some day down the line my husband might decide he wants to live full-time as a female. I am heterosexual, and for quite a while I was sure I could not be in a relationship like that. Now I see him differently; I see the "whole" person. If he were to choose to live as a woman full-time someday, perhaps I'd be able to remain in the relationship. I don't want to volunteer to give up who I am and just go along with it, but I would be willing to deal with the issues and try to work it out so that both of us could be ourselves individually and as a couple.

I don't like secrets—never did, never will. I was tormented by many emotions when I found out, and what bothered me most was the mistrust generated by my husband having hidden the cross-dressing. Through couples therapy and our private conversations I came to truly understand *why* it was a secret. My husband is basically a very honest person. He was tremendously guilty about both his cross-dressing and that he was hiding it from me.

I believe that Mike's guilt about being transgendered is why he has been depressed most of his life. When I found out about the cross-dressing, he went into a major depression and became suicidal. Currently, he sees his psychiatrist only for management of his antidepressant medication, but for a while we were each in both individual and couples therapy as well. At this point, we have worked through the necessary issues. But we know we can return to therapy if other issues come up. The door is open.

That fall when I found out about the cross-dressing, Mike and I researched gender dysphoria, cross-dressing, etc., on the Internet, and read a lot of books. I could tell that Mike was struggling within himself and suggested that he might want to talk to someone about it. He was agreeable, but wanted to go to a therapist who had experience with gender issues. We found someone and Mike continued with her until about May or so of 2002.

Relationship therapy was really helpful. We learned how to communicate more effectively with each other. I don't think my husband ever felt too comfortable with the relationship therapist though. She was not very knowledgeable about gender issues, but we taught her a thing or two.

I believe that therapy is a good thing for individuals and couples with gender issues, but not all therapists have gender expertise, and it's important to see a specialist. The cross-dresser and his wife or significant other each has his or her own issues, and they need therapists who are aware of the specific issues and concerns.

While he was in therapy Mike had questions about his childhood and decided to talk with his sister. He gave her material to read, books, essays, etc. He told her that he often would put on her or their mother's underwear and that later on he would dress in her clothes when no one was home. She'd had no idea. He also told her that he always preferred to play with the little girls in the neighborhood rather than the boys. I remember how deeply touched he was when he came home that day. She told him, "you're still my brother and I love you." Mike told her that it was up to her whether or not she told her husband, which she did, and he also was supportive. Mike's sister did have concerns about how I was handling the whole thing and knew that it must be difficult for me.

We each have children from previous marriages. Mike has a seventeen-year-old son who has not been told about the cross-dressing. I have a thirty-two-year-old daughter whom I told in the early months following the discovery, during the time of Mike's major depression. She was aware that something was going on. She could sense that I was upset about something, so I told her rather than leaving her to fear the worst. I was very proud of her. She told my husband that it didn't change the way she felt about him, that she loved him anyway. She told me that she'd be there if I needed to talk or vent.

My daughter doesn't live close by, and our visits are not as frequent as we would like, but the first time we visited after I told her, both she and my husband were nervous. When we got to her house, after the initial greetings both seemed to relax. This helped my husband greatly. We also gave her information to read so she would be informed about cross-dressing and gender dysphoria.

Mike and I have fun shopping for clothes and joking around. We have a great time together. I'll see something that I think he would like (as a female) and I'll buy it; somehow I've never had any problem in that area. Naturally, Mike needed an entire wardrobe—wig, breast forms, and other items to make him look more female. We enjoy shopping together and he enjoys purchasing items on the Internet. He is free to buy things he likes, within reason. At one of the Tri-Ess meetings a local gender-friendly wig store brought several wigs for the "girls" to try on and purchase. We went together one Saturday, and Mike tried on several and bought one. It was very expensive. I encouraged him to buy it since he looked so pretty in it and I could tell he loved it.

Mike and I are members of Tri-Ess and attend monthly meetings. I have had a difficult time recently with the Tri-Ess bylaws not being honored by some members of our chapter. For the comfort of the wives and the protection of the marriages, Tri-Ess is strictly an organization for heterosexual cross-dressers who are not going further, i.e., taking hormones or embarking on transition. I felt betrayed and angry when I found out that one of our officers was not only starting transition, but had also posted pictures of himself, en femme, on a Web site, with another of our members, and that they were representing themselves as being in relationship with each other, calling themselves "soul mates." I confronted the chapter officer whose behavior was contrary to Tri-Ess bylaws. It is important to me that the group remains true to its promises.

In February of 2003, Mike and I went on a Dignity Cruise with other cross-dressers and their partners. We had never gone out in public while Mike was cross-dressed, so this was completely new. It was my birthday present to Mike. During the early part of the cruise I felt very uncomfortable walking around with Mike while he was en femme. We were getting strange looks. Getting together in a daily group with the other wives and Peggy Rudd, the organizer, was very helpful for me, though. It was comforting to know that other wives had similar feelings.

Our relationship is going well now. I never would have believed I would heal and go on this way when I first learned Mike's secret. All marriages have obstacles. Cross-dressing does not have to make divorce inevitable. If both partners are willing to negotiate so that the needs of both are respected, then happiness can prevail.

Mike did not disclose his cross-dressing to Sally. Instead, he left clues around, which she found. In my clinical practice, cross-dressers whose part-

ners are not aware of the gender variance have told me that they find themselves being "careless." As we discuss their seeming inability to find the right
words and the right time they realize that the "carelessness" is more than
just carelessness. If their SOs confront them about the cross-dressing, they
do not have to bring it up themselves. I urge them to do so, however, since
the likelihood of a positive relational outcome is higher if they initiate disclosure.

Like so many partners, it was difficult for Sally to be sexual with Mike
when she first found out about his cross-dressing. She couldn't will herself to
"block out" awareness of Mike's female side. As I have often heard from
other SOs, Sally believed that if it was possible for her to continue to be attracted to Mike, something must be wrong with her. Some wives can get beyond this belief and others can't. Sally did, and at this point, not even Mike's
shaved body interferes with Sally's sexual attraction to him.

Sally's issues about her physical attractiveness seemed to be exacerbated by the discovery. She credits her personal therapy, in which she had
been engaged since prior to discovery, for helping her to regain the self-
esteem she initially lost when she found out about the cross-dressing.

Only the SO of a gender-variant person would wonder if her spouse or
partner is really wishing he himself were a woman when he looks at her with
desire in his eyes. Despite having grown beyond her difficulty being sexual
with Mike, Sally occasionally finds herself having this uncomfortable feeling.
What wife wouldn't prefer to know that her partner's desire is all about her,
rather than, at least in part, being about his wish that he were more like her?

Sally's difficulties with the behavior of some of her Tri-Ess chapter members are a textbook example of the reason why Tri-Ess has strict bylaws
about membership. I know from my gender-variant clients who come from all
over the southeastern United States that some Tri-Ess members are at least
bi-curious, and that perhaps an even greater number wish they could or intend some day to transition at least partially. I believe that Tri-Ess's bylaws
about heterosexual exclusivity and limitation to cross-dressing are for the
protection of wives and other partners who are uncomfortable *enough* with
the cross-dressing without being confronted with these other possibilities.

Sally has come an incredibly long way. She has moved beyond being
overwhelmed by feelings of betrayal and mistrust about Mike's secrecy. Realizing that hiding his cross-dressing from her had been motivated by shame
made a big difference to her. Sally sees herself as potentially able to remain
in relationship with Mike, even if he chooses to live as a woman full-time
some day.

A Dignity Cruise, what a gift! Peggy Rudd (see bibliography), author and
cross-dresser's wife, has been organizing these cruises within a cruise for
years. A vacation such as this is an opportunity for cross-dressers to dress
en femme in a safe, supportive, fun environment in which partners are welcome. Sally seems to have risen above her initial discomfort with Mike's
cross-dressing, rebuilt trust, and, with her spouse, created a respectful relationship.

Chapter 5

Jo and Cameron/Clarice

Whereas Sally had difficulty with her self-esteem when she discovered Mike's gender variance, Jo panicked when she found out about Cameron's cross-dressing. What concerned her most was what people would think. She was afraid that her family would find out and shun her, even take their children away.

I am the wife of a cross-dresser. Cameron and I have been married for nearly twenty-six years. We grew up just a few miles from each other in very small towns in rural Ohio. After my husband got out of the navy twelve years ago we returned to the area. Our two children are twenty-one and seventeen. Cameron is an electronics technician and I am a homemaker.

Cameron and I first noticed each other when I was just shy of fourteen and he was nineteen. He was in the army at the time, and home for a funeral. He asked about me and was warned off because of my age. Three years later, when he got out of the army, we began dating. A year after that, in 1979, when I graduated from high school, we were married.

Due to the job situation in our area, Cameron enlisted in the navy a year later. We spent six months in a commuter relationship, and then moved to Florida. I have always been a laid-back tomboy type. I had no girls to play with when I was growing up. My mother was never into makeup, etc., so I was a "natural" kind of girl. Cameron always wanted me to wear frilly, lacy, satin, stick-to-you, itchy things to bed. Not only was I not into that kind of lingerie, but here we were in Florida, in a tiny apartment with no air conditioning and I was pregnant and sick.

One day I snapped. I asked why he wanted me to be uncomfortable and miserable. He proceeded to tell me about how as a young teen his

Head Over Heels: Wives Who Stay with Cross-Dressers and Transsexuals
Published by The Haworth Press, Inc., 2007. All rights reserved.
doi:10.1300/5737_05

mother had dressed him as a girl for Halloween and it was a turn-on. He had then begun sneaking her things when he was at home alone for the sexual thrill. I looked him in the eye and said, "You did this as a kid and it caused you to be turned on by these things, right?" Something in my tone told him that if he wanted to keep his beloved wife and raise the baby I was carrying he better say yes, so he did.

Life went on for another three years. He was still in the navy and we were running around the world. Shortly after our fifth anniversary we had a crisis and we had to face some difficult issues. We spent a week crying and talking and barely sleeping while we tried to work the problems out. Finally, we had worked through the obvious issues that had been troubling us. We were standing in the kitchen and Cameron said, "I have to tell you something else." Don't ask what made me say it. Maybe it was the night that we were being silly and I'd made him wear pantyhose and I saw the effect it had on him. I just knew and I said, "You are still doing it, aren't you?" He lowered his eyes and softly said, "Yes."

My initial reaction was sheer panic. I didn't know what to do. We were living in a foreign country, 3,000 miles from home. It was hard not to take it personally. At times I blamed myself, thinking that he wouldn't cross-dress if I were woman enough for him. I also questioned his sexual orientation, but it really didn't make sense that he would be gay.

I was terrified that "big brother" would find out and we would be looking for some way for him to support us with a dishonorable discharge hanging over our heads. I also feared that our families would find out and shun us, or even try to take our children from us. I was afraid that Cameron would decide he was a woman and go off for surgery or something. I never doubted that he loved me, I was just concerned that he didn't really need me because he had "her."

I was very disturbed by Cameron having kept this from me for so long. I have *big* issues about lying and I felt that he had deceived me for all those years. Keeping it secret from the world to protect my children was very important to me. Privacy is always a problem when you have children. The girls were good about keeping it quiet for a long time.

I knew enough about the phenomenon to realize that it wasn't going to go away. He dressed for me one night, and it was the worst experience of both of our lives. I was shocked and he knew it and that hurt him. We struggled for thirteen years with this aspect of our lives. I bought him clothes, I made him clothes, I *let* him dress. We always incorporated this in the bedroom to some degree, sometimes more successfully than others, playing it by ear and never doing anything that made me uncomfortable. I encouraged him to meet with other cross-dressers, even attended some events with him.

I *thought* I was being a wonderfully accepting wife, but he knew I was only tolerating the dressing because I knew it wouldn't go away. My behavior was pushing him away. Finally, after thirteen years, things reached a crisis point and I nearly lost him.

I came to some conclusions in a big hurry. It wasn't that Cameron dressed that bothered me. I knew that this was a part of what made Cameron who he was: a kind, loving, giving man who treasured me; an empathic man who truly felt for other people's pain; in short, the best man I knew. What bothered me was what other people might think if they found out.

Suddenly it dawned on me that if what other people *might* think was the biggest problem with this, then it wasn't worth worrying about. This man was my prince. He was the person who was always there for me, the one who loved me despite my many faults. I was *not* going lose him. I am married to a cross-dresser and that's just the way it is.

This enlightenment came five and a half years ago. Since then we've had our ups and downs. There have been times when I would prefer that it just go away. I get tired of the overcrowded closets. Just because he is in the mood to dress on a particular day doesn't mean that I'm in the mood for him to dress. I guess sometimes my lack of enthusiasm on these occasions shows through. Yes, we still have disputes about the dressing. Sometimes it's a matter of just not hearing each other accurately. Cameron can be sensitive about any perceived slight.

The problem is that if I express any negativity about his cross-dressing Cameron will withdraw. For example, for a long while he wore makeup constantly. I told him that I would prefer that he not wear it all the time. Since he could get away with wearing it to work I wondered if he could leave it off when we were going out together. Since that day, Cameron has only worn makeup twice when he was not fully dressed. We have lots of miscommunications like that.

There was a time when finances were a big deal for us. I thoroughly resented those little pink books, as I called them. They were only a few pages in length, poorly printed, and they cost more than a real novel that we could all read and enjoy. Nowadays Cameron reads stuff online at Fictionmania and other sites of that kind. This was a great compromise for us.

Cameron has never just gone out and blown money on his dressing, although I do tease him about his expensive pantyhose from Silkies. We budget for trips to cross-dressing functions, like Be-All or Paradise in the Poconos. He saves up for big purchases like boobs or corsets. As far as clothes go, we rarely buy anything for anyone in this household unless it's on sale. If we are going through the sale racks and see something for Cameron's alter ego Clarice, we buy it. We find shoes at clearance sales and sometimes more expensive things are purchased for his birthday or Christmas.

Sometimes I'm envious. Cameron can wear things I can't wear because I'm so short. He has beautiful long hair and mine is just a pain. He worries less about what people think of him. I have pretty low self-esteem and I need everyone to think well of me. I wish I could be as nonchalant about myself as Cameron is about himself.

Our daughters are aware of Cameron's cross-dressing. The oldest was gradually introduced to this after I found out about it; the younger girl has always known. She was born a year after I found out. Her dad would get up to tend to her in the night wearing a nightgown. Both girls have shared this with trusted friends who have had no reaction.

We pick and choose those we tell very carefully. We don't share information about Cameron's cross-dressing indiscriminately in our community. This is a major redneck area. We are surrounded by farms and farmers.

We will never tell some members of our families. My mother knows. We told one of my brothers and his wife. One of Cameron's sisters and her children know. We have told a few friends outside the cross-dressing community. Many of the people Cameron works with now are aware that he cross-dresses. So far, there have been no rejections. One of our neighbors has seen Cameron dressed. Her husband chooses to ignore it. His words are, "Keep it at your house and I have no problem with it."

Cameron's sister doesn't want to see him dressed up, but says it's his business what he does with his life. She'd thought our secretive weekends involved swinging. My sister-in-law (my brother's wife) and I were talking about some other topics, and I just came out with it to her. She and my brother had also attached a more sinister meaning to our weekends away—they too thought we were into mate swapping!

Although it doesn't bring me great pleasure to have a cross-dressing husband, I have learned to enjoy the time we spend together as "two girls." I've done things I would never have done otherwise, gone places I never would have gone, and met people I never would have met. Cameron is a wonderful man and a terrific husband. I wouldn't trade him for anyone.

When Cameron first disclosed to Jo that as a teenager he had cross-dressed "for a sexual thrill," Jo seemed not to be ready to hear that he was still interested in engaging in such behavior. Denial may have prevented her from recognizing that Cameron may have wanted her to wear the kind of sexy, feminine lingerie to bed that she found uncomfortable because he was still interested in cross-dressing and wanted to experience lingerie vicariously through her. In a clinical context I have observed SOs whose transgender partners manifest a desire to live fantasies through them in this manner feeling used, e.g., experiencing a disturbing blurring of identity boundaries, and even feeling violated.

Jo panicked when Cameron told her that he was still cross-dressing. Many partners experience fears similar to Jo's: she was afraid that family members would find out, reject them, and possibly even take their children away; she feared that Cameron would receive a dishonorable discharge from the military; she was concerned that Cameron might decide that he was actually a women and would feel a need to have SRS (sex reassignment surgery).

Some wives blame themselves, as did Jo, who described herself as "tomboyish." Self-blaming wives often think that if they were the kind of women their husbands wanted, perhaps their husbands wouldn't cross-dress. Clearly, though, being transgendered is not brought on by anything lacking in a partner. It's vital that wives understand that gender variance resides solely in the transgendered person.

Jo and Cameron have chosen to let their children and certain select others in on their secret rather than excluding them from knowledge of Cameron's cross-dressing. Some couples mistakenly believe that knowing this about their dad would be unhealthy for all children in all families. That position suggests internalized transphobia, that is, shame about gender variance that has not been worked through. Whereas safety concerns sometimes make selective authenticity necessary, it is healthy that Jo and Cameron allowed their daughters to disclose their father's cross-dressing to trusted friends, yet hard to believe that in that "major redneck area" those friends had no reaction whatsoever.

Jo acknowledges that she would prefer that her husband not be a cross-dresser. However, when she realized that she, like so many significant others of gender-variant people, was more bothered by what other people might think if they found out than by her own personal response, she began to move from tolerance to true acceptance. Cameron's many precious characteristics and her love for him motivated her to go out of her way to nurture her marriage.

Chapter 6

Shelly and Marv/Allie

Shelly was concerned that Marv's need for cross-dressing would escalate, and that he resented her for being a "real woman." She had difficulty with the necessity to keep this secret, to monitor herself, thus decreasing her sense of spontaneity in communicating with people to whom they had not disclosed. But, similar to Jo, she was concerned about what people would think.

Early in our marriage we moved around a bit and had three sons. Marv changed jobs several times. He was in the fast food business, and then he went back into construction. After a trip north for a class reunion Marv felt the need to move back home. He said that he wanted to get the kids back into decent schools. I didn't want to go. For the first time in my life I had a very good job, paying an excellent salary for a female. But Marv won. Thinking back, I wonder whether he may have thought that if we moved his urge to cross-dress would stop. I have a lot of "afterthoughts" nowadays (now that I know). Well, the move didn't make it stop. He became very depressed and easily upset; he was like a ticking bomb. Then came the Internet, Tri-Ess, and the Internet list. To top it off, our town looks like a Norman Rockwell painting. It's beautiful; it's also Peyton Place. Everyone knows everyone's business.

I believe that as people mature their identities are still forming. You know, like when you hear older people speak up? They get to the point where they don't care what people think anymore. They figure, what the hell, I'll just say it! Or they're tired of feeling like they're being run over, and they speak up for themselves. It's like they're finally getting comfortable in their own shoes. I'm getting there myself. I'm only forty-three, but what the hell! I'm just saying what I think and what I feel. I'm not afraid of my age, or of who I am. My shoes are

Head Over Heels: Wives Who Stay with Cross-Dressers and Transsexuals
Published by The Haworth Press, Inc., 2007. All rights reserved.
doi:10.1300/5737_06

starting to get comfortable. Hey, I got smart; I'm wearing flats! Beats me why cross-dressers like wearing those high heels. It's beyond me. But in retrospect, they're still going through adolescence. Geeze! Aren't we always waiting for the men to mature? This alone sets us back years in the natural process.

. My husband may think differently, but I do have a sexual identity. Actually, I'm really clear about it. I am a woman, and he is a man. I do not allow him to cross-dress in the bedroom. I married a man; therefore I will sleep with a man. I once told him that if I wanted to go to bed with someone who had breasts, long hair, long nails, and so forth, I'd find myself a woman . . . a real woman!

Despite my confidence about my sexual identity, self-esteem is an iffy issue for me. Sometimes I have it, and sometimes I just can't find any. In spite of that I don't believe that my self-esteem issues have anything to do with Marv being a cross-dresser.

I have some discomforts that seem to be related to Marv's cross-dressing, or to personality traits that are tied in with his cross-dressing. For example, Marv might ask, "Why did you polish your nails?" instead of saying, "Your nails look nice." If he compliments me on a particular article of clothing, I wonder, is he really complimenting me, or is he wondering if it'll fit him? Sometimes I don't know whether I'm coming or going!

Marv and I have some problems with communication. Sometimes it seems that any time I say something negative about Marv he exaggerates the significance of what I'm saying and reacts dramatically. He says things like, "I give up," or "I'll never dress again." Where will that get him? Further back than when we started to make progress. As for me, I won't be silenced. I have to feel free to speak up when something bothers me. It's hard seeing someone you love struggle for self-acceptance. I used to feel this need to fix it all and make it better. But I can't. I love Marv so much, but self-acceptance is something that he'll have to find on his own.

A few years ago, Marv kept me on a pedestal. I remember times when he would profess his love for me openly right on our Internet list for cross-dressers and their wives. Now he rarely speaks. It's all gotten twisted. Sometimes I feel like he resents me for being a woman—like he's jealous because I can be a real woman and he can't. After a cross-dressing event, he used to feel so comfortable with himself and he'd be a much happier person. That happiness would stay with him for days upon days. Now, there's not enough time to be "her." That concerns me. What does that mean?

Our family is pretty unusual. Our sons are twenty-four, twenty-two, and nineteen. Our children are growing up and have their own thoughts and values. Some of them deal with their dad's cross-dressing well, and some of them don't want to deal with it at all. That makes it even more complicated.

We were finally blessed with our daughter, the Queen of the Land, who is eight. It's like having two separate families. Family #1 doesn't like to babysit family #2. I don't like the secrecy that seems necessary every time we go to a cross-dressing event and have to get a sitter. And people get so nosey! Where are you going? What did you do? "I could tell ya, but then I'd have to kill ya," I say to some of them. It makes them forget their question. Also, if by chance I do meet someone at a meeting that I find absolutely fascinating, I can't share it with anyone. It's a secret. Damn secrets anyway. We have learned that once a man comes out of the closet to his wife, he puts her *in* the closet.

I didn't used to have any resentment about Allie (Marv's name when cross-dressed), but I do now. Maybe it's because I'm not so naive, or I'm more mature. At times I feel that cross-dressing is taking over our lives. Some of our dear friends have gone by the wayside. When you're in relationship with a cross-dresser, you can share only so much with your non-cross-dressing friends. There are friends you can't burden with your secret, friends you can't trust with your secret. I do resent that "secret." It's preventing me from getting more comfortable in my own shoes. It puts my mouth in alert status. Not only is Marv/Allie living two separate lives, I am too. And how must he feel? It's hard, really hard.

I've actually gotten some pleasure from being married to a cross-dresser. I've learned a lot. I've seen a lot. I've met some wonderful people whom I wouldn't have met otherwise. I've made some life-long friends. My husband and I have had some personal enjoyment, some real thought-provoking conversations. Also, when Marv's dressed, he likes to assume the more womanly duties of the household. That gives me a mini vacation! Now if I could just figure out how to get him to do it without the skirt!

Shelly raises several common issues. She is concerned about how much Marv's need to cross-dress seems to be escalating. Some SOs notice that what used to please and satisfy their partners eventually ceases to meet their partners' needs. This can seem similar to the way tolerance develops to, for instance, pain medication, so that if a person uses the medicine long-term they may need increasing dosages to offer the same relief.

Similar to Shelly, some wives become concerned that their husbands resent them for being natal women when they can't be. The suspicion often exists that their husbands wish they could be "real women" and are envious. It's best that wives not sit silently with fears or assumptions. Instead such concerns must be discussed and resolved, alone, if the couple communicates well, or if they don't, with the assistance of a professional.

Over time Shelly has become quite accepting of Marv's cross-dressing, although at first she wished he would stop. She also seems to have developed the capacity for self-validation. Shelly is obviously a woman with a sense of humor who has the courage to be true to herself, speaking her mind and expressing herself with great authenticity.

Chapter 7

Bernadette and Gene

Bernadette discovered that Gene was a cross-dresser in a truly shocking way. Whereas Shelly resents the way the cross-dressing has taken over their lives, what made Bernadette angry was not to have been given the information about Gene's gender variance prior to marriage—information she needed in order to make an informed decision about continuing the relationship. Similar to so many SOs, she's concerned about the possible progression of Gene's gender-variant feelings and desires.

Gene comes from a family of ten and I am one of the middle children of a large family—one that takes more than two hands to count. I didn't have an easy childhood; psychologists would probably define my family as dysfunctional now, but I'm not sure they had coined that phrase back then. I made it through to adulthood and I try to be a nice person as I go through life.

Gene and I got married in 1998. This is my second marriage. The first lasted twenty years. Finally, I could no longer put up with someone who was extremely controlling and cheated on me to boot. We did have two beautiful children, both of whom are now out living on their own, and doing pretty well. My son lives about a thousand miles away, so I don't get to see him often. My daughter lives about thirty miles away, and I see her a couple of times a month.

I'm particularly proud of my son since his last visit. He has gone through that phase people often do, between ages twenty-five and thirty, when a lightning bolt hits and they finally realize that they really are adults and it is time to start acting like it! I mention this because I have something else to relate about him later in this little tale.

I chose to stay home and take care of my kids rather than putting them in day care. It was tough financially, but I believe it turned out to be better for us all. In a sense, we had fun "growing up together." When my daughter started kindergarten, I started college. It took me

Head Over Heels: Wives Who Stay with Cross-Dressers and Transsexuals
Published by The Haworth Press, Inc., 2007. All rights reserved.
doi:10.1300/5737_07

49

seven years to get through but I did so with flying colors. I was divorced by the time I finished college. The only really hard time I had with my kids was for a couple of years after the divorce. I did not, nor will I ever, tell them why I got the divorce. He was a bad husband, not a bad father. Suffice it to say I was the one who was blamed by the children for a few years. Somehow they got over that.

After I graduated I got a position that, over the past ten years, has developed into a job I really like. I train people to use computers, write lots and lots of documentation, and create multimedia instructional materials that are distributed over our local network as well as the Web.

In 2000, two years after Gene and I got married, I was diagnosed with a neurological disorder. Gene's response to my illness was not good. In fact, it was really, really, really bad. You would have thought that I had chosen to get sick just to cause him grief and to be a pain in his you-know-what. Medically, however, I persevered, going for many months with nary a problem. I have to stay cool, calm, collected, and make sure I get my beauty sleep in order to remain asymptomatic.

Before Gene and I married we lived together for about a year. During that year I found a suitcase in the basement with a bunch of women's clothes in it. Of course I was furious that he would dare to store some other woman's clothes in my house, and when I asked about it, he did not respond. It was a difficult time. Eventually things got better, but he never did address the issue. The clothes simply "disappeared," or so I thought.

About a year and a half after we married, Gene complained for a few weeks that his T-shirt drawer was too full and he needed some more space. One Sunday afternoon, when he was out, I thought I would surprise him. I cleaned out one of my drawers, and started moving his T-shirts over.

At the bottom of the drawer there was a videotape with the names Gene and Cindy written on the side. Cindy was a woman with whom Gene lived years ago. I figured it must be a tape of events like July Fourth picnics and such. Since I had never seen Cindy, curiosity got the better of me and I put the tape into the VCR to watch. The surprise was on me that day! It was Gene, in all his glory, in various cross-dressed states, in numerous outfits, in numerous locations of his house.

I was shocked. I felt like I'd been sucker punched. I was scared, confused, angry, and disturbed. *My god,* I thought, *I hope this is a response to his breaking up with her and not something he does on a regular basis. Geez, this is just too bizarre for me to deal with! What did I do, marry a wacko?*

I was angry as hell because I felt that at the very least I should have been told before our marriage. I got out of one marriage because of lack of communication and secrets and deception. I had the right to the information I needed in order to choose whether I wanted to be married to a cross-dresser; that decision should not have been made for me!

During the next week or so, whenever there was no one around the house, I screamed and screamed at the top of my lungs. I thought I must have married a real weirdo who didn't even have the common courtesy or guts to let me know about his propensities in life. I had a very sore throat by the end of the week.

I didn't say anything to him that day when he got home. I needed some time to let the reality settle in, and I also wanted to do some research. The next day, I looked at the video again and then when I was supposed to be working, I spent the whole time researching the topic of cross-dressing. Since I work at a college, I have access to a lot of information.

What kept coming up time and again was the fact that heterosexual cross-dressers have a tendency to be absolutely committed to the relationship with their wife or significant other. Since I already had one failed marriage due to a husband's lack of commitment, that particular fact about cross-dressers intrigued me. I decided that I would stick it out with Gene until I found out more about the topic, and that at the very least I should give him a chance to talk with me about the whole thing.

That evening, after dinner, I said, "You know, when I found that suitcase with all the women's clothes in it, I had no idea that they were actually yours." We talked a bit and decided that it was an important issue that we needed to discuss, and that it would take time to get everything sorted out. Over the next few months, we talked often, almost daily, and I believe that we both felt a sense of camaraderie that we had never felt before. Our relationship was better than it ever had been before, or than it has been since during those first few months after I found out.

After a few weeks we started getting our wires crossed and our conversations went haywire. That's one reason why I decided to start writing things down. It was my effort to help us stay on track and to help Gene, who can be very forgetful, to remember the things he had said previously.

About a month after I found out we had a huge misunderstanding regarding my suggestion that we seek counseling. Gene thought I was saying that he needed to be "fixed," which was not what I meant. Basically, I wanted some help in learning to deal with the cross-dressing and I believed at that time (and still do) that Gene needed help in dealing with years and years of shame and guilt. I realized that it was important that in dealing with this "thing that he does" that I never hurt or embarrass him. After a while I also made a request: not to be put in a position where I am publicly embarrassed or shamed. Although I understand that it is impossible to absolutely guarantee this, I thought some steps could be taken.

Cross-dressing is not something that I feel is gross, awful, or disgusting, but it was bizarre to me then, and it still is. When I asked Gene what this thing was to him, he replied, "Private." To me, this whole phenomenon moved out of the private realm on the day he said "I do" to me. And if not then, at the very least the first day he started borrowing my stuff, which he still does without my permission despite the boundary I've set.

I know that Gene was anxious about our relationship, because he repeatedly referred to losing everything, implying that our relationship would not work out in the long run. I wished that I could help him change this attitude. I didn't know what to say or do that would demonstrate my absolute commitment to him, our love, and our life.

As Gene's greatest champion, and the wife and lover of his choosing, given the circumstances as I understood them, I didn't think it was too much for me to ask that we explore all possibilities together so that we could make choices together that would contribute to our having a long and happy life together. I hoped that we could accomplish that without making either of us feel stupid or unreasonable.

I worked very hard at having a clean slate, without judgment or prejudice. I figured that with Gene's help I could write whatever I wanted on it, but he seemed to be attributing the attitudes and prejudices of other people from his past to me.

We spent the next several months going through this big, recurring question-and-answer session. All the while I felt like I was going to fall apart. It was like pulling teeth to get any information out of Gene. On my own, I did a lot of research on cross-dressing. It would actually be quite an interesting phenomenon to look at if I was not so intimately involved.

My health problems arose again, probably because of stress. I have had a number of episodes since I found out about his CDing. Over time, I've become better able to deal with my condition, and I'm having fewer problems. I've been working on figuring out how I can look at my husband all decked out like a woman (sort of, anyway) without it causing me so much emotional disturbance.

I had an overwhelming sense that something was missing, or that Gene was leaving something out of the picture. I am still terrified of being duped once again, like I was by my first husband. I really don't want to go through the experience of feeling like a stupid, naive idiot who refuses to see reality even when it smacks me in the face repeatedly. I've realized that I'm petrified of the unknown.

What I know is that Gene is a man who dresses in women's clothing occasionally. What I don't know is how often he has thoughts that would be considered to be "female." I don't know whether being a man is essential for him. I'm concerned about what the "typical" progression of cross-dressing is, where he fits in, and where he intends to go with it. I honestly don't know how important all of this is to Gene or how pervasive is it.

Sometimes I think the cross-dressing is rather selfish, sort of like a kid on the playground saying "I am going to play by myself." I believe that he and I definitely have a responsibility, individually and to each other, to consider the possible consequences of our actions. What are the consequences for each of us in the short and long term? What if he has a car accident while he's dressed? What might happen if Gene does not dress? Should I see Gene dressed? What are the possible consequences of that? So many questions have gone through my mind.

I felt as though I was going through a massive, unrelenting bombardment of my brain. I tried to document this process through writing, and then expressed all my thoughts, fears, and feelings to Gene. What I didn't know was what he was going through, what was next, where we'd go from here.

I gave a lot of thought to what I needed: being in control of my own actions and of my own life; the ability to express myself without re-crimination; to take a valuable, and valued, part in a relationship; and to achieve goals that seem worthwhile to me and are perceived by others as worthwhile.

I asked Gene to consider why he had this need to disassociate himself. I wondered why "Gene" is not allowed to have these wonderful feelings that the feminine aspect of him has, what enables "her" to have them, and whether there was anything that he could do to better enable, or allow, "Gene" himself to experience them.

At the end of June 2001, I learned about the CDSO (Crossdressers' Significant Others) list online. I joined for a short while. I received over 975 messages from the list that dealt with cross-dressing! I was overwhelmed, but it was a great relief to find other women in the same predicament, and it was a good place for me to vent. The best thing about the list was finding out about the ninth annual SPICE conference. And, even though I found out just a week or so before it actually started, I managed to get both myself and Gene to Cleveland for the conference.

I began to understand a lot about the cross-dressing intellectually, although continuing to have a difficult time processing it emotionally. When I think about Gene's cross-dressing I find it quite disturbing. Since there are so many facets to my reaction I have a hard time sorting them out so that I can tackle them one at a time. Often I've become almost catatonic trying to deal with this intense new aspect of my life.

Gene takes hours to get dressed. He goes the whole route, from tying up the dangling part to toenail polish. He has a really cheap wig that looks pretty sad. No matter what he does to get the special look he desires he still looks like Gene the carpenter, hands and all. Since he likes to get this total look, and because it takes so long, he can't do it often. Six months after I found out I had only seen him dressed six times. Thank God for small favors! When he's ready, looking just the way he wants to look, he changes his clothing—over and over again. I can't believe the amount of underwear the dude has.

One small part that really bugs me is my husband having prettier underwear than I have! When I mentioned that to Gene, he said that we'd fix that. The following Saturday we spent most of the day buying some very nice underwear for me. Then, of course, he felt compelled to dress, and wanted to try on some of my new stuff. Unfortunately we are close to the same size. It pissed me off; I mean, here we were supposed to be doing something for me, and we wound up in *his* fantasy land. And when we go there, *everything* is about him.

Don't they get it how ridiculous they look? Very few men can actually pass as beautiful women. Heck, most women are not truly beautiful—we are just passable—so why do men think it works for them?

The first time I saw my husband get dressed—I got him to show me the whole ritual—I was shaking in my boots from all the disturbing aspects and trying real hard not to crack up and roll on the floor at the same time. I don't know that I'll ever get past the urge to laugh. In a way it's like when my kids were small and they would say the most ridiculous things in a very serious way.

I got the book *My Husband Wears My Clothes* (Rudd, 1999). In fact, Gene read it himself. I am also going to check into the *Brain Sex* book (Moir and Jessel, 1991) that was mentioned on the LISTSERV. But you know what? I really don't want this CDing to overtake my life and it seems like it has—it's become much more central than I want it to be. At least he doesn't have a femme name. He says he can't think of a female version of Gene that he likes—another one of God's little favors to me.

Gene asked me if he could read the mail from the list. My first reaction was no, but then it occurred to me that I wouldn't be here if it were not for him, and maybe it would be good for him to see the varying opinions and see what some women have to put up with.

Since Gene asked and many of the women on the list felt that it was not necessarily a bad idea, I let him read the list messages starting from the time when I signed on. When he was finished, he said he had to go to bed. He did have a smile on his face, so I'm hoping that what he learned will be productive for both of us. It was probably nice for him to find out that other people have the same issues that we do!

The one person I have told about Gene's cross-dressing is my son. I really needed to talk with someone before I busted a gut. His immediate response was, "Mom, are you aware that cross-dressing is usually a result of child abuse?" And I told him that I'd read that, and other conflicting research as well. Then there was about a thirty-second delay, he took a deep breath, and said (and I will never forget it), "Mom, I hope that you can learn to appreciate, and more important, love this very special aspect of his personality." What a great kid! I am think-

ing that I did a good job as a mom. Now, I guess, whether I would
have chosen it or not, I have to figure out how to do a good job of being a cross-dresser's wife.

Bernadette found out about Gene's cross-dressing in a very disturbing
way. It's one thing to discover clothes or a Web site trail, but it's shocking on a
whole different level for one's initial exposure to her husband's gender variance to be seeing him live or even on video cross-dressed. Such an upsetting mode of discovery contributes to the intensity of a partner's initial reaction, and, in many cases, to ongoing difficulty with her distressing feelings
about it. This is particularly the case if the partner has a traumatic early history, which I suspect Bernadette did, given her mention of her dysfunctional
family of origin, and her betrayal by her first husband's infidelity. Bernadette
seems inured to being treated poorly. I found her description of Gene's reaction to her illness disturbing.

Similar to Bernadette, wives are often irate about not having been told
prior to getting involved, or at least before marriage. After all, even if disclosures are only on a "need-to-know" basis, gender variance is certainly
something a person needs to know in order to make an informed decision
about whether to marry someone. But, as I have discussed previously, many
transgendered people seem to be unable to disclose prior to marriage.

Amazingly, Bernadette bided her time, researching cross-dressing prior
to revealing to Gene that she had seen the videotape, affording herself
some measure of control. Two things seemed to open the door to healing.
First, Bernadette found in her research information about cross-dressers
tending to be very committed to their partners. Second, she and Gene began communicating regularly about this issue, which opened the door to a
new sense of connection for them.

Having been deceived by Gene initially, and by her first husband as well,
Bernadette was exquisitely sensitive to the possibility that Gene was keeping other secrets from her. Similar to many natal women in relationship with
cross-dressers, she is, quite naturally, concerned about where Gene might
be going in his gender exploration. She worries about where he will ultimately find himself on the transgender spectrum and whether he might
eventually **"go TS."**

She is anxious about behaviors of Gene's that she sees as thoughtless,
such as the possibility of having a car accident while dressed, or risking exposure in their community. She also complains, as do many wives, about the
self-centeredness that her husband displays. Bernadette again went
through a difficult time when she and Gene began miscommunicating a lot,
and she suggested counseling, which Gene misunderstood and refused.
I've noticed that SOs refuse joint counseling urged by transpeople more often than the reverse.

Bernadette tends to be quite introspective, and she is aware that she has
a need for control over her life. She finds it difficult to achieve that in her relationship with Gene, but has tried nonetheless via various means. She wrote
in her journal, and she expressed her feelings to Gene, but she couldn't

seem to get him to reciprocate. She joined an online support group and even got herself and Gene to a SPICE conference, where she learned more about cross-dressing and gained understanding of Gene. Although Bernadette's son asserts that child abuse causes cross-dressing, I know of no research that supports a causal link between abuse and gender variance.

Bernadette has worked very hard at avoiding judgment and prejudice. She has tried to communicate to her spouse her absolute commitment to him, their love, and their life together. She has put great effort into acceptance of Gene's cross-dressing and dealing with her fears. But again, this seems like a relationship in which the significant other is carrying more than her share of the responsibility for ensuring the relationship's well-being and stability.

Chapter 8

Joan and Don/Lucy

Joan has coped with Don's cross-dressing for a very long time. Her primary concern was that her role in the marriage would be usurped. Her acceptance of this activity as part of their lives was likely fostered by Don's having voluntarily disclosed that he is a cross-dresser. Joan does not share Bernadette's concerns about the possible progression of Don's transgender feelings and does not seem to be holding much anger. The latter is also probably related to Don having disclosed rather than Joan having discovered the gender variance, and the length of time that Joan has known about it.

Don and I have been happily married for forty-seven years and coping with cross-dressing for forty-four of those years. When Don first told me about his need to cross-dress, my first reaction was, "Just leave *my* things alone." I hoped never to hear more on the subject, and certainly never expected it to become such a major factor in our lives.

It was tough during the beginning years because there was very little information on the subject and I kept trying to put my head in the sand, hoping it would go away. We had years of discussion, going round and round in circles. Since we had no one in whom we could confide, we had to rely on each other.

When I realized that this issue was here to stay, our discussions became more of a two-way street. I don't ever remember not being willing to talk about the subject; rather, I got tired of not having any substantive answers. We had to find our own way, and it took many years to find our comfort zones, but never did I say he could not cross-dress, and when I saw him it bothered me that he didn't always look his best. Consequently, as money and time permitted, we began getting Lucy, Don's femme self, shaped up.

Even today when I'm tired, hungry, or just emotionally worn out and Lucy wants to emerge, my reaction is "no." However, give me a little time to rest or eat and my whole perspective will change. Then I

Head Over Heels: Wives Who Stay with Cross-Dressers and Transsexuals
Published by The Haworth Press, Inc., 2007. All rights reserved.
doi:10.1300/5737_08

become a whole lot more receptive. As Don says, it's all a matter of timing, and neither of us always gets it right.

I don't see much difference in personality, as such, when Don is in Lucy persona. However, his voice and gestures are softer and I can get his attention much more quickly when he is dressed as Lucy. People have asked me whether Lucy's feminine gestures and voice cause problems in our relationship. They do not. I'm glad that when dressed as Lucy, my partner's gestures and voice are feminine. However, when it comes to romantic moments, I'm glad that Lucy can go away and leave me with Don. He's very good at knowing when I need Don and when Lucy can come forth. Plus, we discuss all our outings well ahead of time so we know exactly what we are going to do.

When we are out together and Don is dressed as Lucy, sometimes people say that they don't know which one of us is the genetic female. I'm always very glad of this because that means Lucy is doing a good job projecting her femme persona. I also feel good that all the time we spent helping her learn how to express herself is paying off.

Although Lucy does a good job projecting her femme persona, I don't think it is possible for her to have any idea how a genetic female feels. She tries, but when we were growing up, society maintained a gap between male and female, keeping us so far apart that it was difficult even to try to comprehend the others' feelings. Now we both try to understand each other, and I think we come close, but can never fully hit the mark.

When we are out together as two women I really enjoy being with Lucy. It's as if we're best friends (which we are). She has some great ideas for things to do and places to go. There are times, however, when I really do enjoy being escorted by Don. Lucy is very good at letting this happen frequently with me and with our children and grandchildren. They enjoy his being their buddy, mentor, and friend.

Over all I have come to enjoy Lucy, even if at times I wish we did not have to deal with issues related to cross-dressing. But if there were a pill he could take to make it go away, I would *not* want Don to take it because it would mean a change in his personality, and I don't think I would like the person who was left.

I would not like Lucy cross-dressing full-time at all. I'm concerned that we would miss out on a lot of wonderful times with our children and grandchildren. I believe that some of our friends might not be the least bit understanding.

A lot of people misunderstand cross-dressing. Some people say that men who wear female clothing are making a mockery of femininity. I don't agree with this in the least! I think a cross-dresser is only dressing to express his feminine side. This is something that our society has denied, and a cross-dresser needs to express it in the best possible way.

To me, cross-dressing is both a blessing and a curse. When we were younger and had no one to talk with except each other it seemed as if this was a curse. I worried that if he did not **pass,** we would be discovered and we would lose everything. As time has passed and we have made a lot of wonderful friends in the CD community, Don's cross-dressing has turned into a beautiful blessing. At this point I can say that I truly enjoy Lucy as much as Don.

I have no sense that our relationship has suffered in the least because of cross-dressing. In fact, I think ours has actually been strengthened as we have struggled with the cross-dressing issue. We have become closer to each other, and have learned lessons from the cross-dressing experience that have helped us in all aspects of our lives. I only wish I had been able to relax and enjoy Don's cross-dressing sooner. Perhaps I would even have helped our sons to acknowledge and accept it sooner.

I also wish we had told our sons about the cross-dressing sooner. I think it would have been easier on the entire family not to have the "big secret" in our family for such a long time. We have always been a family that felt that communication between us is very important, so it was difficult for me not to be able to be up front about their father's cross-dressing. But there was no help out there for us and we had no idea how to tell the boys or help them to understand. So, we just kept putting it off. We finally decided they needed to know, and when each one decided to leave home for college and jobs Don took them aside and explained how cross-dressing affected him and our lives. It was a bit surprising to us that each one independently told their dad that it was no problem for him, that it was Dad's thing and they understood.

However, both of them said that they would prefer that their future wives not know, and both of them said that they had, and still have, no desire to see or meet Lucy. Furthermore, each of them said that if they decide to tell their wives they will let us know if it was to be in the open or not. We both think the wives know, but we do not broach the subject—it is never discussed—because we have agreed with the boundaries they set and they have not changed them.

There was never a change in our relationship with the boys or with their families. Both of our sons are still very close to their dad and hold him in high regard. They come to him for advice, ideas, and information. Because they do, so do our grandsons. The one person who the grandsons always interview for school projects is Don.

I think we have a very special relationship with both our sons and daughters-in-law. We communicate openly in all areas except this. I wish the cross-dressing did not have to be ignored, but I will not upset the balance by trying to force anything out in the open. We have complete access to our grandsons and have a healthy relationship with them, so for now I am content to leave it alone and not upset the apple cart.

I'll tell you a funny story. On a recent two-week cruise, Don, who is good at passing as a woman, presented as Lucy the whole time. As far as we know we were the only CD and wife on the ship. My only regret was that as we were, ostensibly, two women, we were not able to take advantage of the excellent dance music that was being played each evening after dinner. Several times one of the hosts who the cruise line had hired to dance with the unescorted ladies asked Lucy to dance, but each time she very sweetly declined.

Then one time, when we were visiting with another lady, the host who had been showing such an interest in Lucy appeared, took Lucy's hand, and said, "Please dance with me." Lucy again graciously declined. The lady sitting with us said, "Go ahead and dance with him; he's an excellent dancer." I couldn't help myself. I too encouraged Lucy to dance. I only wish I'd had a camera with me. The dance was a rumba. Lucy does not know how to rumba, nor had she ever wanted to dance with a man. So I will leave to your imagination the scene on the dance floor. I still quake with laughter every time I think about it. It was my small revenge.

Don disclosed his cross-dressing to Joan when they had been married for just a year. This relatively early disclosure, and the information coming to light via disclosure rather than discovery, certainly contributed to Joan's ongoing comfort with Don and his femme self, Lucy, whom she sees as her girlfriend. However, more than forty years ago, when Joan first learned Don's secret, a paucity of available information on the subject existed. No means were available for Joan to educate herself.

One regret Joan mentions is that they did not disclose the cross-dressing to their sons earlier. This would have made it unnecessary for them to have a big secret from the children, and instead the whole family could have been in on this private aspect of Dad's life. Then they could have been a family with a secret.

Joan mentions an issue that troubles many cross-dressers' partners. When Don first told her about his cross-dressing, she said, "Just leave *my* things alone." Partners' attitudes about cross-dressers using their clothing, jewelry, and makeup often go beyond possessiveness or territoriality. Their feelings extend into the sensitive area of identity. No one wants their identity appropriated. Some SOs are even sensitive about household tasks. Whereas most women would be delighted if a partner showed any interest in doing domestic chores, the wives and girlfriends of gender-variant natal males may feel as though their feminine roles are being usurped.

Joan and Don do not bring the cross-dressing into the bedroom. Joan is clear that when it comes to physical intimacy she wants Don, not Lucy. People of their generation, given the era's tendency toward socialization into strict gender roles, are less likely to feel free to experiment with gender fluidity in their sexual lives.

Admittedly, Joan wished Don weren't a cross-dresser in the early years, and now sometimes wishes she didn't have to deal with issues related to cross-dressing. However, even if she could snap her fingers and make the cross-dressing go away, Joan would not do so at this point. She reports that she actually enjoys Lucy as a girlfriend and takes pleasure in the time they spend together. She believes that cross-dressing has brought her and Don closer to each other and that they've learned lessons that have helped them in all aspects of their lives.

Chapter 9

Julie and Dan/Diana

Julie had a more difficult time with the disclosure than did Joan. When Dan first told Julie about his cross-dressing, she was terrified. Hit hard by the news, she had difficulty sleeping and got sick. Dan reassured her, and as she experienced his respect for her limits she felt that she was regaining some sense of control.

I am the significant other (SO) of a cross-dresser. I have been married to Dan for a little over forty years. We have two daughters, both grown. I have known about my husband's cross-dressing since 1987. At that time one daughter was in college, the other in high school.

When Dan first told me about his cross-dressing, my reaction was, "Are you gay?" (And I never knew?). He said "No, I just like to dress like a woman." My second question was, "Do you want to be a woman?" Again, he said, "No, I just want to dress like a woman."

So began many conversations between us. I was, as are most SOs, bewildered, puzzled, embarrassed, and most of all terrified, as I did not know what this meant and I wondered whether my husband was out of control. I couldn't sleep, and I got sick! I told him that I could not go on this way and he promised that he would do nothing without my permission. That helped me to regain a semblance of my life, and I was able to sleep without worrying that he was going to go out gallivanting while I was asleep.

With little to go on at that time, I remembered that I had seen a show on cross-dressing on television. The show was very well done, and I remembered that I had learned that there was no cure for cross-dressing. I wrote to the show for a tape in order to obtain information on Tri-Ess, a national organization for cross-dressers and their families, which had been featured on that talk show.

Head Over Heels: Wives Who Stay with Cross-Dressers and Transsexuals
Published by The Haworth Press, Inc., 2007. All rights reserved.
doi:10.1300/5737_09

In time the tape came, and we wrote to Tri-Ess and found out that there would be a convention in our area. I encouraged Dan to go since I believed that he needed to meet other cross-dressers and find out what all this meant. He was a bit reluctant to go, but I said I would also attend for a couple of days.

We went to the conference and he was in seventh heaven, of course, meeting other cross-dressers for the first time. I had a great time as well which surprised me since I had no idea what to expect. But I met the greatest group of men ever—intelligent, sensitive, caring, and interested in what I had to say.

When we came home we were both in tears as we realized that these friends we had made were now flying back home, perhaps even out of our lives forever. But we did find out about a local group. That scared both of us since we weren't sure we were really ready for anything close by.

But after a few months we got up the courage to contact the local group, and eventually went to some meetings. In time, we told both our daughters. Their main concern was for me and how I was handling the situation. Since they have both graduated from college and are no longer living at home, they are not involved in that part of our lives, but they have seen pictures of "Diana," and they know we are active.

Over the next few years we became very involved with support groups. Diana went on to become a founder of a support group in our area, and I became an activist for significant others. I began writing articles from a SO's point of view, and these articles have been published in many newsletters, on the Internet, and in gender magazines such as *The Femme Mirror* and *Transgender Tapestry.*

I have cut back my involvement with the community in the past couple of years, but we are both part of a couples group, and I participate in an online support group for significant others. I continue to write monthly articles for Diana's support group, and I have a hotline number listed for other wives/partners new to the phenomenon. My goal is to help other couples integrate the cross-dressing into their relationships in a positive manner.

Personally I have found that my relationship with Dan has deepened significantly since he told me about the cross-dressing. He has always been a very kind, considerate, and generous person, and I think there is a direct correlation between his personality traits and his desire to cross-dress.

This is not say that I like everything about the cross-dressing. There are times when I feel it impacts our lives too much; but Dan, being considerate, will back off a bit when I mention this. We have learned to compromise. We have learned what each other's boundaries are. Early on my husband realized that he did not want to bring his "femme" side into the bedroom, so I have not had to face the same sorts of sexual issues that some other wives face. I have no problem with what my husband wears to bed. He could wear a gorilla suit if he wanted to; that would not turn him into a gorilla! But I don't care to kiss lipstick and he respects that. So when he is cross-dressed, he is my friend, not my lover.

Like most significant others, this is not something I wished for, nor is it something I really like. But I have come to learn that cross-dressing is not a choice. I believe it is a biological condition that impacts more men in our society than most of us know, and it is this biological condition that has made Dan the wonderful person I believe he is.

And so we continue day by day working on our relationship. We have our ups and downs, but that is normal in any relationship, not just marital relationships, and not especially relationships between cross-dressers and their spouses.

Early on, similar to many wives, Julie had a strong reaction to Dan's disclosure of his cross-dressing. She was terrified, had trouble sleeping, and became ill. She experienced the common fear that he might want to become a woman. For many wives this is a key concern. All too often they feel deceived because their husbands concealed their cross-dressing. Given this deception, it's no wonder that they suspect and fear that their husbands are withholding more information from them, and it's not surprising that so many wives have grave concern that the truth of their husbands' transgender nature lies beyond cross-dressing, in the more intense realms of the gender spectrum.

When Dan reassured Julie that he would do nothing without her permission, Julie felt that she had regained some measure of control. Then she was able to seek information about cross-dressing and to find support for both herself and Dan. Yet again it seems that it was the wife who did the work. Julie researched and made contact with support resources.

Involvement in support groups and investment in helping others is one of the commonalities among spouses who reach an exceptionally high level of acceptance and comfort. That, and the increased openness between them since Dan told Julie about his cross-dressing deepened their relationship. What a delight it is to hear stories in which relationships improve due to the communication generated by the cross-dressing.

Chapter 10

Holly and Jack/Jackie

Jack did not disclose his cross-dressing to Holly. The fact that she discovered it herself has made trust more of an issue than it might have been had he volunteered the information as did the Joan and Julie's spouses. Holly has concerns about what else Jack could be hiding and whether his gender variance is more intense than he admits.

Jack and I have been married for twenty-four years. He's fifty-one and I'm forty-four. Jack is retired military, and for twenty years of his thirty-year career I was the anchor that kept things going on the home front. He was in special ops, and that meant that he was gone either training or in real-world situations six to nine months out of each year.

Our two sons are out of the nest. Neither knows about Jack's cross-dressing. We have good relationships with both of our sons. I honestly believe that some day, when Jack is ready to be open with them, we will disclose his cross-dressing to them. Our sons are very loving and open-minded, due partially, I think, to being raised in a military household. We have had all types of friends in many different places.

During the last year of Jack's career he had back surgery. While he was recuperating he discovered the Internet and lots of other guys who were cross-dressers. He has told me many times that he knew he could not be the only one, but he sure didn't think he'd ever get to know so many other people with whom he had this in common.

I stumbled onto his Internet connection in 1998. Once we sorted out the facts from my fears we were able to relate to each other in total honesty. It seemed as though that first year we developed a whole new relationship. We were closer than we had ever been before. I grieved his having lived for so many years concealing half of his identity. I felt very sad that "rules" made up by society made such a loving man feel like less than a whole person.

Head Over Heels: Wives Who Stay with Cross-Dressers and Transsexuals
Published by The Haworth Press, Inc., 2007. All rights reserved.
doi:10.1300/5737_10

Jack was so relieved that I didn't reject him. Discovering that our love and lives were being enriched by the deepening of our knowledge of each other, Jack went through a period of euphoria. This euphoria was primarily expressed through shopping, shopping, and more shopping! It almost seems as though an expression of the caveman hunting instinct drives his shopping. Unlike a caveman, though, he always buys things on sale, thank God!

The year after I found out about his cross-dressing I went through *my* "euphoria." Thanks to Leah *[see Chapter 13]* and the other wonderful ladies in my online support group I realized three very important facts: I could dislike certain things about Jack's cross-dressing without rejecting him; the best relationships are fifty-fifty, even when they include cross-dressing; and I could and should have my own space.

I have never felt threatened by "Jackie." My husband is the same loving man no matter what he is wearing. But I had lots of difficulty and still have occasional small setbacks on issues of trust. Even though in my head I truly understand the self-preservation instinct that drove his concealment, I still can't help but be awed by how good he was at it. Being aware of that, sometimes I ask myself what he could be hiding now. I also have periods when I wonder if there may be another level—transsexual issues—looming ahead. Jack seems very content with his opportunities for dressing at this point. In fact, he doesn't seem to want to dress all that often. Yet I still wonder whether he is as content as he says he is. My goal is to stop second guessing everything all the time.

When we lived in Florida and were only able to go to Tri-Ess meetings in Atlanta once or twice a year we both enjoyed the weekends very much. They were an escape for us and we always had such wonderful times. I felt especially free because there was little or no chance that we would run into anyone who would recognize me.

Now that we've moved to Vegas, it's very different. Although we have more access to the meetings and have met some wonderful folks, neither of us is enjoying our Tri-Ess weekends nearly as much. We have to be more cautious, and that is tedious. In fact this brings up the only thing I would change about the cross-dressing: the need for secrecy. I am not, nor will I ever be, good at this. Heck, I'm one of those people who have blabbed Christmas gift secrets since I was a child!

Someone once said that when the cross-dresser comes out of his closet, his wife goes right into hers. I don't like feeling separated from good friends and family members. In some ways, we have more honest friendships with people we have never met face to face and only know online than we have with people we have cherished for years. Jack and I both agree that we are not willing to risk rejection from these folks right now. So, we keep living two lives.

I don't have any issues about his cross-dressing in the bedroom. We have lots of fun playing together, and there is no problem with gender issues there. I like the feel of silk and lace on him too!

I find it ironic that the things we disagree about and have minor spats over are not cross-dressing related. Our big issues are occasional lack of constructive communication and what I see as the occasional explosion of his male tendencies toward selfishness and laziness. Fortunately, when we open up and talk honestly we are able to work things out. I really get angry when he erects a wall around himself and won't share with me, but I recognize that this is a family thing. He got it from his father, God rest his soul, who was like a turtle in a fire, closed up tight! But with our love, and if he will just accept that Mrs. Right's first name is Always, we will live happily ever after.

Holly, like so many cross-dressers' partners, has a hard time with secrecy. It's as though she has to lead a double life. A huge contrast exists between the honesty of Holly and Jack's friendships with their Tri-Ess and Internet friends and the need to keep secrets from old friends and family. Some couples who live with cross-dressing choose not to tell the significant people in their lives. Therefore, they find it necessary to monitor what they say to friends and family who don't know about the cross-dressing. They have to make up stories if they go to Tri-Ess meetings or conferences. Holly mentions a theme common to many SOs who find this closetedness awkward, cumbersome, and a threat to their sense of integrity.

Holly mentions that their sons are not aware of Jack's cross-dressing. She sounds ready to disclose the cross-dressing to the kids as soon as Jack is comfortable with them knowing. She anticipates a caring response from them. It may be that Jack has concerns about how this knowledge might impact his sons' image of their dad. This is not an unusual concern for gender-variant people. After all, given the perception of transgender among the general public, it seems natural that even a caring adult child might see his father in a different light knowing that he enjoys expressing his feminine side. Holly claims that their upbringing in a military household has made them open-minded, yet a military environment can also engender stereotypical attitudes about gender roles.

Holly has benefited a great deal from her online support group. Her friends in that group have helped her to deal with the mistrust that continues to arise occasionally because of Jack's skill at concealing his cross-dressing. As with so many other cross-dressers' partners, Holly still has some concern that Jack may be hiding something else, and particularly that he may really be transsexual. Holly is working on rebuilding trust and accepting that what Jack is telling her now is the whole truth.

Holly was open to informational input from Jack that calmed her initial fears. She was compassionate about the shame Jack had felt because of societal disapproval of cross-dressing. Just as with some other couples, such as Julie and Dan, Jack's revelation of his secret contributed to increased emotional intimacy between him and Holly.

Holly's discovery of Jack's cross-dressing does not seem to have damaged their sexual intimacy. Holly reveals her enjoyment of exploration of gender play in the bedroom. The fact that she enjoys the feel of silk and lace on Jack too suggests a capacity to access the arousing synergy that can occur when people are able to allow their sexual identities to be fluid.

Chapter 11

Angie and Tommy/Charla

Angie has been very supportive of Tommy's cross-dressing. Although Tommy disclosed his cross-dressing to Angie (albeit on the heels of her discovery of his "cyber affair"), Angie, similar to Holly, has a concern that Tommy will some day decide that he is living in the wrong body.

I met Tommy when I was nineteen. I'd been raised in a very strict and sheltered environment; my dad was career army. It was the first relationship for each of us, and before long I was pregnant. When I found out that Tommy was only seventeen and still in high school I broke up with him and decided to raise the child alone.

We met again several years later and we were still strongly attracted to each other. We were married in December 1988. He didn't tell me about his desire to dress like a woman. Before long we had another daughter, who had a severe medical condition. She lived until just beyond her third birthday. Our third child was a son, Jim.

For a number of years we had various houseguests and roommates. Sharing the expenses made things easier financially, but privacy was an issue that had us on edge. Tommy and I began arguing a good bit.

I was really pissed off when I found out that Tommy had found female companionship on the Internet and had had a "cyber affair." At first he denied it, but eventually we got it all out in the open. I was so upset and hurt. Then he told me about his cross-dressing—I guess he figured he had nothing to lose. Boy, that news hit me like a ton of bricks! I have a brother who is bisexual who was even into cross-dressing when he was younger, but I never would have guessed that Tommy was "that way." The night he told me, I asked the usual, "Are you gay?" Of course I knew better, but felt compelled to ask.

When I asked him about makeup he told me that he had only tried it twice, and that he didn't feel right in it. I was still angry, but I put

Head Over Heels: Wives Who Stay with Cross-Dressers and Transsexuals
Published by The Haworth Press, Inc., 2007. All rights reserved.
doi:10.1300/5737_11

makeup on him. Now picture this: he was sporting a mustache and a goatee. He *didn't* look good! It was kind of funny. I told him that if this was what he wanted he would have to shave, which he did. But even then, when he fixed his hair and applied makeup he didn't look right. It bothered me, so we went to Wal-Mart and bought one of their Halloween wigs for Tommy's female persona Charla to wear, so I would feel better looking at him. I told him that we would do this together since we both had a lot to learn. I was determined to work at forgiving him for deceiving me.

We began using the Internet as a resource. Some sites were helpful and some were scary. Neither of us knew the difference between cross-dresser, transgender, and transsexual. Since then we have been communicating more, and I've learned more about transgenderism than most nontransgendered people do in a lifetime. I've made time for Charla, to come out and have freedom. We've joined support groups, which have helped me in terms of understanding and accepting Charla. I still have days when I am confused, but I feel for him having to hide this all his life.

Eventually, after our son Jim began school, we told my brother Bubba our secret so "Charla" could come out of our room. Tommy didn't want to feel that he was constantly "in the closet," so to speak. One night after we'd been out as Hubby and Wife, we came home, showered, and my Tommy became Charla. I did his makeup since he sucks at doing it, and fixed his hair. I picked out an outfit for him, and he had to wear cowboy boots since at that time we hadn't found any women's size 14 shoes.

Bubba volunteered to stay with our son who was asleep, and we went to Wal-Mart, both of us scared to death. I gave Charla a pep talk. I told him walk with his head high; to not stare at people and they wouldn't stare at him; and to breathe, walk slow, and take small steps. I stressed that holding hands was out of the question since it would look weird. We picked up a couple of more wigs. I needed the wigs to help me mentally separate my husband from Charla. We did okay in Wal-Mart; no one said anything, not even the cashier. Our first night out with no glitches!

I tried to teach Tommy to do his own makeup, but it was hopeless. He always made up his eyes too dark, so he looked French. I decided that I would just do all the makeup. I also tried teaching Tommy how to walk in a more feminine way, but it didn't work; he still walked like a guy.

Then I recalled that when I was younger, Mama taught us girls the book method. That's when you place a heavy book on your head and try to walk without dropping the book. It builds up your posture. It takes a lot of practice, but practice makes perfect. So I taught Tommy to walk with a book on his head and we laughed a lot, but practice we did. Now, when he is Charla he can hold his head high and walk like a lady. "Remember," I tell him, "always take small steps, not long strides." Tommy decided that he didn't want to try to talk like a girl when he is Charla, so he just talks more softly when we are out in public.

We had a talk about making Halloween 2000 a night for Charla to come out. I decided that Tommy needed some kind of breast forms instead of stuffing his bra with socks. We went over to Fort Worth, and at Victoria's Secret we found a reasonable pair for $50. We also bought Charla some panties and a bra; she can't wear mine since I am a bigger cup size than she is (after all I did give birth to three kids).

On Halloween morning I transformed Tommy into Charla. This was the first time our son Jim saw Charla, and he wouldn't go near his dad. While I was dressing Jim, Charla had to run down to the supermarket around the corner. We know everyone who works there, including our brother-in-law's sister Sue Ann. While Tommy was in line he said hi. Hearing his voice, Sue Ann was looking all around for Tommy, so he waved. At first she freaked, said she'd never have known who it was. Her comment that he made a pretty woman made him feel really good.

We took our son trick-or-treating, with Charla wearing a black checkered dress. Our first stop was at Tommy's mom's work. Charla walked in first, and his own mother didn't recognize him. Charla said, "Mom, it's me, your son." I thought his mom was going to have a heart attack! When she calmed down, she too told him that he made a pretty woman.

When we were finished trick-or-treating we ended up at his other sister's house, where everyone laughed at first and then stared, because they couldn't believe it was Tommy. His sister Daisy has two teenage boys, twelve and thirteen at the time, and they had a blast asking all kinds of questions. Now you have to realize this is a really redneck family, so this was a challenge and an adventure for both of us.

Sometimes I have to set boundaries if Tommy wants to do something I don't want to do, but things are getting easier with time. I still can't seem to call my husband a "she" very often, but that's me; some people may have an easier time with that. I think it's fine to take baby steps if need be, but we have to keep communicating.

My sister Corrie sometimes went on the road with her trucker hubby, Dale. We were all living together. One day, after Tommy and I had another argument about telling her, I blurted to Corrie, "Okay, you really want to know the big secret we are hiding?" "Yes!" she said. So I told her the whole story, and her only response was, "So, your husband has a female side to him. So what? I kind of figured that out when I found more female panties than male underwear in the wash, especially some I have never seen before." We busted out laughing. Tommy was so happy that he didn't have to hide around her anymore. She wanted to meet Charla, so we did our transformation, and Corrie met Charla. When she told him how pretty he was, you could just see the pride in his eyes.

Tommy was riding high, but I was still having days when I didn't want any part of it. During an argument with Tommy one day I commented that he didn't have the balls to tell his own mother. He stormed out of the house, went over to his mom's, and told her. Her first words were, "But you're married!" Tommy told her that I knew, and that he wasn't gay, that he just loved the female clothes and being able to express his feminine feelings.

His mom told him that when he was born she used to dress him in girl clothes, since that was all she had, because she thought she was going to have a little girl. She also told him she was suspicious when he was a teenager because her clothes would be rearranged when she got home and he was the only one there. His mom told him that she was okay with his cross-dressing as long as he didn't do it in front of our son. And at *that* time, he didn't.

We do a lot of talking whether my husband is presenting as Tommy or Charla, but I am still not at the level where some partners are who consider their men their "girlfriends" when they are cross-dressed. The intimate talks we have are between Tommy and me, not between Charla and me. I need to see him as having two separate people in one body. That's hard to explain, because he only has one brain.

At first it really bothered me that Tommy was involved in an Internet LISTSERV that includes both cross-dressers and transsexuals. I asked him what his true intentions were, and if one day he might decide that he was living in the wrong body. He said that if he ever decided to **"go full-time,"** then he would lose Tommy, and that wouldn't be right. He assured me that he wants to be able to express both sides of himself and doesn't want to kill off the male in him. I was relieved to hear this.

The feelings Tommy shares with me are real to him, whether he is in his male or female personality. The feminine part of him, now that it's been released, should never have to bear the torture of being locked up again. When Tommy talks to me about Charla I can see the pain in his eyes from having endured keeping her locked away all those years and not dealing with this issue head-on. It pains me for anyone to live with such heartache and fear.

Tommy's a trucker. When he was home from being on the road we were going to church as a family. We were talking about our feelings like never before, but I was still really moody. I couldn't forget his cyber affair; I'd bring it up during arguments, but really all that I wanted was a reason why. Why would he do this to us? He couldn't answer me. He had once told me while in "Charla mode" that she (Charla) tried to warn him and stop him. At that point, I threw up my arms and hollered, "Hel-LO! You and Charla are ONE!"

Tommy joined an online forum, where he was getting replies from other cross-dressers. I couldn't seem to get any help, though, so I became jealous of the relationships he had with these guys. I was scared, too. He wanted more freedom to go out dressed, and I felt uncomfortable about that. One night, he was **clocked** by my boss, who began razzing me about Charla.

That year Tommy spent part of Thanksgiving as Charla, and on Christmas Eve Charla and I spent the evening together. We did the Santa thing, and all of a sudden our son Jim got up and saw his dad looking like a totally different person. He didn't freak, but the cat was out of the bag. We had to make him promise us that what happens in this house is our business and no one else's.

During the year 2001 we finally told my sister Corrie's husband, Dale, about Charla. Dale is a redneck through and through. At first he thought Tommy and I must be into S&M, but then he just said, "Okay." When he and Tommy were alone Dale started asking Tommy about Charla. Tommy even showed Dale his pictures on our Web site. The next day we asked him if he wanted to meet Charla. He said,

"Sure." After seeing Tommy all dressed up and looking nice, Dale said, "That's still Tommy," but at least he's never said anything bad about my husband.

By 2002 we had become members of a lot of transgender groups and had met a lot of people both on the Internet and in person. Tommy recognizes more each day that he isn't a freak and he isn't alone, and I believe that knowing Charla has enriched my life.

There are a lot of wives who just tolerate this side of their husbands. They have a hard time really accepting the cross-dressing, but the need—and it is a need—to cross-dress doesn't go away. I've noticed that the more stressed my husband is, the more he wants to relieve his stress by being Charla. It isn't easy for nontransgendered people to understand transgender issues, but recognizing that it took a lot, and I mean *a lot* of guts for them to come out and tell us what had been bothering them for years—to include us in a world we never knew existed, is a good beginning.

A couple of years after my sister Corrie found out about Charla she had several strokes. At this point, Corrie's condition that resulted from her strokes is much tougher to deal with than Tommy's cross-dressing. Corrie is my younger sister and I helped to raise her. Now I feel like I'm raising her all over again. She remembers some of her adult life, but her short-term memory is gone and her mentality is that of a five- to seven-year-old. She's in a nursing home near us and we take her home every Sunday for dinner and a movie.

I love my husband despite all the pain and hardship we've endured. We've become more honest and loving, and we have had the best sex since we met eighteen years ago. He's more alive now. It's been confusing and downright scary at times, but one thing I have learned from all of this, is to talk. If we don't discuss our feelings, we never get over them, and they tear us both up. We don't want that; our love for each other is too strong. I want to learn as much as I can so that I can help myself and other women like me. I put my story online and chat with other partners of transgendered people, and in the end, after reading my own words, I realize that I have been helping myself.

Tommy voluntarily disclosed his cross-dressing to Angie. Unfortunately, however, Tommy's disclosure came on the heels of Angie finding out that he was having a "cyber affair." Even so, that he volunteered the information about his cross-dressing probably had a positive influence on Angie's feelings about her spouse, his gender variance, and their marriage.

Typically, relationships have a greater chance of surviving and thriving if the transgendered person reveals the truth to a spouse rather than inadvertently being found out. Before they become willing to disclose to their partners or bring their partners into therapy sessions, I often coach transpeople, sometimes role-playing with them, giving them the opportunity to "rehearse" the sometimes terrifying act of disclosure.

Angie became supportive relatively soon after Tommy told her about his cross-dressing. The couple demonstrated good partnership skills when they began using the Internet as a resource, where before, when Tommy had used it to have his "cyber affair," it had been a threat. Angie arranged for Tommy's female persona, Charla, to come out and have some long-awaited freedom. Angie was much less reluctant than many partners of gender-variant people about her spouse going out in public en femme. She was also amazingly willing to accompany and coach Tommy about presenting acceptably as Charla. Some wives never go out in public with their partners when they are expressing another gender presentation.

Joining support groups seemed to make a significant difference in Angie's capacity to understand and accept Charla and Charla's needs. Telling Tommy he would have to shave and going with him to buy wigs for him to wear helped Angie to survive the deception and gave her a sense of authority in the relationship. Using the wigs to help her to mentally separate her husband from his femme persona demonstrated Angie's capacity for creative problem-solving strategies that help to keep her feeling safe. Angie was a generous and caring keeper of the secret in many ways. She looked ahead and saw to issues of safety.

Similar to Angie, many wives reject the notion of embracing their husbands' femme personas as their "girlfriends." She is clear that she doesn't want to consider Charla a "bosom buddy" in whom she confides. It is marvelous that Angie and Tommy talk about their feelings together. Angie only engages in intimate discussions with her spouse, however, when he is in masculine mode. Seeing the husband and the femme persona as separate people is a coping strategy that works for some wives better than for others. For some women this tactic can exacerbate any existing jealousy about "the other woman" (the femme persona) who captures so much of the transperson's attention. For Angie, though, it seems to work well. Compartmentalizing Tommy and Charla enables her to remain clear that Tommy is still her husband despite his personality having a feminine facet. Thus, she minimizes any disturbance she might experience as a result of being married to a cross-dresser, and she also holds on to her own femininity as a coping tool for herself. Thus, the compartmentalization helps Angie to avoid discounting Charla's significance to Tommy while clearly honoring her own limits. It must be comforting to Angie that Tommy clearly states that he does not wish to "kill off" the masculine part of himself. Many cross-dressers' wives become anxious about such a desire arising.

With great good humor and a generous heart, Angie is reaching out to help other women like herself. She is sharing with them the relationship skills she has learned. She encourages other SOs in her online support network to be sure that while being supportive of the transgendered partner they remember that it is vital to take care of their own comfort level and to avoid resentment by setting limits. Although she has boundaries about Charla's activities, Angie's attitude toward Tommy is extremely compassionate. She empathizes with the heartache and fear he has experienced and the anguish that was the result of locking Charla up for years. As she writes, it seems, without being said, that Angie also has compassion for her own feelings, vulnerability, and limitations as she seeks to create a balance for the feelings, needs, and enjoyment she and Tommy can have together as a couple.

Chapter 12

Rita and Bill

Bill disclosed his cross-dressing to Rita on their first date, just when their friendship was being transformed into a dating relationship. Similar to Angie, she was curious about her spouse's cross-dressing.

I met Bill when I was fifty-four years old and had been divorced for twenty-five years. I had been celibate for three years and was definitely not looking for a husband. We became friends, then married three and a half years later.

Bill told me that he was a cross-dresser on our first date. I had no idea what this meant at the time, but he answered every question I asked. Of the many qualities that endear Bill to me, his honesty is at the top of the list. Because he is the kindest man I've ever met, and because I am a bit of a liberal, I didn't run.

My initial reaction to his being a cross-dresser was curiosity. I heard what he'd told me, but early on in our relationship I saw him only dressed as a guy. I look back now and wonder why I wasn't shocked the first time he wore his breast forms, but I wasn't. In fact, I've borrowed them a few times when we've gone out. They're rather impressive.

The first time I saw Bill completely dressed as a woman was when I dressed him in my dress, my shoes, and my makeup. I was amazed at how cute he was. This was the first time I actually considered the possibility that he could pass as a woman. That scared me for months and months. I was afraid he would decide to live life completely as a woman and I had already fallen in love with him.

My own identity and sexual orientation have never been in question, even though there are times during sex when we will play at being "lesbian lovers." There are also times when he prefers me in a

Head Over Heels: Wives Who Stay with Cross-Dressers and Transsexuals
Published by The Haworth Press, Inc., 2007. All rights reserved.
doi:10.1300/5737_12

dominant, almost masculine role. I like sex to be fun and playful. This includes some role-playing.

We have some challenges with family, friends, and the community. Bill had a very public, nasty divorce trial, in which cross-dressing was a big issue. It was especially a strain on his relationship with his children. At the time his daughter was twenty and his son was sixteen. His relationships with them were extremely fragile for many years, but now they seem very good once again. My point is that the cat was out of the bag, so to speak, in a very public way.

Me? I'd be happy if the topic never came up with any of our children again. My son and daughter-in-law do not know. They are thirty-six and thirty, respectively. I have asked myself whether I'm embarrassed about Bill, and I don't believe that is the real issue. If my children, my family, or my work associates found out about the cross-dressing we would deal with that. I just don't believe that it is any of their business. It is a very personal subject.

Bill feels that since his friends and family already know, eventually so will mine. I'm not ready for that. I'm not sure what this says about me. We have several mutual friends that already know because of the divorce, but the subject is never talked about, nor is it an issue, as far as I know. The same is true with his family.

We work on nurturing our relationship. We discuss any issue that arises and arrive at an appropriate decision together. When Bill dresses I usually comment on the size of the breast of the day. He will occasionally get "dressed" for his morning biscuit run and less often when he just plans to stay around the house. He does like to wear lipstick. When we go out together, if there is something that he is wearing or doing that is obviously feminine I will point it out if it makes me uncomfortable. On the other hand, I will try and make him prettier when he wants to dress around the house.

In our four years together I have experienced no resentment or jealousy. We take pleasure in each other and enjoy our time together. We have a wonderful relationship, and we feel blessed that we met. I consider myself the luckiest woman on the planet.

Unlike so many partners of gender-variant people, Rita experienced no deception. Therefore there was no sense of betrayal. Her primary initial response to Bill's disclosure of his cross-dressing was curiosity rather than shock, pain, or anger. This is at least partially attributable to Bill having told her so early on, at the point at which their friendship became a dating relationship. Early disclosure typically predicts a more favorable outcome for the relationship if the nontransgender partner is willing and able to see herself in relationship with a gender-variant person.

Rita's only fears seem to be that Bill might want to "go full-time," with the concomitant possibility of people in her world finding out. Each of these concerns is common for wives of cross-dressers. Given her awareness of how uninformed and judgmental many people are about gender variance, it is understandable that Rita would prefer to keep the cross-dressing private.

Rita brings up the issue of their children by previous marriages. She prefers that they treat Bill's cross-dressing as private in terms of her son. Bill's adult children know because it was an issue in his divorce. It is likely that the fragility of Bill's relationship with his children stems from the divorce trial being public and nasty. Many children can deal well with a parent being transgender, particularly if disclosure is handled in a thoughtful manner, with age-appropriate explanation. This is rarely the case when the issue arises in the context of a divorce.

Rita is very open-minded about her erotic life, and is willing to experiment with the kind of role-playing that would delight many cross-dressers and, for that matter, some transsexual women. She may very well be exploring her sexual identity with curiosity and delight. Perhaps she is one of the lucky wives who has the capacity to access that magical synergy that some women describe with their gender-variant partners that can be so arousing: the liminal adventure of erotic play at the boundaries of gender and sexual orientation.

Chapter 13

Leah and Frank/Franki

Leah herself discovered that Frank cross-dressed. Unlike Rita, who experienced no deception, she felt hurt and betrayed. She was also angry with herself for allowing herself to be "duped."

I met my Frank just over eighteen years ago. He had been in the military, and did two tours in Vietnam. Frank has one child from a previous marriage. We met at work, and now own our own company. I had been through two failed marriages and several relationships, having spent most of my adult life as a single parent raising three children. We've been married since 1989.

I was forty years old when I met Frank. I had totally given up on men by that time and had decided never to get involved again, but it didn't take long for me to realize that he was different. He was so kind and gentle; he didn't expect me to be something I wasn't. I couldn't help but fall for him. We have a very strong relationship. We are lovers, partners, soul mates, and best friends. We have all the things that were missing in my previous relationships: caring, consideration, companionship, and compassion. I had never felt so secure with anyone. We have been through good times and bad, all strengthening our bond.

During our first three or four years together Frank and I never had an argument. It was almost too perfect to be true. Only one problem surfaced early on, and it didn't seem like a big thing. Although Frank is a terrific lover, he didn't seem to want sex very often. Sometimes we would go months without making love. It was frustrating for me, and I began to feel as though I wasn't good enough for Frank, as though something was wrong with me. I felt inadequate and undesirable.

Head Over Heels: Wives Who Stay with Cross-Dressers and Transsexuals
Published by The Haworth Press, Inc., 2007. All rights reserved.
doi:10.1300/5737_13

What made this even worse was that we are both extremely shy. We can't seem to talk about sex. When I tried to discuss the infrequency, he got defensive, seemingly interpreting what I was saying as though I didn't think he was a good lover. He would seem hurt at first, and then get argumentative. I didn't want to hurt him so I just quit trying to talk about it. This didn't work either because keeping it bottled up inside made me edgy and bitchy.

Frank and I have a very trusting relationship. His work requires him to be on the road a lot. You have to have total trust to be married to a man who spends most of his time away from you. I did trust him, and there was a time when I thought I knew everything about Frank. Boy was I wrong! The summer before our tenth anniversary I began to suspect something wasn't quite right. For the first time, I felt as though he was keeping something from me. We had recently gotten online and I noticed that he was deleting his Internet history every day. If I walked into the room while he was surfing the Web he would jump off the site he was looking at. He was becoming so secretive that I began to worry.

I hated to break our trust to check up on Frank, but I had to find out what was going on in order to save our marriage. When I discovered that he was checking out X-rated sites I was shocked. Although I'm not a prude, knowing that he was looking at such graphic pictures hurt me because I was so dissatisfied with our sex life. I was angry because I thought he was substituting those pictures for sex with me. It made me feel even more undesirable.

We fought about this, and finally Frank said that he had only been curious and wouldn't do it again. But he did—over and over and over, he just got better at hiding it. A real problem with trust had developed: he was lying and I was snooping.

Then his Web surfing turned down a new avenue. He began looking at a lot of transvestite sites. Due to my inadequate knowledge of gender issues—not understanding the distinction between gender identity and sexual orientation—I began to wonder about his sexual orientation, and thought that maybe he was using me to mask his interest in men. I was confused. He showed his love to me in every other way, but there was this secret side of him that seemed to contradict everything. I didn't know whether our marriage was going to make it.

I started looking more closely at the sites he was surfing and reading some of the pages. My research led me to suspect that Frank was a cross-dresser rather than a homosexual. This puzzled me; cross-dressing was totally inconsistent with my husband's interests. However, I knew that his brother was a cross-dresser, as was his father. Other than possibly his mother, Frank is the only person in his family who knows about his father. I wondered if he was researching something because of them.

Then I found some women's clothing in his duffle bag. Because his work requires a lot of travel, Frank's bag is always packed. My first thought was that he was cheating on me, but in my heart I knew this was not the case. I knew my husband loved me. He couldn't be cheating on me. Then I realized that this was some of my discarded clothing. I put two and two together and decided he was trying this "cross-dressing thing" himself.

My initial reactions were shock, fear, worry, insecurity, and then, all within a few days, understanding and acceptance. At first I was hurt; I felt betrayed. Frank hadn't been honest with me. He was keeping secrets from me! I was afraid that he might be hiding other things from me. I was scared that our friends and family would find out, and concerned about what their reactions would be. Most of all, I was afraid I was losing Frank. I was angry too: at him for keeping secrets and at myself for having allowed myself to be "duped."

I was also angry with myself for not being able to control these feelings. I know my husband very well. I know he loves me, that he would never intentionally hurt me. We have always had a very strong relationship. So I was angry with myself for doubting his love and for failing to trust my own strength to deal with this.

I spent a couple of weeks researching cross-dressing. I learned as much as I could, and then confronted Frank with my suspicions. At first he denied it. Then, after another trip, he said that he had tried it but decided it wasn't for him. Finally we sat down and really talked. He told me he was a cross-dresser. He claimed that he had only dressed a couple of times in the past, but he had been drawn to cross-dressing from an early age. He had suppressed the urge for most of his life. Now that he realized there were many others like him, who enjoyed wearing women's clothing, he was beginning to accept this side of himself. He made it clear, however, that if I couldn't accept it, then he wouldn't do it anymore.

Prior to reaching a point at which I understood and accepted Frank's cross-dressing, I had questions similar to those of other cross-dressers' partners. Is my husband gay? Is he bisexual? Will he want to actually become a woman? Will he want to go out in public dressed? Will others find out? Am I not enough? Why does he want to do this? But even though I asked these questions I knew Frank was no different than before. He was still my wonderful husband. He still loved me. Therefore, I knew what the answers would be. I really had very little trouble accepting this new part of our relationship, although I did and still do have bad days along with the good, as do all marital partners.

When Frank finally admitted the truth to me, we had a long talk. He said that he wanted to try cross-dressing in earnest. He wanted me to go with him to buy some women's underclothes and a nightgown. At this point we both thought of this more as a sexual enhancement than anything else. Although I still felt hurt, angry, and afraid at times, I thought I owed it to him to at least try to accept it. Why not? It didn't hurt anyone. No one but the two of us had to know. There was even a chance that cross-dressing would add some spice to our intimate life.

For two years after Frank came out to me we had a whirlwind sex life. Not only was it great, it was *every* night. This was more than I could have wished for. After seeing Frank dressed for the first time I realized that no matter what he was wearing he was still my husband, the man I fell in love with and married, and I was still me. There was a time when I was afraid that my husband's dressing might make me feel like a lesbian, but it doesn't. I do not see another woman in the bedroom. I see my husband, the man I love!

We had fun! We went shopping together. We shared a secret that kept us whispering and giggling like lovesick teenagers. It was "a dream come true." We talked like we had never talked before. I told him how I had felt before: alone, abandoned, undesirable, all because of his lack of interest in having sex with me. He promised me that it would never be like that again.

But guess what? After about two years of bliss, the novelty seemed to wear off. Our sex life began to subside like a tide flowing back out to sea. And now, although the quality is still good, we're back to having sex only occasionally. I'm beginning to feel less desirable again. My self-esteem is falling and I don't know what to do to perk up our sex life again.

I know that his line of work, which is extremely tiring, causes part of our problem. But that's not all of it. I wonder if he is into self-gratification. When I've asked him, he's denied it. This seems to be a pretty normal pattern, according to other wives of cross-dressers I've spoken with. Cross-dressers seem to have less sex drive than other men. Once they come out to their wives or partners they have a rush of sexual desire. After a period of time, however, their sex drive diminishes.

What bothers me most is that even though they have little desire to have sex with their partners, many cross-dressers still look at X-rated sites, buy sexy clothing for themselves and their wives, read provocative stories, etc. I don't know whether the dressing is a substitute for sexual satisfaction with another person, or if they just prefer self-gratification. Whatever it is, the lack of physical intimacy is destructive to the relationship. No matter how much Frank really loves and cares for me, I feel undesirable, unloved, and unwanted.

This is the one issue that talking about it hasn't helped. It remains unresolved. Frank may make the effort on the night we talk, but then it's back to the same old thing, so I feel as though he only had sex with me because I "pushed it," not because he wants me. I really don't know what to do about this.

I used to feel as though I were competing with another woman. At times when Frank has been so intensely involved with the dressing I have felt pushed aside. His "femme self" seemed like another physical being who was more important to him than I was. My husband seemed to need something I could not give, something he could only get from "the other woman." Many of the signs and feelings of betrayal were just as strong as if there were a physical "other woman." I felt inadequate, unsure of my place in the relationship, afraid of losing my partner, and no longer needed as a woman.

I used to be jealous when Frank dressed and admired himself in the mirror. When he browsed the Web looking at other cross-dressers I wondered if he would rather be with someone like himself than with me. When he admired my new blouse I wondered whether clothes were all he saw when he looked at me. When he took me shopping and looked at pretty things I wondered if he would rather get them for himself than for me. If he bought me a new outfit, jewelry, flowers, I wondered if he bought me these gifts out of guilt rather than because I was the most important person in his life.

I wondered why Frank wouldn't share his thoughts with me, why he wouldn't or couldn't stop dressing for me, why I was no longer "the only woman" in his life, how I could live a life of deceit, secrecy, guilt, and unfocused anger without falling apart. He was out of the closet—I was in. The "other woman" doesn't exist in reality, of course. It's a creation of my emotional reactions. The problem is that with no physical being on whom to focus my anger like there would be if Frank were actually having an affair, in my frustration, I focused my anger on the cross-dressing and on my husband.

It helps that Frank's personality doesn't change when he's cross-dressed. He's still the same wonderful guy I fell in love with and married. Another thing that helps me with the "other woman" issue is my refusal to call Frank "she," or to refer to him as a "lady" when he's dressed. As far as I'm concerned, I'm the woman in this relationship and I will address my husband by his femme name, but that's it.

One of my pet peeves is cross-dressers who insist that the women in their lives call them she, girls, or ladies out of respect, or in order not to hurt their feelings. I will not refer to any man by any femme term other than his chosen femme name. I was born a woman and deserve the title of "she" and shouldn't have to share it. I give cross-dressers acceptance. I allow them to sample my world. But I don't want to be expected to see cross-dressers as "real women." Women who work on cars, build cabinets, remodel homes, go hunting or fishing are expressing their masculine sides, yet they don't ask to be called "he." I say to cross-dressers, "Play your parts, enjoy the freedom to express yourselves, as you see fit, but don't try to become what you are not."

There are other bits of advice I give to cross-dressers: Let your wife know that she is still the woman of the family. Compliment her when she looks good. Let her know that she still has a place in the marriage; make sure she knows that her place isn't being taken away from her by the "other woman." Show her that she is loved and that this "other woman" is not a replacement for her but another side of your own being.

Someone asked me recently whether I participate in the cross-dressing. I don't know. We shop together. I've helped him with make-up. He dresses in my presence. I accept, support, and even encourage Frank in his cross-dressing, but isn't cross-dressing a personal thing? The way I see it, it's not a team sport. I can't exactly join in. Wives can be the cheering squad, but we can never be players. The personal nature of cross-dressing is what sometimes makes wives feel left out.

Even when I felt left out, I knew that Frank must still love me, maybe even more for my total acceptance. Yet I still had feelings of betrayal, jealousy, abandonment, loneliness, and fear of not being "enough of a woman" to totally please him. For the most part, we have dispelled these bad feelings by talking, listening, and learning not to be defensive. Frank listened to what I had to say, giving me an outlet for these feelings. He moved slowly and made concessions, not pushing me into any aspect of this way of life that I could not, or was not ready to, accept.

Frank recognized that I was not trying to control him; I was only trying to find peace within myself. He let me know how much he appreciated what I was able to accept. By giving me the space I needed, Frank made it possible for me to move forward one step at a time until we were satisfied, confident, and happy with our places within the relationship.

Now I can look across the room at Frank when he is dressed in feminine clothes and a wig and it doesn't bother me to see him that way. He is still my husband no matter what he is wearing. Yet despite my level of acceptance, I still have days when I feel totally alone and completely inadequate, days when I would like to shove "the other woman" back in the closet so I can have my husband all to myself again, days when I need my husband to tell me yet again how important I am to him and show me how much he loves and needs me—and he does.

As a young girl I had very low self-esteem. With age it has improved, although it's still something I have to work at. When my husband first started dressing I thought perhaps it was because I was not "woman enough" for him. But now I realize his dressing is not about me. In some ways, my self-esteem has actually improved. Now I take better care of myself—I wear nicer clothes, and I do more things for "me." That has made me feel better about myself.

While researching cross-dressing and talking to my husband about "who he is" and what it all means, I did a lot of self-examination and soul-searching. This gave me new insight into who I am and what I want. I found that not only do I love and accept my husband as he is, but I also love and accept myself for who I am. I have recognized that it takes strength to accept cross-dressing in a relationship. I realize I am strong enough to deal with all the issues Frank's cross-dressing triggers in me. Yet, believe it or not, I think our relationship is better now than it ever was.

We negotiate decisions about cross-dressing the same as any other decisions: together. When we have a decision to make, I state my ideas, Frank rejects my ideas, we discuss options. Then, after time, he comes up with a great idea that we agree on. (Guess what, it's the same idea I'd originally offered.) Isn't that the normal way to handle a man? Just give him the seed and let him think it was his idea to start with. Okay, I'm just teasing. But really we make decisions, especially major ones, together. We talk things over then do what's best for both of us. If necessary we compromise.

The most difficult issue for me, even now, is having to deal with the fact that when Frank is dressed he can't take out the garbage or feed the dogs or whatever outside chores there are to do. I am the one who does all these chores when he is on a trip. I enjoy having him take them over when he is not on the road, but sometimes he gets up in the morning and dresses. Then I either have to continue to do these minor chores or wait until he is ready to change. This bothers me at times, but it would also bother me if he didn't dress at home. I would feel "left out." I want to be included in this part of his life. Balancing the dressing with the other parts of our lives can be tricky. Too much of one, and I feel smothered; too much of the other, and I feel abandoned.

I can't say yet, since we haven't ventured out of the house except for the occasional drive, but I believe my biggest challenge will come when and if my husband decides he wants to venture out dressed. We'll face that *if* it comes up. At this point Frank dresses any time the mood strikes him since we live alone, and that seems to be enough. Of course there are some mad dashes to the bedroom when the kids or friends pop in unannounced.

We've agreed that other than in the anonymity of the LISTSERVs on which we are active, no one is to know but the two of us. My biggest fear now is that someone will discover "our little secret." I know I can cope with whatever happens. I am much stronger than I once thought, but that doesn't mean I want to have to cope with problems caused by discovery. We live in the heart of "redneck" country. It could be devastating to our life and livelihood if Frank's cross-dressing became common knowledge.

I do believe my children would accept it. They love my husband as if he were their own father, yet we don't believe there is a "need-to-know." If our friends found out and didn't accept it, then as far as I'm concerned they weren't real friends to begin with. We would just move on and make new friends, true friends. We live in a small southern town. We would very likely have problems if this came out in the open. But if that ever does happen I will stand beside my husband. We will do whatever it takes to keep us both safe and happy.

I have learned a lot from coming to terms with Frank's cross-dressing. I've come closer to understanding who my husband is and what he wants. I also know more about who I am and what I want. I didn't even know what cross-dressing was before it became a part of our lives. I've learned to be more tolerant and open-minded. It takes a lot of love to see your husband in full dress mode and see the person inside the clothes without feeling shame or fear. I've learned to listen more closely. I am stronger than I had ever realized. I know now that my husband is more than a cross-dresser or a man or what he does for a living. He is a unique individual with whom I'm very pleased to share my life.

Leah's insightfulness and ability to articulate her thoughts and feelings offer us a window through which we can view many of the issues faced by partners of gender-variant people, particularly those who identify as cross-dressers. Therefore, my commentary about this story will be particularly extensive.

From reading her story, it appears that after the shock of discovery wore off, Leah moved, with amazing rapidity, from fear, worry, hurt, betrayal, and anger, into understanding, acceptance, and integration of the new and disruptive issue of gender variance into her marital relationship. Intense feelings related to her spouse's cross-dressing did, however, arise from time to time.

Frank's interest in Internet porn also may have challenged her values. Women who discover that their spouses are gender-variant often have to confront differences between their long-held values and beliefs and the behavior of their spouses. They may have to return to a developmental stage in which people make personal decisions about what they see as good and bad, right and wrong.

Her story suggests that Leah as with some other partners did all the work, rather than it being a more mutual effort undertaken by her and Frank. She did independent research, an activity made much easier for partners by the advent of the Internet. This technology has offered partners the opportunity to educate themselves, rather than depending upon libraries (which had a paucity of information about gender variance until recently) or information the gender-variant person chose to share.

It is not uncommon for women to find out that their partners are gender-variant, rather than having this noteworthy information voluntarily disclosed to them. Often, suspecting that something is going on, significant others check up on their partners, as did Leah. Not understanding that gender identity and sexual orientation are separate aspects of sexual identity, Leah asked herself the almost ubiquitous initial question, "Is he gay?" Usually wives quickly realize that this is not the issue. They may be confused, however, since most people are not informed concerning the distinction between gender identity and sexual orientation.

When transpeople deny the truth or tell half-truths when asked about their gender issues, as Frank did, their partners are likely to become angry about the dishonesty when the truth finally comes out. Issues of hurt and betrayal are even more severe. SOs focus on secrets that have been kept, and, similar to Leah, may be anxious about what else their partners might be hiding. Mistrust is generated. It's natural in a situation of this kind for a woman to become somewhat paranoid, and to be come diligent in her attempts to detect deception. Marital counseling can be quite helpful for such couples. Gender specializing therapists, while validating a significant other's feelings, can help her to understand the deep shame and fear that often motivates the dishonesty.

As often happens when an SO finds women's clothes in her partner's possession, Leah wondered if Frank was having an affair. Later, when Frank began to cross-dress with more frequency and openness, Leah felt as though she was competing with another woman. She, similar to many other cross-dressers' SOs, experienced her husband's femme persona as a rival . . . a rival who was more important to him than she was.

Women in relationships with gender-variant people must learn that they are on a journey too. Women experience acquisition of knowledge and adjustment to this new element in life at different rates, based on their childhood and family of origin dynamics, their adult history, and other individual factors. Leah brings her history into current time with her remarks about her very low self-esteem in childhood. This raises questions about what drives her current dynamics.

Leah discusses the advice she gives cross-dressers about how to relate to their wives and her strong feelings about the inappropriateness of cross-dressers ever expecting to be called "she," "girls," or "ladies." Here Leah reveals her anger, perhaps due to unfinished business yet to be addressed for which counseling or therapy might be helpful. It's interesting to note that Leah tried her best to stay in control of her own experience vis-à-vis Franki, and seemed to find some measure of comfort and safety regarding the issue of language. Leah seems to empower herself via her refusal to refer to cross-dressers as if they were females.

Leah mentions her fear that someone will discover "our little secret." It doesn't seem that she and Frank have worked out a plan to prevent that happening. Although Leah is invested in Frank's cross-dressing staying private, she also seems resentful of having to do minor chores when he is cross-dressed. It might be productive for them to deal with this issue at some point, coming up with strategies that respect Leah's needs as well as Frank's.

Although initially a couple's sex life may be enlivened by the shared secret about gender variance, the original lowered level of desire and frequency of sexual contact sometimes resumes, as it did in Leah's marriage. My clinical experience suggests that the incidence of low libido in **MtF** transgendered people is higher than in the general population of **natal males.** The disinterest in sex, intense involvement in cross-dressing, and what their partners interpret as vain self-absorption of some of these gender-variant individuals may leave partners feeling unloved and undesirable. Several of the wives in these pages report this experience.

A woman in this situation is called upon to be quite good at self-validation. She must constantly remind herself that her spouse's behavior is not about her. Even if she manages to hold on to her self-worth, she may still contend with a level or frequency of physical intimacy in her relationship that is far from satisfying for her, if not totally lacking. Communication about their sex life is extremely important, yet it is one of the most difficult topics for many couples to discuss. Therapeutic work may be of great assistance in improving communication in general, and in particular about erotic issues.

Masturbation is a common and natural part of the sexual repertoire throughout the life cycle, and partnered people typically masturbate more frequently when their work requires regular travel away from home. Leah, however, mentions the suspicion that Frank may actually prefer self-gratification to physical intimacy with her. No other women in this collection raised this concern, but I have heard it from many clients and have discussed this issue with other mental health professionals. A wife who believes that her husband may be shutting her out sexually in favor of what amounts to an affair with himself might consider mentioning her feelings about this to her husband. He may be oblivious to this behavior's effect on her. If a constructive dialogue does not ensue, perhaps a therapist who understands the transgendered person's issues would be able to facilitate open discussion of the sexual needs of both parties.

The transperson may have arousal issues stemming from the gender variance. It is common for a cross-dresser or an MtF transsexual to enjoy (at least some of the time) playing a more stereotypically feminine erotic role. They may express, or wish they could express, their desire for their partners to engage in role reversal with them in order to have the opportunity to experience a more receptive role. For some natal women this temporary gender role exchange for erotic purposes is arousing. Others wouldn't consider it. This can range, for example, from being more passive in various ways related to initiation and being more the recipient of caresses to where on their bodies and how the TG person would prefer to be stimulated and even fantasizing being a female rather than a male during intercourse.

We do not know whether this is the case for Frank, but for some gender-variant people, challenging mental gymnastics are required in order to become aroused and experience orgasm with a partner. Guilt concerning focusing on the fantasies rather than on the partner during sex can also impair a gender-variant person's sexual functioning.

Some SOs may be even more disturbed about the sexual issues if they understand these dynamics. Others may be able to accommodate some of the partner's desires and needs as they may fit within her own newly awakening gender exploration. It may be a time of curiosity and experimentation for her. Focusing totally on the gender-variant person's sexual needs to the exclusion of her own is not, however, advisable.

Leah has done an effective job of negotiating about the cross-dressing. She and Frank have worked on communicating without defensiveness (a challenge in any relationship). Frank was willing to move slowly and avoid pushing Leah to accept anything new for which she was not ready. Together, they have created compatibility, although it appears that Leah has done most of the work.

Leah made the significant leap from thinking that Frank cross-dressed because she was not "woman enough" for him to recognizing that his cross-dressing was definitely not about her. His cross-dressing actually motivated an increase in her self-care, self-acceptance, and self-esteem, whereas some partners' responses are quite the opposite. Instead of berating herself for her feelings, Leah now recognizes the strength it takes for her to deal with all the issues the cross-dressing triggers in her.

Chapter 14

Cheryl and Jerry/Marge, and Mark/Lora

Cheryl's story in unique in this collection. She was involved with Jerry (Marge), whose cross-dressing she discovered in an unusually disturbing way. Jerry's gender variance was more intense than had originally been admitted, and, ultimately, it resulted in transition, which came about in a way that was very painful for Cheryl. Some time after their relationship ended Cheryl got involved with another gender-variant individual. Mark's gender issues seem less intense than Marge's.

1978 was a very traumatic year for me. The man I had been with for twelve years (ten of them as husband and wife) decided to leave our three children and me for a new lover. I was ill-equipped to survive with three small children, the oldest eight and the youngest two. I worked as a waitress in a small-time restaurant making enough to supplement an income but not enough to be the main provider. I was terrified. How could I possibly manage?

About a month later, in September, I met Jerry at the restaurant. He had come in several times before and I had talked with him while he was sitting at the counter. I was so glad to see him walk through the door. Maybe I needed to validate my femininity. I'm not sure. We had a quiet dinner together there at the restaurant and then went to the movies. That was the beginning of a whirlwind romance.

With Halloween approaching, Jerry and I were still dating even though I was not yet divorced. It looked as though my relationship with him would be permanent. We had carved a pumpkin for the kids and were excited about spending time together. One afternoon I came home before picking up the kids and found the pumpkin smashed against the living room wall. Someone had broken into my apartment but stole nothing, just broke the pumpkin. The next day I arrived home to find the door wide open and the heater on the fish tank turned off. I was scared out of what little wits I had left. Within minutes of

Head Over Heels: Wives Who Stay with Cross-Dressers and Transsexuals
Published by The Haworth Press, Inc., 2007. All rights reserved.
doi:10.1300/5737_14

calling him, Jerry was there. We grabbed what little we could and we moved into his home.

Moving in with Jerry was quite an experience. He lived in a small two-bedroom house, full to the brim with junk. There was not much room for four more people and a dog. The kids slept on a king-sized mattress on the floor in the small bedroom. Needless to say, we looked for a new house.

Having had no children from his first marriage, Jerry doted on my three. He especially seemed to love my son and even wired a Tonka fire engine with flashing lights and siren. The kid sure loved it. He wrestled on the floor with all of them and took them everywhere. I thought life was perfect. My divorce was final December 12, and we were married in a quiet evening ceremony December 27, 1978.

Problems didn't arise until the birth of our daughter in May 1980. All of a sudden the other three kids didn't exist for him. He dropped them like a sack of hot potatoes. Our daughter became the center of his life. He would get up at night with her and hold her for hours. He took her everywhere—to the fire station where he worked, to work on boats, to the store. If he left the house, only she was with him. Of course, the others resented it. All the talking in the world could not make him see what was happening.

Our fighting was almost continuous. The kids were terrors and life was miserable, to say the least. Jerry couldn't or wouldn't keep a full-time job. I was making next to nothing. Figuring that I had to do something to change our situation I decided to attend nursing school during the day while working evenings.

Summer of 1986 was the time of awakening. My son's team was in the city's softball tournament, and, of course, being a typical mother I wanted pictures. However, I neglected to bring a camera. After dropping him off at the field I returned to the house. It was too quiet. When we had left, Jerry was there and had not indicated that he was going anywhere. With a feeling of unease I started searching. As I went through the house calling his name, more misgivings arose. Where was he? Was he all right? I finally went down into the basement. From behind some boxes he came forth. Like in a nightmare, I saw my husband dressed in a full-length white formal, staring at me. (It wasn't until years later that I realized how silly he looked, a stocky, dark-haired man with a mustache in a sleeveless formal.) My life came crashing down around me. What had I done to deserve this?

Numb, I ran up the stairs and out the door. I don't remember driving to the ballpark nor do I remember the games. I do know that afterward the three oldest children went to their father's for the weekend. I sent my youngest to the babysitter's. Jerry had gone to work before I got home. Alone in the house I went into the bedroom, shut the door, and downed a bottle of pills.

I vaguely remember the hospital intensive care unit and yelling obscenities at my husband. I recall someone asking me if I wanted to be treated as an outpatient or admitted to the local psychiatric hospital. Into the psych hospital I went. For six weeks I hid from the world and opened my soul to my friendly "shrink." It was strange going home. I felt so fragile, when actually I was stronger than I had ever been.

Jerry and I did a lot of talking—all of which centered on his cross-dressing. I found out that he had been dressing since childhood and that our daughter knew about it. She had been told so he could dress when I wasn't around. He assured me that none of the other children knew.

After a lot of discussion I agreed to give the situation a chance. We mutually set limits that he almost immediately broke. He was like the proverbial kid in a candy store. The more he got, the more he wanted. First the mustache went, then he dyed his hair and grew it longer, his nails were done, he started on electrolysis, took hormones, went out en femme (even with his "boobs," which he insisted no one would notice), and wore my clothes without asking. There was no stopping him.

During this time he joined Alpha-Omega, a local Tri-Ess Chapter. For some crazy reason, I was still determined to save the marriage. So I started attending with him. At my first meeting I was met at the door by Gloria (the president and a **CD**) who took me under her wing. By the end of the evening I was actually starting to feel somewhat comfortable. For the next couple of years that was my life—trying to slow Jerry down, working nights, being a parent, and attending chapter meetings. Other members befriended me and helped me to deal with the enormous stresses forming at home. More and more I came to depend on the people in the chapter for my sanity.

The end came in the fall of 1994, when I got the next big shock of my life. One afternoon I came out of the bathroom after taking a bath. Wrapped in a bath towel I was confronted by a TV camera and reporter who wanted to know how I felt about the news. The news? It seems that my husband had announced to the world that he was a TS (transsexual) and had legally changed his name to Marge. All of this was news to me. I showed both the camera crew and my husband to the door. It was time for a divorce.

The time immediately after Marge (formerly Jerry) moved out was traumatic. It seemed as though the news media took delight in adding to the turmoil. Everywhere we went they followed—work, school, friends' homes. We were always in the public eye. We even made the newspapers in Florida. I had to change our phone number and make it unlisted. I had to send our daughter to stay somewhere else and not go near her for almost six weeks in order to protect her. When we most needed to be together, we were apart.

At school her life was hell. She was taunted and tormented. Fortunately the school staff was supportive. She arrived at school late and left early so that she had minimal contact with other students. The school counselor was available to her at all times. Whenever she was overwhelmed, she could leave class and talk with him. Over the four years of high school the taunting decreased, but the damage had been done. A vibrant, lovely girl had been turned into an angry, headstrong teenager. She missed the high school activities that all students look forward to—she went to no proms, no clubs, and she had no friends. She said that her father was dead and buried in the backyard but actually she was the "dead one"—a child forced into adulthood by circumstances that no one understood.

The media persisted in chasing us for almost six months. We even heard from Montel Williams and, of course, Jerry Springer. Finally they left us alone, but too late. Family bonds were broken and anger was all around us. My daughter and I no longer knew how to reach each other. We were strangers.

I cut myself off from all connections to the CD world. I no longer attended my local Tri-Ess meetings, nor did I communicate with any of the members including my friends. I thought that since I was no longer in a relationship with a CD I could no longer be a member. Ironically, it was like a purge. Months flew by. I was miserable. I didn't have anyone to talk with who could really understand what I was going through. How could they? They hadn't been married to a CD turned TS. Their private lives hadn't been broadcast throughout the city. I was alone in this.

Finally one day I'd had enough. I felt emotionally crippled. My life was in shreds and I knew I had to find some answers. I reached out to the only person I felt close enough to—Gloria, the CD who had taken me under her wing at my first Tri-Ess meeting. She had helped me before; would she now? I should never have doubted. One of the first things she mentioned was my attending the meetings. It was like a ray of hope. Could I really? Maybe there I could find some peace. She and I talked for hours but she couldn't convince me. Tri-Ess was for "heterosexual cross-dressers *and* their significant others." I felt that I didn't qualify anymore. I had no cross-dresser in my life; therefore, I wasn't an SO. By this time, I really wanted to attend. In fact, I was beyond wanting to, I needed to. I had to regain some sense of my own self-worth and I had the feeling that somehow, in the chapter, I could.

Finally the decision was made, and I returned for my first solo meeting. I was just as nervous opening that door as any new member. Would anything be said about my not belonging? Would I be shunned or accepted? As I look back, a smile crosses my face. The members who had been there before greeted me with hugs and expressions of love and concern. They allowed me to talk and cry freely. Each person welcomed me.

The next four years were very lonely in many ways. I had no special person to be with, although frankly, the idea of becoming involved with someone scared me. I managed to keep busy. In April 1997 I started using my son's computer and became a chataholic. What a fantasy world! I spent hours each day in various chat rooms, using them as a social substitute. The next April, my father, who was suffering from multiple myeloma, came to live with us. Taking care of Dad severely curtailed my chatting, but by then I was becoming bored anyway.

I had purchased a new computer the previous December and was having problems (going from a Macintosh to a Compaq is not exactly easy) with some of the programs. Lora, a CD who was a member of the Tri-Ess chapter, came to my rescue. It became a matter of routine for her to come over on Sundays, watch an old movie with us, have dinner, and troubleshoot the computer. It made no difference to either Dad or me whether Mark/Lora came en femme or en homme. She/he was always welcome. I began to really look forward to her visits. Life was exciting again.

Between work and taking care of Dad, there wasn't time for outside activities. I didn't feel comfortable leaving him since I was already gone all night working and slept much of the day. Lora's visits became important. It was like bringing the outside world in. Besides, she fascinated me.

At the chapter meetings Lora reminded me of a little lost sparrow. She dressed kind of dowdy—dresses below her knees, light makeup, simple shoes, a brown wig with no style. Nothing flashy, just clothes like Grandma would wear. She hung behind others and was very quiet. In her quietness, she captivated me. I wanted to tell her "everything was okay" and that she was safe. When she started visiting us, she was quiet and just seemed to fit in. I found myself wondering what to wear, what to cook, and watching the road for his/her car. I figured that I had found a friend who didn't care that my house wasn't the cleanest or that dinner wasn't the fanciest. I had found a friend with whom I was comfortable.

In August my dad developed some problems. His pain was no longer controlled by medication, and he couldn't keep food down. We decided to go to the hospital. I didn't know that he would not be coming home ever again. Eleven days after his seventy-second birthday he was gone. I was devastated. I was barely functioning, but I managed to make the funeral arrangements. The night before his funeral I was no longer able to cope.

After I washed the same dish at least three times, my daughter took me aside and said that I needed a break. Whenever I'm extremely stressed out, I go to Niagara Falls and stand at the crest for hours. I take all the problems that I can't solve and mentally throw them over the falls. In effect, I'm turning them over to my Higher Power. But this time I couldn't do that. It was late, there was no time, and I had to go to the funeral in the morning. My daughter persisted and convinced me to go.

I needed to do a favor for Mark on the way, she said. He needed a compact disc he had left at the house. Would I drop it off on the way? I didn't want to, but I did. I arrived at his place to find him waiting for me. He moved me out of the driver's seat and drove me to the falls. Neither of us was thinking clearly—he had on just a light jacket. But he never said a word while standing in the cold mist of the falls. I cried more tears than I thought I had in me, with him standing quietly beside me.

Finally I was cried out and needed to rest. We looked for a hotel and finally found one that had a vacancy. A vacancy! They only had one room with a double bed. I figured we were adults—just friends—and could behave that way. After all, we had never been on a date, never kissed other than as friends do, and never said a word about any kind of relationship. We lay on the bed with our heads toward the TV and our feet at the head and flipped through the channels. Something on the Disney Channel caught Mark's eye. It was one of my favorite programs that I loved as a kid—*Zorro*! He, being twelve years younger, had never seen it. So we watched it, and it was followed by *Spin and Marty*—another program he had never seen. I leaned over him to explain who Annette was when he said, "I love you." I looked into his blue eyes and realized that something magical had happened over the months during which we had known each other.

This kind, gentle man had managed to talk to my heart and make it blossom, all without my realizing it. Looking at his face, I felt warmth and comfort. His hands in mine took the loneliness out of my life. I had found love without looking for it, and knew that I gave it in return. I had a feeling of excitement steal over me. I was in love and it was great! The world was right again!

I've tried to understand why I don't mind Lora when I had such a difficult time accepting Marge. I came to the conclusion that it was a matter of choice, trust, and caring. I chose to allow Lora into my life. I knew about her from the start. She wasn't suddenly sprung on me, and we care for each other. If Mark needs to be Lora, it's okay. If I need for Lora to stay away, I know that all I have to do is be honest and tell him. My feelings are important too. Choice, trust, and caring make all the difference in the world.

On July 29, 2000, Lora and I were married. She wore the bridal gown and I wore the tuxedo. On August 26, 2000, Mark and I had our second (and legal) ceremony. This time I wore the gown and he wore the tuxedo. Two separate, distinct ceremonies to show that we accepted all "sides" of each other. Four years later, we are still at peace with Mark's cross-dressing. I use my experiences to work with the wives of CDs.

Daily I thank Dad for his final gift to me—my darling husband! I felt that it was Dad who brought us together. He was the catalyst. Mark came over to help Dad and it was during those times that we grew to know each other. Dad didn't die until Mark was ready to be here for me. It was like a change of command. I wasn't left alone. In a way, my dad lives on in the relationship Mark and I have.

As I have mentioned before, if a woman finds out rather than being told directly about the gender variance, the relationship has less chance of recovering. Cheryl was traumatized by the way she found out about Jerry's gender identity issues. There are other modes of discovery that are also very difficult for a partner. Seeing one's spouse on the street or in the mall is even worse than discovering him dressed in the home. Being told by a "well-meaning" friend is crushing. Perhaps the most humiliating form of discovery would be for a woman who had no clue to see her transgender partner on a program like Jerry Springer "in disguise."

In Cheryl's relationship with Marge, a fear that is almost universal among cross-dressers' wives turned into a reality for her. Although Jerry initially presented to Cheryl and to their Tri-Ess group as a cross-dresser, ultimately Marge decided to go further . . . to begin transition. Jerry may have originally identified as a cross-dresser, but Cheryl's story suggests that Marge had always been at a more extreme point on the transgender spectrum. It sometimes happens that, purposely deceptive, transsexuals present as cross-dressers to their partners. More often, a transsexual who is confused about her gender identity may at first think she is a cross-dresser, and then, over time, begin to self-identify more accurately. Most cross-dressers, however, are just that—cross-dressers. At a less extreme point on the gender spectrum, they are satisfied with occasional expression of their feminine side, and have no need to transition.

Although she had found great comfort there, in some ways it is remarkable that Cheryl was able to bring herself to return to the Tri-Ess group she and Jerry attended. Yet return she did, at a very lonely point after her divorce. Amazingly, Cheryl fell in love with another cross-dresser. However, a huge difference existed between her relationships with Jerry and Mark. In the latter instance, there was foreknowledge, honesty, and a growing friendship, trust, and caring that blossomed into love. Cheryl was even able to acknowledge and celebrate the masculine side that exists within all women (Jung, 1953).

Chapter 15

Katherine and Paul/Petra

At first, Katherine's biggest concern was that being gender-variant wasn't "normal." Then she became fearful that the more feminine Petra became, the greater the likelihood that she would want to prove that she's a woman by being with a man instead of with Katherine. Since Paul/Petra admitted the truth, Katherine has faced her own sexual orientation issues and now admits that she prefers women. Therefore, she is enjoying her relationship with Petra and is comfortable with the fact that Paul "is rarely around anymore."

I didn't know that my partner was TG before getting involved. It was actually November 2000, three months after we got married that Paul told me. It started after I confessed to him one night after several drinks that I had always been attracted to women, and that it was a big fantasy of mine to be with a woman. So, he said that he wanted to help fulfill my fantasy, and he would "dress" as a woman for me.

It started as a sexual game that we both loved. I never thought anything of him doing it; I just thought he was doing it for me. Then he started wearing hold ups and women's knickers under his clothes when we went shopping. He said it was for me and that it was just a game, but he began doing it more and more often. Soon he was wearing women's underwear more than men's and I started to wonder what was going on.

I confronted him one night, and that's when he confessed everything to me. He said that he had felt different as a kid, that he never fit in, and that he used to wear his mum's and sister's clothes when they were out, the usual stuff. Trying hard to deny it like most do, he joined the army. I was the first person to whom he had ever confessed his feelings; his first wife still doesn't have a clue about this. He denied it for so many years, and did not dress at all. It was only when he confessed to me that he admitted his feelings to himself. Petra came to life.

Head Over Heels: Wives Who Stay with Cross-Dressers and Transsexuals
Published by The Haworth Press, Inc., 2007. All rights reserved.
doi:10.1300/5737_15

My initial reaction was one of complete shock and devastation. It was fine as a game, but this, this was something else. I really didn't know how to handle it. A lot of my discomfort was a result of the fact that I simply didn't understand. There were lots of tears and plenty of talking over the months that followed. We spent ages looking on the Internet, learning what this was all about. We both joined groups in which we talked to others in similar situations, and eventually the crying stopped. I knew that I loved him/her no matter what, and that I would stick by my partner.

The biggest thing that kept going through my mind was that this wasn't "normal," that society wouldn't accept it. I think that's why talking to others helped. It made me see that it was more common than I had thought and that others had gotten through it and were happy. While I was coming to terms with being married to a TG person, I was also battling my own feelings. I knew that I had always been attracted to women, but this was making it all so real that I had to accept the feelings that I'd had for years.

My definition of my sexual orientation has changed completely. I mean, before Petra I saw myself as completely straight. Yes, I'd had fantasies about women, but I'd told myself that was all they were since I'd never acted on them. Now, although I won't openly say to people that I am a lesbian, I have told several people that I prefer women. Deep down, I know that I am, and probably always have been, a lesbian. It took Petra to help me realize that.

It all makes sense now why, over the years, I never was that interested in men. I followed the path that society wanted, denying any feelings that I had. After a failed marriage, I told myself that I was finished with men. Somehow though, when I met Paul, I couldn't stop myself from falling in love with him. I had never experienced love like that before, and now I know why. I fell in love with Petra even before I knew about her.

I have never felt threatened by having a transgendered spouse, except for my fear that the more feminine Petra becomes the less likely she is to actually want me. The possibility that she may want to prove she is a woman by being with a man rather than me scares me too. The only other thing I have ever really been concerned about is that I am holding Petra back—that without me and our daughter Pamela she would be able to do what she wants. She may want to go further with this, and I wonder whether the only thing holding her back is her fear of how people would treat Pam and me.

Telling people has always been a big issue for me. I've always been scared of how people will react and that everyone will treat us differently because of this. However, now I have told close family and friends, and I haven't had any negative reactions from my side at all; they have all been brilliant. The only big negative reaction has been from Paul's mother, brother, and Gran. As far as close family and friends are concerned, if they really care about us, then they will love us no matter what and will support us in this.

We live in a small village in England, and I still worry about how the people in our village would react if they found out. I have been scared about Pam being teased at school, but there will always be something that kids can be teased about. Pam is fine about Petra, even calling Petra her big sister. Pam adores her.

Through contending with this I have learned not to judge people without getting to know them first. You can't go by appearances. It's the person inside who counts, and it takes a while before you can really know that person.

Any decisions as far as Petra's gender issues are concerned have always been made jointly. Petra would never do anything without consulting me first, and I think that's why this works so well, because we compromise, and everything is agreed on first.

My biggest challenge so far has been to accept myself and learn to love myself no matter what I am or what I feel. I've gained happiness with such self-acceptance. I've also learned that at the end of the day it's our feelings that count and if we are happy, who is anyone else to judge that or try to destroy that happiness that we share.

The biggest challenge though is yet to come, which is being completely open with everyone about us and ignoring any rude or nasty comments that we are bound to get from people who just don't get us or don't want to. I'm prepared to deal with this, though, because our relationship has only improved. Petra and I are so good together. Paul is rarely around any more, and my love for Petra just grows more and more.

I must admit that in my experience, it is unusual for a gender-variant person initially to act out cross-gender identification as a sexual game "for the sake of the partner." This is, however, the experience Katherine reports with Paul/Petra. She was shocked to find out that her spouse was actually transgendered. Katherine enjoyed the erotic playfulness, but initially the actuality of the gender-variance devastated her.

As with many other partners of transgender people, Katherine was extremely uncomfortable. Her belief was that transgender is just not "normal." Therefore she was concerned that maintaining a relationship with a gender-variant person would be seen by others as aberrant. This is an issue for which education is particularly helpful. In this instance, both partners worked together toward education and resolution.

Through talking with others, reading, and watching some of the well-presented television programs now available, partners may see that gender variance is more common and acceptable than they had originally thought. They may learn that trans people have existed throughout history and across many cultures. They may realize that other couples have dealt with the issue and have gone on to live happy lives together.

Katherine shares a concern with a number of partners: the possibility that the more feminine the transgender spouse becomes, the more likely it is that she will want to experience sex with a man. This is sometimes the case. The gender-variant individual may simply want the experience out of curiosity, she may want to have the experience as evidence that she is really a woman, she may crave being desired by a man, or her sexual orientation may change, possibly influenced by modifications in hormone levels. I have come to the following conclusions based on some of my clinical observations. First, while numerous transwomen originally oriented more toward women temporarily experience a new attraction to men, this often fades over time, and they return to their primary erotic interest in women. Second, permanent shifts in transwomen's sexual orientation more often entail an evolution from being attracted exclusively to women to a more bisexual inclination. Therefore, if the relationship is strong, the couple can deal with any developing bisexuality in a way that is in accord with their value system. Many couples have at least one bisexual member. Bisexuality does not necessitate nonmonogamy.

Despite her initial devastation, Katherine decided that she loved her partner enough to stay in the relationship, no matter what. This decision was made easier by experiencing her relationship with Petra, which allowed Katherine to finally acknowledge to herself her true sexual orientation. Petra and Katherine seem uncertain about how far the transition will progress. She cares so much about Petra that Katherine doesn't want to hold her partner back from going further.

Katherine has become quite autonomous and self-validating, realizing that no one has the right to judge her or her relationship. She feels good about the way she and Petra process decision making, consulting together and compromising when necessary. Katherine has evolved out of her devastation with courage, strength, and determination making her nontraditional relationship work.

Chapter 16

Celeste and Ed/Edy

Celeste is glad that she did not know about her spouse's gender variance until more than thirty years of marriage. Edy is further along on the transgender spectrum than most of the gender-variant people whose wives have told their stories thus far. Edy no longer wears any "real" men's clothes, and Celeste believes that if it were not for her and her income, Edy would probably live full-time as a woman. Unlike some of the couples whose stories appear here, Celeste and Edy do not seem to be working together to make the relationship work. Edy has made unilateral decisions with which Celeste has been uncomfortable.

My name is Celeste, and my husband told me of his cross-dressing activity when we had been married for thirty-one years. I've known now for about two and half years. I cried for hours when he first told me. If I had known that it would affect my sexual desire for him and our daily conversations, if I had realized that I would never again see him in "real" men's clothes, if I had foreseen watching him obsess with jewelry, colors, and materials, matching this with that, I probably would have cried for months instead of just hours.

My husband is quite **"out."** He has his own church, seamstress, and the usual places where he runs errands. Since I have my own business, I'm gone a good bit of the time. He is probably cross-dressed constantly when I'm not around. He **passes** well enough, has friends as "Edy" (his feminine name), and even has a small art business in which he engages while cross-dressed.

Ed has an unimaginably large wardrobe. He and I both wear the many clothes he buys. He just "likes to look nice," he says. Ed doesn't spend much money on his cross-dressing. He mostly buys thrift store clothes, but he's good at selecting them and does look "very together." Women tell him they wish they were as tall as he is. Women

Head Over Heels: Wives Who Stay with Cross-Dressers and Transsexuals
Published by The Haworth Press, Inc., 2007. All rights reserved.
doi:10.1300/5737_16

stop and tell him he looks nice; they are totally comfortable with him. What could be better for a cross-dresser?!

During the first year or so I went to several transgender conferences, choosing to attend the ones that were in interesting cities I wanted to visit. I flew cross-country with Ed "dressed" too, but I no longer attend. At this point I'm clear that I consider the cross-dressing his activity, and I refuse to be drawn into it in ways that take up my time. I resent the time Ed puts into matching clothes. He spends hours looking for the "perfect" whatever to go with some article of clothing.

I do not resent Ed for waiting so long to tell me; those were the best years of my life. But I do resent the way he treated the children. Earlier in our sons' teen years my husband was hard on them. He behaved as though their having long hair and earrings was the end of the world. Now, look who has both! Two of the children know about their dad's cross-dressing. They discovered it themselves. They're smart kids. However, he doesn't know they know. I've considered the possibility that we'll all talk about it at Christmas, but why ruin the holiday? No one else in our families knows. It would be an absolute shock.

Ed is moving all his "Edy" clothes, jewelry, and other stuff to another room after the holidays. I would prefer not to see him "dressed" anymore, and we have agreed that he won't dress much in my presence. Despite this, though, I am constantly reminded of his cross-dressing. If I close my eyes, sometimes I see him as a "lady." This happens because of his walk when he's dressed, or the way he speaks a little softly, or his eyes looking different after he's taken off the makeup.

Unfortunately, this all came along at about the same time as my menopause. Living with a cross-dresser is not getting any easier for me. I may think a bit less of him than I once did; my respect for him seems to have diminished. The way I see it, the world is a serious place with lots going on, and he's dwelling on *this!*

I've realized that Ed would do this full time if it were not for me. He says he stays because of me. Occasionally I'm ready to say, "Don't bother." But I know and he knows that if I ever stopped working, our financial situation would be very difficult.

I'm not sure whether my sexual desire or interest is diminished because of my hormonal level or because I'm disinterested in him due to his female side. I've told him that he's a turn-off for me at the moment and he says that I'm not a turn-on for him either. I think we may be at a standoff. I accept the fact that being a cross-dresser is in the genes, but that doesn't help me like it.

The cross-dressing is, of course, important to Ed, since this is who he is, and I do not want to downplay the importance of anyone's journey. There's a four-year-old boy in our preschool who likes to touch the little girls' soft clothes, wrap scarves around his head, and play with the dress-up clothes we have. His mother is starting to question this and nervously laughs about it. I'm certainly torn, but I tell her to allow him to do these things.

Ed and I are aware of each others' good and bad points, and are pretty honest with each other. We talk all the time. We're working on the relationship, and hoping that we can regain our intimacy and stay together. Our partnership is important to both of us.

With her spouse, Celeste is dealing with a greater depth and breadth of involvement in cross-dressing than many of the women whose narratives are presented here. Although self-identifying as a cross-dresser, Edy may be closer to the middle of the gender spectrum. Edy no longer wears men's clothes. She is out in the world creating a life for herself. She even runs a business en femme. Although it is difficult to say without actual imput from Edy, to me she sounds more like a transgenderist than a cross-dresser.

It can be very difficult for a woman to deal with the knowledge that her husband would live full-time if it weren't for her. Similar to Celeste, she may deal with an inner conflict. Focusing on her spouse's needs, she may feel as though she is holding him back from true happiness. Attending to her own needs, she may live in fear that her spouse will throw caution to the winds, leaving the role of "husband" behind once and for all. A therapist might help Celeste to balance these competing needs.

Celeste is dealing with Edy's gender variance at a very difficult time. Going through menopause herself, she may be prone to increased emotional sensitivity and discomfort with her moods. This may be exacerbated by the insecurity about their own identities as women that many females experience during menopause.

Celeste's story suggests that Edy is not taking her wife's feelings into consideration to any significant degree. It seems almost as though they are living separate lives while sharing a home. I do not hear any evidence of consultation or compromise, and Celeste may have found that the only way she is able to empower herself within the marriage is to set limits at home and to stop attending gender conferences. Despite her major concerns, Celeste is still willing to invest energy in improving her marriage. According to Celeste, Edy claims that she too is willing.

Chapter 17

Nicole and Bob/Bobbi

As was the case for Celeste, Nicole was angry because this was not what she signed on for, and disturbed by the escalation of Bob's gender-variant expression. Eventually she had to deal with Bobbi's exploration of the possibility of transitioning from male-to-female.

Bob and I were married in 1992. Our daughter was born in 1994. In 1996, Bob and I cross-dressed as a gag for a Halloween party. As far as I knew, that started Bob's experiment with cross-dressing. I found out how far my husband's gender issues had progressed when, in February 2000, he wanted to find a therapist who specialized in gender issues. At the time I thought it was something that would just go away. It hasn't.

I lost my mother in May of 1996 and I've been fighting depression ever since. Although Bob said that he understood that he was changing the rules and knew that I had not signed on for this, I couldn't help but feel that he had *no* clue. He didn't understand that my depression stemmed from more than my mother's death. He didn't get why I shut down sexually. For me, from 1996 until 2000, grieving the loss of my mother and my husband as I had known him, dealing with the cross-dressing, and coping with depression was a struggle that kept getting more difficult.

At first, Bob was just cross-dressing right here at home. It made me uncomfortable, but given how much stress he was under at work, I didn't think it could hurt if he kept it strictly private. As time passed just cross-dressing at home wasn't satisfying whatever need Bob was having. He started to crank it up a little more, wanting to go out in public that way, despite the somewhat rednecked, yet affluent, area we live in. Unless you're in San Francisco, the Northern California

Head Over Heels: Wives Who Stay with Cross-Dressers and Transsexuals
Published by The Haworth Press, Inc., 2007. All rights reserved.
doi:10.1300/5737_17

Bay Area is *full* of conservative Republicans who aren't the most, shall we say, diversity-friendly people.

Because of where we live, I was naturally concerned about people in the neighborhood and how they would react to an obviously cross-dressing male. I was worried about violence against us, expulsion from our church, and discrimination at Bob's work. He works for the federal government, and his boss is paranoid about security.

I was especially worried about our daughter. We didn't tell her about her dad until two years ago. She's handled it quite well. But then, she was eight years old when we told her, and they say that before puberty and after puberty are the times to spring something like this on kids.

My biggest problem was (and this is still something I'm struggling with) that this was not part of the deal when I married him/her. I married a male. Bobbi (Bob's new name) seems, to this day, not to understand how that can mess up a person's thinking.

Now, I have to cope with the very unsettling situation of being married to a man who wants to change genders. When Bob/Bobbi first started this transition I found that there were precious few resources for straight spouses in my predicament. I had hoped that would change, but I don't see that it has.

We still love each other very much and want this relationship to work. Our daughter loves us both, and our family wants to stay together. One of our daughter's godparents has severed the relationship with us after a thirteen-year friendship because I decided to stay and try to work out this relationship. We didn't tell our daughter this immediately, but when she was told, she was just as angry at her former godparent as I am.

My biggest fear was about Bob's job. After all, this is the same federal government that doesn't really want gays and lesbians in the military. Bob had a habit of getting in trouble at work. I was very concerned that Bob's boss and his assistant would try to come up with any kind of excuse to fire him. Bob learned, though, that the government has a very strict policy of anti–sexual harassment. This meant that if he got fired as a result of the transition his boss could lose his job. Bobbi has since settled down from being the trouble-magnet that Bob was to being a more content, happier employee. She still wants out of the government, but isn't trying to hatch all kinds of airheaded schemes in order to do so.

I'm a very feminine person. I also see myself as a somewhat broken person due to having been molested as a teenager. In order to survive the sexual abuse I developed the habit of allowing my identity to be shaped by whoever I was with. I am fifty now and have been discovering who I really am only in recent years.

I see myself as 99.9 percent straight. However, when I was in my early thirties, I wondered whether it was possible that Mr. Right might in reality be Miss Right. That thought never bothered me, which, I figured, indicated that I had bisexual tendencies. That was perfectly all right with me, but when I fell in love with my partner, at the time, she was a he, and I figured that ended the debate.

We have yet to work out our sexual relationship; however, the desire is there, which is major progress, I think. I don't believe for one moment that my staying in this relationship makes me a lesbian any more than it could change my blood type. I'm just finding a way to love this person I've chosen and with whom I want to spend the rest of my life.

In February of 2000, when Bob found a therapist who specialized in gender issues, the proverbial shit really hit the fan. My self-esteem hit lows I wouldn't have believed possible. Despite having grown up in the sixties and having watched the women's movement arise I had the traditional habit of tying my self-esteem to the men in my life. So, when Bob announced that he wanted to explore the possibility of **HRT** and living full-time as a woman, I was absolutely devastated. I thought it was the end of my marriage. I spent a lot of time driving around our small town, crying.

The year 2000 was the worst in our marriage. Bob couldn't make up his mind what he wanted, let alone how he would go about it. He waffled about the HRT, and was even more ambivalent about sex reassignment surgery. In September of that year, I had about all I could take and told him I couldn't live with someone who is half man, half woman. I told him to "pick a gender and stick with it!" I thought he would stay with being a male. I really thought the transition stuff was a ploy on his part to get fired. I also thought it was another way for him to indulge in his favorite pastime of shocking the hell out of his family. He was very secretive around this time, which increased the tension between the two of us.

Bob went so far as to have a conference with his boss and all the office staff without my knowledge. I didn't find out until several months later. Bobbi told me that she was afraid that it would be the final straw and that I would take our daughter and split for parts unknown. In fact, at the time, that was a real possibility. I was pretty close to leaving. I had even looked around for a more economical place to life. His/her secrecy has kept us from being equal partners.

There was no support group for me, except over the Internet. The slender thread maintaining my sanity at that point in time was the few friends who knew and the TransFamily of Cleveland spouse e-mail list.

Because of my contact with that e-mail list, I'm aware of the difficulty a member of the list and her partner had finding an accepting congregation. In fact, they were asked to leave a church because they were perceived to be a lesbian couple. This concerned me deeply because we are practicing Catholics and wanted to raise our child in the Church. During one of our conversations, Bobbi told me that one of the things that attracted her to me was my deep faith. She was quite concerned that it might have changed drastically when my mother died. So, more to save my marriage than any desire to get involved, I joined this ministry at church, teaching the children various parts of our Mass while Mass was going on. After teaching one session, the troubles with my marriage intensified. I informed the pastoral associate that I had to step back and why. He was incredibly supportive and understanding. That's how special this church is. In Lent of 2001, I entered training to become a Eucharistic minister. I had the most incredible feeling the first time I served at Mass. It was only dwarfed by the way I felt when my daughter made her First Communion.

Shortly after I received the nasty letter from our daughter's godparent, I thanked our pastor for not asking us to leave. His response was one I will never forget. He very quickly replied, "I would have no right." Bobbi found two ministries she wanted to pursue: outreach, whose members serve monthly meals to a homeless shelter, and social justice, a more political ministry, currently working to establish affordable housing, reminding the people in this affluent area that not everyone is so blessed.

As for the parish's reaction to Bobbi's transition, she has been met with the best example of unconditional acceptance that one could possibly hope for. This is pretty phenomenal considering that this is a Roman Catholic church we're talking about!

I've also been very concerned about our homophobic community. I worried about how people would react to what they would perceive as a little girl parented by two people in a same-sex relationship. I assumed that our friends would be as confused as heck, but I was confident that these people who have seen me through lots of problems over many years would stand by me.

I have been delighted that our child has been lovingly accepted and supported by the teachers and staff at her school. It hasn't made any difference to my child's best friends that her daddy was becoming a woman. We have taken our daughter to a therapist to make sure there aren't issues she isn't mentioning, and we have been assured that nothing is out of place. After all, her father has been cross-dressing since she was two. Our daughter has become very private about who she tells about Mom (as she now calls Bobbi—I'm Mommy). She is aware that her principal and all the teachers she's had so far know about Mom.

I have felt threatened when Bobbi has come home with the rare story that she has met a male she finds attractive. At first I was quite worried that Bobbi's commitment to me would change. I have seen other relationships fall apart when the MtF transgendered person has found another mate—usually a male. We talked about this, and Bobbi assured me that her commitment to me would continue, but I have needed to see this for myself.

Sometimes I feel threatened by Bobbi's lifetime friend Calvin. When I met Calvin, he was a she and her name was Callie. It's not the fact that he too is transsexual or that he is transitioning that bothers me, what feels threatening is the fact that sometimes Bobbi shares information about my marriage with Calvin before she lets me in on it. They're like siblings, and I'm intensely jealous of Calvin's role as confidant in Bobbi's life.

We've had financial difficulties at various stages of our marriage. In November of 2001 Bobbi received a five-figure sum as part of her mother's estate. She was itching to get more clothes so we could throw out all of Bob's clothes. I told Bobbi that because that money was from her mother's estate, although we would discuss how to spend it, the final decision was hers. After all, it was *her* mother. Naturally, we spent a lot of the money on clothes for all of us. I had started to prefer Bobbi to Bob anyhow, having discovered that there was a big difference between them.

I guess you could say that was when we kicked Bob out. We took all the clothes Bobbi didn't want any more, put them in plastic bags, and immediately put them in the car to drop off at a thrift shop. To this day, when we get mail for Bob, we throw it away since he doesn't live here anymore!

By February of 2002, although we had spent it wisely, the money was gone. Bobbi decided which of our creditors would get paid and how much. I write the checks because of Bobbi's disability. She's been legally blind since early childhood and writing checks is too visual. We have new checks now with my name and Bobbi's on them.

People's perceptions of Bobbi have been a constant challenge for me. In November of 2001, while shopping for clothes, we found a few items for Bobbi and me. Because I'm too close to the situation to see whether Bobbi truly passes as a woman I was worried about the reactions of the women in this very crowded dressing-room area during a big sale. I was concerned that we'd be kicked out; but what happened was the exact opposite. Not one word was spoken. Maybe that was because Bobbi, our daughter, and I were all sharing a dressing room. Maybe the other women were too busy to notice. Whatever the reason, it made shopping a little more pleasurable. As we go out more in public, I'm less concerned about how well Bobbi passes. It's more important to me that the employees of the restaurant or store treat us with the same respect they give to any other customer.

I still have problems from time to time shopping for Bobbi. I'm used to being the one who gets feminine underwear or tights or dresses, but I've learned that we have pretty much the same taste in clothing. Our similarity in taste has made us shopping buddies, something we were not before Bobbi began transition.

Early last year Bobbi and I were meandering through a Macy's in an affluent, conservative California community. I wasn't sure how well Bobbi was passing, and I wondered how salespeople would approach what they might assume was a lesbian couple. We were nosing around the women's shoe department, hand-in-hand, when a salesman asked us, "How are you ladies doing today?" It came across totally friendly and accepting. We said that we were fine and continued on our way, feeling encouraged.

I've been quite pleased by how respectfully we've been treated. Recently, when I was called for jury duty, I asked to be permitted to respond to the usual jury selection questions by the judge and attorneys privately. The prosecuting attorney followed my lead, referring to Bobbi as my partner. The defense attorney, however, took it up a level, calling her my "life partner." A rather interesting choice of words, I thought.

Recently I had a car accident. While talking with the insurance agent I informed the agent of some minor injuries Bobbi sustained in the accident, referring to my partner in the feminine. After putting me on hold briefly, she told me that since California does not recognize same-sex marriages, they couldn't recognize Bobbi's injuries. We couldn't care less about how GEICO felt about our union. The woman was so apologetic; it struck me as incredibly funny! So I explained the realities of our marriage.

We can be pretty assertive about the way we want to be treated. After the aforementioned car accident the police officer wanted to talk with us to get our side of the story. He kept referring to Bobbi as my "friend." When we got out of the intersection and into a nearby convenience store, both of us corrected him, saying, "partner!" He got the message and used the proper title and pronouns. Bobbi still giggles when she thinks of that policeman. He only saw the dress, long hair, earrings, and nail polish, not noticing the day's growth of beard Bobbi didn't have time to shave off that morning.

Our relationship is on a truly equal basis now. Bobbi is learning to tell me what's on her mind and I'm learning to deal with having a more outspoken partner. Bobbi and I have the ability to make each other laugh. That's one of the reasons why we married. While our daughter is in dance class on Saturday mornings we have breakfast in town and reconnect with each other. We are trying to heal our relationship by finding things we can do together.

When I sent Nicole her edited narrative for final approval, she told me that everything had changed. She sent me the following update.

When we first got married, it seemed that we supported each others' dreams. Bob wanted to be a writer, so I supported him in following that dream. But, over a period of the past year or so, everything began to turn sour. It took me a long time to realize that all the support was going in one direction: from me to my spouse. I looked up one day and realized that I was married to a complete and total stranger. The sweet, considerate man I fell in love with and pledged to spend the rest of my life with had been replaced by a self-centered, self-obsessed, immature individual.

From the beginning of the transition, it was all about Bobbi's dreams, wants, and needs. Even Bobbi's sister noticed how selfish and self-absorbed Bobbi had become. Financially, we couldn't manage all of us getting everything we needed, even with me working three part-time jobs. It seemed that every spare cent was going for what Bobbi wanted, with our daughter and me doing without.

In January of 2003 Bobbi told me that she had been fighting depression and suicidal thoughts and had even attempted suicide a couple of times since the previous November. I didn't know how this could have been going on without her having told me—without my having noticed. Then, Bobbi had a complete emotional breakdown. I took her to a hospital and she was admitted for the weekend. She started taking Prozac, and improved so much over the weekend that she was discharged on Monday.

In March of the same year Bobbi was admitted to another psychiatric facility. She gave the staff at the hospital the idea that her psychiatric problems were the result of our relationship. She made it seem as though everything that ever went wrong between us was my fault. The doctor said that she could not be discharged to home and so instead, Bobbi had to stay with a friend. While she went through an intensive outpatient psychiatric program, she insisted that life with me was so bad that it made her want to kill herself.

Bobbi eventually moved back in with us. In May she began telling me all the things I do to hurt her. She also said that I smell bad, even right after a bath, and that it doesn't feel good when I touch her. The worst thing she said was that although she knew that some day she'd be intimate with someone, it wouldn't be with me. That was my sign from God that I had done everything in my power, and that it wasn't enough.

We decided to separate. In July 2003 my daughter and I moved in with my seventy-nine-year-old father. I'm happy with my work as an interpreter for the deaf in a small town in Northern California. Bobbi and I are trying to maintain a friendly relationship for the sake of our daughter. On the day when our divorce is final we are planning to call each other and celebrate.

Originally I had intended to limit this volume to the stories of women whose relationships had remained intact. When I heard from Nicole that she and Bobbi had separated, I decided to amend and include her story. It does contain some threads common to relationships that involve gender variance. For instance, wives often mention the gender issues not being part of the deal, not being something they "signed on for." This is one way they express their sense of betrayal, their anger about having been deceived, led to believe that their spouses were "just regular guys."

Nicole mentions several fears that are more common for partners of people whose transgender expression becomes public. First, she worries about violence against Bobbi and her. Given the number of hate crimes targeting gender-variant people, this is certainly a valid concern.

Second, she is concerned about discrimination by her spouse's employers. Bobbi works for the federal government. Gender-variant people are often not protected by law in the work environment, and even employers who fear lawsuits can find ways to dismiss or make the work day miserable for employees who do not fit their mold.

Third, Nicole is apprehensive about the possibility of expulsion from their church. She mentions that they attend a Catholic Church, and although some churches in this denomination are more accepting than others, a good chance exists that a transgender couple might experience rejection or shunning in the congregation of their choice. This can be extremely painful. People seek support, guidance, and nurturance from their spiritual leaders and members of their congregation, but may instead be wounded by lack of acceptance. Fortunately, Nicole and Bobbi continued to be welcome at their church, in which they were quite active.

Finally, Nicole is anxious about how Bobbi's gender issues will affect their daughter. She reports that the child, who was eight when she was told, is handling the issue well at this point, but she is uncertain what may unfold in the future. Kudos to Nicole and Bobbi for having their daughter's adjustment to Bobbi's transition professionally evaluated.

Nicole has dealt with many issues in conjunction with her spouse's gender variance. In addition to grieving the loss of her husband as she knew and loved him, she grieved the loss of her mother, and dealt with depression. Her difficulties coping with Bobbi's disclosure may have been compounded by her having been molested as a teen. She has been retraumatized, albeit in a different way, and her self-esteem and mood are suffering.

One thing that Nicole was clear about was her sexual orientation. Unlike some natal female partners of transwomen, she never doubted her heterosexuality, despite her willingness to stay in relationship with Bobbi. I like the way she put it: "I'm just finding a way to love this person I've chosen and with whom I want to spend the rest of my life."

Nicole seems to have tried her very best to make the marriage work. She really wanted to keep the family together, and appeared to be working hard to create an environment in which her daughter would not experience discrimination. Nicole is a woman who was willing to stay with her transgendered spouse. It seems that in this case it was the transgendered spouse who was not interested in continuing in relationship.

Chapter 18

Ellen and Alfred

Ellen found out about Alfred's gender variance little-by-little. At first she thought her spouse was "just a cross-dresser." Eventually, Alfred told her that he would like to start hormones and eventually have sex reassignment surgery. She was devastated. As did Nicole, Ellen had many valid concerns.

My husband Alfred has not been one to come right out and tell me the whole truth. Instead, I have learned little bits about his other "persona" as he lets me. Near the end of our seventh year of marriage I discovered his makeup. That's when I first learned of his secret life. He told me, when I confronted him, that he liked to dress in women's clothing. It made him feel sexy; he would masturbate. This didn't worry me, as I figured it was just a dress up game and it didn't hurt anyone. His dressing didn't interfere with our life.

I didn't know anything about cross-dressing, but that didn't concern me. What was there to know? I did not tell any friends. It would be embarrassing for him; besides, my belief is that what happens in the bedroom stays in the bedroom. All our friends were in the military, and I did not want Alfred's cross-dressing to get back to his superiors or peers.

About two years later, when we went back to Canada, we got the Internet and our lives revolved around cross-dressing. We spent hours in chat rooms and going from site to site looking for information. My husband began to dress around me. He told me of his fantasy that I would make love to him while he was dressed as a woman. I tried it twice. I did not like it. We ventured out in public twice. Once we went to the drive-in and once we went shopping, to dinner, and to the movies.

During the past three years my husband has become obsessed with cross-dressing. A day has not gone by when Alfred didn't have on

Head Over Heels: Wives Who Stay with Cross-Dressers and Transsexuals
Published by The Haworth Press, Inc., 2007. All rights reserved.
doi:10.1300/5737_18

something feminine. As a result, our sex life became nonexistent. I felt lost and got more and more depressed. I also started to suspect that he was not "just a cross-dresser."

As fate would have it, Alfred was transferred to headquarters in Ottawa, four and a half hours away from where we live. This was bad news. Decisions had to be made and made quickly. I own and operate a business, and our daughter was just starting high school. We decided that since it would only be a little over a year before my husband could retire, he would go to Ottawa alone.

My depression and apprehension worsened as the time grew nearer for him to leave. Because he seemed so calm about it, I assumed that he was welcoming being away from us. Finally I asked Alfred if he felt that he was really TS and was looking at becoming a full woman. He assured me that he would never cut off his penis. The day he left I cried uncontrollably and could not even face my daughter for the rest of the day. She had to fend for herself as I lay in bed as though I were in a coma. In my heart I knew that this was the last time I would see my husband as I knew and loved him.

A month after Alfred went to live by himself in Ottawa, he started to change his appearance and behavior drastically. He shaved off all of his body hair and began a radical weight loss program. He became preoccupied with his looks. Again I asked him if he was considering a sex change. At this point he admitted that he would like to try having breasts. Three months later, he told me that he would like to start hormones as soon as possible and eventually have SRS.

When Alfred first told me this I was distraught. Then I internalized all my feelings in order not to hurt him. I wanted to die. I wanted him to die. I felt guilty for feeling this way. But after all, he was the one who had lied all this time. He didn't deserve to live. Finally I became angry with God for putting another massive hurdle in the way of my happiness.

As time went on I got angrier and more depressed. I knew that my husband needed to talk and so I let him, but inside I wanted to die. I felt like a total failure. What kind of woman can't tell a woman from a man? Am I a lesbian subconsciously? Did he marry me because he saw something in me that I didn't . . . that I was a dyke? What kind of a wife am I that I end up turning my husband into a woman? What a failure I am that I can't even pick an appropriate husband? If I leave him, what does that say about me? I have always told my daughter not to follow the crowd but just be herself. I'll be a hypocrite if I don't support my husband in being who he needs to be. What will happen to my daughter and me if I let go of Alfred? Who am I without him? So many questions—my head was spinning.

I then started looking at women to see if any of them aroused me sexually. Am I unconsciously a lesbian? I must be because I married a woman in disguise. As hard as I tried to let it happen, I didn't become aroused by women. I continue to mourn the loss of sexual intimacy. To stay with my spouse meant that I would be giving up everything from hugging to sex (I am very uncomfortable hugging women, and always have been).

I have had low self-esteem most of my life. With my husband, I slowly came to realize that I was an intelligent, beautiful woman and that I had a lot to offer to society. He made me feel like I was the best woman in the world. Since his coming out with the "full" truth, I've gone back to feeling like a stupid, ugly, fat failure.

The more Alfred primps and preens, the less I feel like a woman. More questions and fears arise. What will it say about me if he looks prettier than I do? My business is sure to go down the drain when it gets out that he is TS. I'll have to move from our small community and uproot my daughter once more. How will we survive? I'm sure to lose my family. My parents are very bigoted. Once more I will be a failure in my family's eyes.

Alfred says that he loves me and that he wants us to be together "until death do us part." He says that he stopped making love with me not because he doesn't love me but because I can't accept him as a woman. He says that he'll stay with me, even if it means that we are just best friends. Personally, I think he's just using me for support. Once he's set up his own new support system, he will no longer depend on me. I don't think that he'll be able to accept a life with no physical intimacy. I'm afraid that Alfred will begin to look for it elsewhere. I'll lose him all over again.

In March of this year, we told our fourteen-year-old daughter that her father is transsexual. I don't know whether or not it was wise, since she is searching for her own identity and is confused. But honestly, I needed someone to talk with on a regular basis. Alfred is out of the closet and we are in it. Our daughter has bottled up her feelings. She'll only talk to me when she explodes. She refuses to tell her dad anything. She believes that if she says what she really feels, she will be betraying him, and then she'll no longer be the "perfect" daughter. Just recently she told her best friend, who took the news very well and has agreed to keep it a secret.

Alfred's therapist has encouraged him not to come out to anyone else until he appears more feminine. That way it will be easier for people to accept him. At least this is what he told me his therapist said. I've told the one person that I consider a friend. She hasn't been too supportive; she thinks that my husband and I will part ways eventually. Not what I want to hear right now. Other than her, I have no friends. I've cut them out of my life in order to avoid a slip up.

I used to be very community involved, to the extent that my husband always complained that I was never home. Since last year, I have taken myself off all but three committees. These I have to keep because of my business. I just don't have the energy to face people right now. Alfred's transition seems to be sucking the life and energy out of me!

I'm jealous that he seems so at peace now. He's making new friends and has a life outside of "us." Alfred has turned my life inside out and closeted me so that he can have a life. It just seems so unfair! For years we were all each other needed, and now it's as though I'm not enough.

We are no longer lovers, but despite it all we are still best friends. I have never felt the need to have a close friendship with anyone else. When something good happens in my life, Alfred is the first person I think to tell. When something goes wrong at work, he's my sounding board. He's there when I need him. I can count on him to help me with anything manual. He's funny; he makes me laugh. I enjoy going on walks with him and talking to him. We have always been good at talking. We've agreed not only to keep our lines of communication open, but also to be completely honest with our feelings and thoughts, no matter how painful it may be. All transition decisions will be made jointly from now on, and my husband will take things at *our* pace and not push me.

This is a very difficult time for all of us. We are trying to figure out who we are as individuals as well as how we fit together as a family. I still hold a lot of anger and resentment. Mostly I resent his having put us into the closet. I resent Alfred for being willing to risk losing a perfectly good marriage. I resent his having taken my dream and thoughtlessly smashed it. I resent his having lied repeatedly and told half-truths, damaging my capacity to trust. I resent his tendency to think of himself first. I resent that he has thrust me into a world of stares, finger-pointing, and people talking about me behind my back. I resent him for not having the courage before we were married to tell me he had a problem. I resent his manipulation. I resent his having friends, a support group, and a therapist when I do not.

To help my growth I have gone back to keeping a journal and writing poetry. This helps me to see my feelings more clearly and to communicate better with my Alfred. I have also taken to reading everything I can online about marriages and transition. It gives me great comfort to know that my daughter and I are not alone in our feelings. Others have worked through this and so will we. We will not be victims!

It is not unusual for people to find out little by little, as did Ellen, about their partners being transsexual. In some cases this happens as the truth unfolds in the consciousness of the gender-variant individual. In other instances, the transsexual tells as much at a time as s/he dares, hoping that incremental disclosure will avoid scaring the partner away and make it possible to "have it all." Some transsexuals actually take actions such as starting hormones, changing their names, and going full-time at work without discussing these major transitional milestones with their partners in advance.

Partners to whom the whole truth is not disclosed at the point when the transperson becomes aware of it may find it very difficult to accommodate to the gender variance. They often have a great deal of anger, resentment, and mistrust to overcome. These partners may feel disregarded, disrespected, and invalidated by their unilateral decision making and failure to take their feelings and needs into consideration.

When Ellen first discovered Alfred's makeup, and Alfred admitted to cross-dressing, Ellen was quite accepting of what she thought of as a harmless erotic activity. More recently, however, it became obvious that Alfred's gender variance was more extensive. Ellen was willing to experiment sexually with her spouse, facilitating actualization of Alfred's fantasy, but the experience was not pleasurable for her. Ellen's depression and her negative feelings about the extent of her spouse's feminine presentation led to an extreme diminution of their sex life.

While Alfred initially told Ellen that she was "just a cross-dresser," Ellen suspected that that was not true. Finally, Alfred began to modify her appearance in more drastic ways, and then admitted that she wanted hormonal treatment and sex reassignment surgery. Ellen's story suggests that her spouse did not include her in the process of decision making at all, instead, simply announcing intentions.

Ellen is engaged in an intense emotional struggle without adequate support. She seems extremely disturbed by every aspect of her spouse's transition. She is another example of a wife who is doing more of the work in her marriage with less support and fewer resources. Despite her pain, she loves Alfred (for whom she provided no femme name) and is working toward finding ways to continue the relationship. She is learning to set limits and is committed to honest, direct communication, whether or not Alfred reciprocates.

I do wonder whether Ellen communicated all the questions and concerns she mentioned to Alfred and if she did, how Alfred responded. Ellen mentions her resentment of Alfred having a therapist and a support group and she having neither. I believe that therapy would be extremely beneficial for Ellen and for their daughter. If I were involved in a therapeutic capacity with this family, I would help Ellen to recognize and change her complicity in her self-isolation. Although it is valuable for intimate partners to enjoy a close friendship, Ellen's isolation seems extreme. She and Alfred may have fallen prey to a common syndrome in transient families in which they become islands unto themselves, not making friends outside the dyad only to have to let go at the point of the next transfer. In addition, I would want to address the parentification of the daughter and her use as a confidant. Ellen is seeking education about marriage and transition, and despite her obvious ambivalence and the way she has been left out of the process, she wants to keep their marriage intact.

Chapter 19

Angelita and Tom/Theresa

As with Ellen, Angelita learned of her spouse's gender variance incrementally. After fourteen years of marriage, Angelita found out that Tom was a cross-dresser. Five years later her spouse admitted to a desire to transition.

When my husband and I celebrated our twentieth wedding anniversary in September 2002, it brought tears to my eyes: both tears of joy and tears of sorrow. Tom and I spent the day shopping. I got a coat and he bought a skirt for himself. There will only be a few more anniversaries with my husband. He is not dying or leaving me. You see, my husband is a **pre-op** transsexual. He has decided that he needs to transition from male to female to feel at peace within himself, to stop living a lie.

A couple of months before our anniversary, we went to see his doctor to begin the process of taking female hormones. I wanted to go because I had a lot of questions for the doctor. I was a complete wreck during the week leading up to the appointment. My heart ached so badly. As we got closer to the doctor's office, I was starting to shake and cry. Now this transition was beginning for real!

I couldn't believe what would be happening a few years from now. My life ahead of me looked like a blank piece of paper. I had a sinking feeling in my gut as if someone had died. What am I going to do? I am angry and sad. I am also strong. I have an "I can do this" attitude, along with a "How in hell am I going to survive?" feeling.

My husband was very sensitive to my feelings and concerned for me so he tried to hide his glow of pure happiness as we left the doctor's office. This emotional roller coaster has been exhausting for both of us. So, as we often do when we need to escape, off to the shopping mall we went.

Head Over Heels: Wives Who Stay with Cross-Dressers and Transsexuals
Published by The Haworth Press, Inc., 2007. All rights reserved.
doi:10.1300/5737_19

Because of the hormonal changes Tom would be experiencing we decided to tell our two teenage sons about the transition. They handled it better than a good share of the adults we have told. Yes, they hurt, but they showed a great deal of compassion for their dad. They knew that he would always be there for them no matter what his outer appearance might be. I was surprised that telling our children gave me a feeling of relief. No more lies, and I no longer had to hide my feelings. At that point, we had our own little support group.

It's been seven years since I discovered that Tom was a cross-dresser. We had been married for fourteen years. That was what he thought he was at the time. It took five years for him to come to terms with being transsexual.

I really love Tom. He has been a wonderful husband and father throughout our marriage. That is why we plan on staying married and living in the same house. After the transition to female, though, "she" will have her own bedroom and bath. The only good outcome of this is that I get more closet space (thank God I still have a sense of humor).

But the reality is that I am losing my husband. I won't have that man in my life in the same way, to hold me and to take care of me. I won't have that security. That "in love" intimacy will no longer be a part of my life. But although my future holds no husband, I will still have the best lifelong friend anyone could have. At this stage the pain is stronger than ever. Am I angry? Yes, at the situation. I have as little control over it as if I were being widowed.

As for how I found out, nine years ago, I began suspecting that something was going on. Tom always looked guilty, and I sensed that he was keeping something from me—about what, I didn't know—but something wasn't right. I was thrilled that we had recently bought a computer and gotten Internet access. Sometimes when I came home from work Tom would look guilty and sign off the Internet very fast. I started getting paranoid. This brought on little fights that ended up with me feeling bad about myself, and my self-esteem began to suffer.

What I didn't yet know was that Tom had signed on to the Internet with a female persona, nor did I know that he had opened some credit card accounts that only came to him at work. He used these for buying feminine things for himself. During this time I guess Tom was talking to the transgender community online in chat rooms. That is how he was coming to terms with himself. He found that there were others out there like him. But I was still totally in the dark about all this. I just knew that I felt uneasy and suspicious.

I started to go through his pockets and his wallet, finding nothing. My gut feeling was that he was hiding something I wouldn't like. I just knew that he was thinking about another woman. I was struggling so much; I didn't know what to do. So I cleaned. In the process I found a duffle bag filled with all the necessities for dressing up as a woman. There were breast forms just like the ones you find in the back of magazines. I stared at them forever in disbelief. There was even an invoice with his name on it. He had actually bought these!

I went through the rest of the stuff, pulling out shoes, skirts, underwear, pantyhose, and makeup. The things that go through your mind in a split second can be so weird. I envisioned him dressing as a woman to pick up women he had met on the Internet. In my mind, that was a pretty bizarre thought. It must have been at least a year before I could set foot in that garage again.

I called Tom at work and asked him about this stuff I found. He immediately came home and we sat down together and talked. I asked question after question. He tried to answer as best he could. I was totally devastated. My whole world turned upside down right then and there. It seemed that everything I thought was real had been a lie. My trust in my husband was gone. It felt like I had a stranger in the house, that I didn't know who I was married to anymore. I felt very alone in the world.

My anger and disbelief were so overwhelming that I couldn't cope. We decided to see a counselor together and also individually. I had never given a second thought to my sexual identity or orientation, until the therapist asked me if I might be bisexual in any way. Wow! Was that strange! Did it make me a lesbian because I was attracted to a cross-dresser? Could I be attracted to other women since I was attracted to my husband? I did wonder about myself briefly; but I am as straight as can be. That was pretty scary. I had always considered myself quite open to the gay community, but now that it was in my own backyard I found myself very uncomfortable.

Looking back at this, I laugh, because cross-dressing was really rather simple compared to the transsexuality I'm facing now. Maybe this six-year journey laid the foundation for both of us. Faced with this situation, I looked deep into my soul to see what I was really made of. I think that is what frightens people most when a loved one "comes out of the closet." You have to take a good, hard look at yourself before you can judge others.

Instead of thinking of myself as part of a couple, I have had to learn who I am as an individual. I used to enjoy our closeness and the feeling that Tom found me sexy and attractive, and it saddens me quite a bit to lose all that. Shopping and eating ice cream together now replaces the physical intimacy we once had. The more he becomes a woman, the less I find him sexually attractive like I used to. This is tough to work through and I will miss him, but we are adjusting to being best friends. At my request, my spouse now has his own room and bathroom, which has made me more comfortable.

I have concerns that since there will be no more husband/wife love, no romance or feeling wanted, that he will want or need to find someone else. I really feel insecure that one of us will leave the relationship. I know that we love each other, but I don't know what the future brings for the two of us. The unknown is what frightens me the most.

As for my self-esteem, I have none, zilch, zip, nada! I am starting from the bottom and working my way back up. I am setting goals for myself and adjusting priorities so they work out in my favor. It sounds selfish, but I have to look out for me right now; I need to survive.

Tom now wants to be called Theresa. We have spent or saved an incredible amount of money for Theresa's new wardrobe, hair care, electrolysis, and hormones, not to mention SRS, and also possibly a hair transplant. This is a big financial burden. I try not to be resentful, instead seeing it as just like any other medical catastrophe. Theresa has been living as a female full-time and at work only her supervisor knows of her past. She knows that her past will eventually catch up with her, but for now, she is flying under the radar.

Shopping has been wonderful fun. Theresa has very good taste in clothing, and since he knows me so well he helps me with selections as much as I help him. (As you can see, I'm having a hard time with the pronouns.) We have a good time when we shop and grab a bite to eat. That is one of the first things I have felt really comfortable doing with him since I found out. I have only done this while he was in "boy mode." I haven't done a whole lot with "her" yet. That is still difficult because I don't want to be recognized by someone and have to make up some lie about who I am with or why my husband is dressed like that.

I am grateful that the four of us, Theresa and our two teenage kids, all have wonderful senses of humor. We tease and laugh a lot—often at Theresa's expense—but it is all in fun. That is the way we are all coping with this. You have to laugh.

More than a few transsexuals believe that they are cross-dressers before recognizing their transsexuality. This kind of confusion most often occurs for people who are not at the extreme ends of the transgender spectrum. For example, an MtF who has been tempted to mutilate her genitals (and the temptation—even the act itself—is not as rare as one might think) would be unlikely to mistake herself for a cross-dresser. That transsexuality can temporarily masquerade as a less intense form of gender variance makes it difficult for the SOs of transgendered people to feel safe in trusting that their partners are "just cross-dressers." Professional assistance can help people with gender confusion to reach accurate conclusions about the extent of their gender variance and what, if any, physical/medical interventions are necessary.

Angelita's questions about her own sexual orientation surfaced only after a therapist raised the issue. Ultimately she realized that she was aware of no capacity for erotic attraction to a woman. Angelita's decreasing sexual attraction to her spouse as Theresa feminizes supports her perception of her sexual orientation. Some natal female partners find it imperative to avoid any erotic experimentation in order to avert sexual orientation confusion in their own minds or in others' perceptions. Others, being at the extreme heterosexual end of the sexual orientation continuum, are incapable of becoming aroused in response to a person they perceive as feminine.

Angelita mentions two powerful desires that are now unfulfilled in her life. It was important to her to have a man to take care of her, and she treasured the physical intimacy she and her spouse shared. Despite her pain, and while grieving her losses, Angelita is choosing to stay with Theresa. Similar to some other SOs who stay, she values her relationship with her best friend enough to relinquish eroticism in her future. At least she feels that way now. Angelita is, however, uncertain about whether being in an asexual relationship eventually will cause them to go their separate ways.

For now, however, they seem to be making their platonic relationship work, and their two teenage sons appear to have adjusted well to their father's transition. They seem to be the exception to the commonly held belief that adolescents have a difficult time coping with a parent's transition. Angelita has been relieved not to have to keep the secret from their sons. Some families operate better without the parents holding this kind of secret. Some children of transgendered people claim that even prior to their being told they knew something was going on, and that they prefer knowing what it is to living with the vague unease elicited by a parental secret. Since Angelita submitted her story for inclusion in this book, Theresa has moved forward in her transition and had SRS. They appeared together on the *Oprah* show, on which they discussed issues relevant to couples who stay together.

Chapter 20

Melissa and Steve/Stephanie

When Melissa had to deal with Stephanie's transition, similar to Angelita, she valued her relationship with her best friend and decided to stay. She wanted Stephanie to be happy, but felt as though she was sacrificing her own happiness for that of her spouse. She found it difficult to validate her own difficulties dealing with the transition, instead seeing them as petty.

Stephanie and I celebrated our fourth wedding anniversary in May of 2003. It is only through sheer love and determination that we remain together, as Stephanie's transition to becoming a woman takes center stage in both our lives. Ours is an evolving relationship that began when we met in 1996. Each new revelation about the woman trapped inside Steve has required many adjustments on my part. Steve/Stephanie has been forced to make some hard decisions.

I was his soul mate, his confidante, the love of his life. Steve didn't know how to tell me the secret that could very well break the bond between us. This was the predicament he faced just before our wedding. Steve gradually told broke the news to me. Since then, we have been coming to terms with Steve's being transgendered—born male, but feeling like a female inside.

Prior to our moving in together Steve had amassed a fair assortment of women's clothes and such. Our move-in date was Steve's first purge; he threw it all in the garbage. He figured that with his love for me, he could overcome his gender confusion. But his mental state started sliding. He had been diagnosed with moderate clinical depression. He found a new doctor and started taking medication. The problem was that he was repressing what was causing his depression—his gender confusion.

I finally convinced him to tell me what was wrong. He wrote me a letter focusing on cross-dressing, telling me about his confusion. I

Head Over Heels: Wives Who Stay with Cross-Dressers and Transsexuals
Published by The Haworth Press, Inc., 2007. All rights reserved.
doi:10.1300/5737_20

was floored; I felt numb from the shock. I didn't know what to say, other than, "Oh, that's all it is?" I was afraid that anything I said might come out wrong, so I kept my feelings inside. We had been together for about a year and a half when he told me about the cross-dressing, and I promised him that I wouldn't tell anyone. I felt very much alone. I had no one to talk to about it; nobody I knew would understand what it was like to live with a man who cross-dressed. At first, I thought that dressing up in women's clothes was all that he would need to make him happy—that, and my love and support.

Since at least age nine, Steve had known that there was something different about him. Eventually, he realized that he was transsexual— born biologically male, yet wired with a female brain. He was raised in challenging circumstances by his single mother. His sister, Etta, is two years younger, and his brother, Bill, is eleven years his junior. They lived in many places and faced many hardships, mainly financial. As the oldest child, and a male to boot, Steve was kind of forced to be "the man of the house." When he grew up Steve continued playing the male role, working at male-dominated jobs, and engaging in male activities.

Steve originally told me that he liked to wear women's clothes when he was at home, but I soon learned that he wanted to cross-dress all the time. He wasn't comfortable in traditional men's clothing, and seemed to loathe having to wear men's clothes to work and when we went out for dinner. I took the news better than Steve expected.

Just knowing that I knew about his desire to dress as a woman seemed to lift a lot of Steve's depression. I didn't have time to really wrap my mind around his disclosure before we went shopping to pick out some female clothes for him to wear around the house. I was so worried about what people would think if they saw him looking at women's clothes with too much interest that I freaked out when he finally found something he could wear. I was jittery because, at that time, we were living in an area that isn't exactly a good place to be "different." Plus, I was still reeling from his confession.

Then, a little over three years ago, Steve's drive toward transition went nuts. We were working on moving to a larger city so that I could take a job there. On one of our road trips Steve gave me a letter. The letter said that cross-dressing wasn't enough. He wanted to begin the steps toward transition. He wanted to live full-time as a woman. He said that he really needed my support, and wanted to have me with him forever.

I was extremely angry at him because he hadn't told me about his desire to transition sooner. I felt as though he had lied to me about this so that I would marry him. I was so angry that I was close to tears. I didn't know how our relationship as husband and wife would change once Steve started transitioning. I wasn't even sure whether I could stay with him. After a while, though, I realized that I *wanted* to stay with him, despite knowing that our relationship would never be the same.

I was accustomed to him wearing female clothing around the house, but when he took to wearing a bra when we went out, it took some time for me to get used to that. I became very confused and felt betrayed. I wanted Steve to be happy, but it felt as if I was sacrificing my own happiness for his.

For a long time I couldn't bring myself to call Steve "her" or "she" because I married him as a male. I thought we were on the same page when he asked me to marry him, and it seemed that we *were* for quite awhile. At first I thought that if I showered him with love and helped him prove his manhood he would no longer desire transition. I was wrong. I've slowly come to realize that no matter what I do, he's going to become, or already has become, Stephanie in his/her own mind.

Steve began therapy in January 2001, and since September of 2002 has been under the care of a doctor who is well versed in transgender medicine. He began antiandrogen therapy, taking Spironolactone and Proscar. The reduction of his testosterone level has helped a lot with his anxiety, depression, and mood swings.

At first all of Steve's decisions were based on how I'd feel more than on what was right for him. Then, for a long time—and still upon occasion—I felt as though it didn't matter what I wanted in our relationship. It seemed that he was going to transition with or without my support. We got into couples therapy to try to work out our problems, and I'm coming to accept Steve's transition more and more each day.

After all, I know that for Steve, it's a path of no return. Even in the first two months after he started taking testosterone suppressants we noticed changes in his body structure. His facial hair growth slowed down and his scalp hair began growing again. His breasts started to round out and he started to grow hips. His sex drive decreased, which isn't necessarily a bad thing.

All I can do right now is love him and support him through transition much as he's supported me through thick and thin. We have certainly had some difficult times. I had a nervous breakdown in January of 2002 and was hospitalized for eight days. I haven't been able to return to work since then and we've been financially strapped. But Steve keeps going to work so we can have food on the table and pay our bills. I'm very grateful for that.

The process of coming out to me wasn't easy, but coming out to family and friends has had more destructive results. Stephanie has come out to her immediate family: her brother, sister, and mother. She chose to come out to them first because she expected the most acceptance and best support from them. Stephanie was disappointed when she lost her mother and brother when she came out. I lost what had been a very good relationship with her mother.

What Stephanie has experienced with her family has made it difficult for her to continue coming out to others. If some of the people that she loves and is closest to seem to be abandoning her at one of her times of greatest need, she wonders what is going to happen with those with whom she is not so close.

I've never kept my desire to have children from Stephanie, and I had hoped that by now we would have at least one of our own. However, when she started taking the antiandrogens, the doctor took baseline testosterone levels as a reference point. We found out that her testosterone levels were very low for a biological male. The levels were so low that she was probably infertile. Although I had told her that her transition would be easier on me if I knew she was sterile to begin with, the reality of her infertility was actually another slap in the face to me.

My acceptance of the sterility has been a journey in and of itself. The sterility issue doesn't bother Stephanie, because she hasn't identified as male for a long time, if ever. I know there are other ways for us to have children, but I would really like to know what it feels like to have a new life growing inside of me, and I wanted the child's father to be my spouse. I've really been grieving about this. Fortunately, we have continued to discuss parenthood and our options. With the help of our therapist and our ever-strengthening relationship we will get through this challenge together.

Stephanie's antiandrogen therapy is progressing well. Her mood has become much less erratic, with the exception of an increased likelihood of crying. The feminization she has experienced just through suppressing her male hormones is amazing. We continue to explore and embrace these changes. Stephanie has become much calmer and easier to live with.

Another change has to do with Stephanie's name and choice of pronouns. Although I have been slowly becoming accustomed to using female pronouns and her girl name, I've pretty much reserved that for private situations. Stephanie has requested that her therapist and doctor, as well as others to whom she has come out, begin referring to her in the feminine. She's also started signing e-mails to her siblings with her girl name.

At one point Stephanie and I actually began "cycling" together. It's true! We were both "PMSing." Sometimes, not even chocolate quiets our bodies down. Stephanie's going through her second puberty with the breast growth and her shifting mind-set. She's just now finding out what her body may do once she starts taking estrogen.

It was difficult finding the money for Stephanie to start electrolysis, but we knew she would have to do that eventually. I don't like hearing her complaints. I hear about it when her breasts hurt. Imagine when she willingly allows herself to be electrocuted to get rid of her facial hair. Yikes!

This is kind of sick and twisted, but I actually laugh, in a rather evil way, when Stephanie complains about her breasts hurting. It's not because she's hurting, it's the way she says it. Her inflection ranges anywhere from wonder to complete exasperation. Her breasts have been growing since April of this year, but just about every night she forgets and just flops down on the bed on her stomach, suddenly realizing that, oops, that hurts! I can't help but chuckle, because in that way she's still male in her thinking. She just doesn't learn.

Stephanie keeps asking me if my breasts hurt when they were growing and I tell her that was twenty-five years ago, and quite honestly, I don't remember. The closest I can come to what she's feeling is the pain from breast reduction surgery I had ten years ago. While I was healing it hurt like hell.

It bothers me that we are forever concentrating on Stephanie's transition issues. Sometimes it feels as though my problems dealing with transition are petty compared to hers. I feel like I'm being left out of this. She just keeps referring to herself and her feelings. I have to remind her that it is we who are going through this, not just her. She is changing and as her body and psyche change, our relationship is changing too.

During August 2002, Stephanie was obsessing about how we were going to afford her transition. I finally got tired of hearing her go over and over the same things again and again and I told her in no uncertain terms, "It's true that we can't afford electrolysis, we can't afford to build your wardrobe, and we can't afford any surgery right now. But you also haven't been working on your voice or your makeup technique, and those things are free." She couldn't argue with that logic.

I'm not usually the logical or practical one in our relationship, but I have sensed a bit of a shift on my part toward those two traits. I don't want to completely take over the male role in our relationship—hell, I don't even want to think about that at all—but someone's going to have to wear the pants in this family.

At one point Stephanie and I came to a lull in her transition. At that point my biggest concerns were keeping our relationship together, supporting Stephanie through transition, and completing my master's degree. In October 2004, though, Steph's name change went through and she began working toward going full-time on her job.

Stephanie has always told me that she loves me and is going to stick with me throughout this transition. I've thought a lot about how our relationship is going to change once she finally starts living full-time as a woman. I don't know that living as a lesbian is going to bother me, because Stephanie and I have always had a loving relationship; the only thing that will be different is that "he" will be a female. I want whatever makes Stephanie happy, and I want our relationship to grow.

Melissa is dealing with a number of issues that are common threads in the fabric of the lives of transsexuals' partners. It seems that in order for Stephanie to be content, Melissa has to sacrifice her own happiness. Only one of them can have what she truly wants, and in this instance, Melissa is allowing Stephanie to be that person. Melissa wanted a man and thought she had one, albeit one who enjoyed cross-dressing. The SO of an MtF transperson often dreams of having her man back, but rarely can that be. So, a woman who wants her relationship to remain intact may let go of her preference for being with a man so that her beloved can have her heart's desire:

congruence between internal mental gender identity and external anatomy. The partner may experience a huge loss that must be grieved.

As with so many SOs who are in similar situations, Melissa often feels as though she is being left out. She tends to minimize the importance of her own feelings, construing her problems dealing with the transition as petty. She reports saying only, "Oh, that's all it is," when Steve first admitted to his gender confusion, despite being shocked. She kept her feelings and the secret inside, attending much more to her spouse's feelings than to her own. If I had the opportunity to work with Melissa, I would support her learning to validate her own feelings and needs more.

Women continue to be socialized to take care of others, so it's not unusual for a woman to focus more on others' feelings and needs than on her own. Pressure on women to be selfless is not as pervasive today as it was for women who grew up in the 1940s, 1950s, and 1960s, and this facet of female socialization is no longer supported by the culture as a whole.

Sometimes Melissa gets tired of concentrating on Stephanie's transition issues. It's vital that when one member of a couple is transitioning, both recognize that the gender-variant individual is neither the only one going through a transition nor the only one having a difficult time. Many challenging issues arise for SOs, and if the relationship is to endure the transgendered person must attend as much to the partner's concerns as to her own. Transsexuals must also avoid the expectation that their lives will revolve totally around the transition, leaving out everything else.

Melissa had many things to adjust to, including Stephanie's sterility. Some couples, prior to beginning HRT, store sperm for later insemination. It sounds as though that was not a possibility for Melissa and Stephanie. Despite everything that has happened to date, and the inevitable changes to come, Melissa wants the relationship to continue and flourish. To that end, she and Stephanie have engaged in couples' therapy.

Chapter 21

Sandy and Mandy (formerly Mark)

Whereas Melissa felt numb when her spouse disclosed the gender variance, Sandy's initial response to her spouse's disclosure was hurt. It was stressful for Sandy when her husband went back and forth between presenting as Mark and as Mandy. She was relieved when Mandy began to present as a woman full-time.

Mandy and I have been married now for more than twenty-two years. Becoming aware of my partner's gender issues has been gradual. Before we were married I was aware that he had cross-dressed once for a short period of time. I didn't know the extent or frequency of this until several years later. He cross-dressed secretly for a few years after we were married, before the difficulty of keeping it secret became too much. Even at that point, he didn't let me know the intensity of his gender dysphoria. That has only become apparent, perhaps to both of us, over the course of several years.

My initial reaction to his disclosure was hurt that he had lied to me. I thought that a lot of our closeness must have been a lie. I wondered how much more of what I thought we had together was also a lie. I wondered, "What now?" I struggled with feelings of being rejected, unlovable. It seemed to me that he must not have valued me very much as a person to be willing to let me live a lie, to ask me to live a lie for him.

Surprisingly to some, my sexual orientation was never an issue. I've always viewed my sexuality as rather fluid, and inasmuch as I've ever adopted a label, have called myself bisexual. I haven't minded the changes in how we perceive our relationship, or in the way we are perceived.

The way I relate to my partner sexually has actually improved. We had always been completely sexually incompatible. I wanted emo-

Head Over Heels: Wives Who Stay with Cross-Dressers and Transsexuals
Published by The Haworth Press, Inc., 2007. All rights reserved.
doi:10.1300/5737_21

tional closeness and tenderness. He was only able to become sexually aroused through escapism—blindfolds, being tied down, and elaborate role-playing—sex games. I didn't *mind* the games, but didn't find them arousing or fulfilling. A lot of this has changed, particularly since Mandy has gone on hormones. Now she talks about the "testosterone poisoning" she used to fight.

I think my partner's rejection of the powerful sexual urges she judged to be incompatible with her sense of self was responsible for our inability to relate well sexually. Now I believe that she is a little afraid of what her sexuality will ultimately be when she completes transition and becomes comfortable in her new "skin." She is starting to feel some attraction to men and wonders if she will ever be in a relationship with one. But, at the same time, we'd like to stay together. So, the future is a big unknown.

As a female couple we are closer emotionally than we were, although we are still a ways from a completely satisfactory relationship. My self-esteem has been battered in this relationship. But at the same time, my partner has always given me the room I need to do what I need to do.

The biggest stressor in our relationship is the amount of time and energy gender dysphoria and the transition process take from our relationship. I often run out of patience with not being able to discuss/address/participate in other areas of life that to me seem to be more important (family, friends, social issues, politics, etc.). It seems that we are way too inwardly focused. I know that transition is a tremendously big and stressful change, and that attention to this process is only natural, but that knowledge doesn't make it any easier to live with. I often feel like my only role in this relationship is to be support for "the big decision."

I also experienced a lot of personal stress when my partner went back and forth all the time between presenting as a man and a woman. I think it is significantly less difficult for me now that she is always presenting as a female. We are getting on with telling everybody and learning to lead our lives this way. But the stress of worrying about who had seen us which way, or wondering whether we'd run into people from one world while we were living in the other was awful. I think it got to me most because my partner got to choose how she presented, but we both ran into the consequences. She really resented it if I indicated a preference for the way I'd like to present as a couple for any particular occasion. But, I felt as though I needed to have some say in the relationship and the timing of our disclosures.

Now she truly identifies as transsexual, and she is completing her transition. It will be easier for me when it's all over, but at the same time I don't want her to rush into the decision, and I worry that my frustrations are pushing her.

It has been difficult knowing how much and when to tell people. We have no children, so that is not an issue. We are most of the way through discussing the transition with family members. Of course, we chose first to tell those who were most likely to be supportive. We have also told those whom we would have to see in situations in which they would figure something (maybe not the right thing) out for themselves if we hadn't told them first. There are still a few people whom we don't know how to approach.

We're concerned about Mandy's dad. He appears to be accepting things gradually, and we have not forced a confrontation, but we worry that any sudden disclosures could result in things being said and done that would be hard to undo. He is naturally grieving the loss of his only son. He told me that out of five kids, only one was male, and now it looks like even *that* Y chromosome didn't take! My dad is pretty near death and is often delusional. We have avoided stressing him with "revelations" that might never have to be made and might not be understood. Yet we still wonder about the rightness of that decision.

My brother and his wife are working class, and some people might call them "rednecks," although perhaps they are not so much prejudiced as they are living in a very different, very hard world. I don't think there is much room for gender change in their experience of reality, yet my brother called on his fiftieth birthday and told us that we will always be family and welcome in their home. It took my brother a year to think about it, and it sounded like a couple of good, stiff drinks before he could make the call, but the important thing is that family won out even though he'll never really understand.

My sister and her husband are fundamentalist Christians. Although they are aware that we are going through this together, trying to honor our marriage vows like the church taught us, it's very difficult for all of us because we all *know* that they are thinking about how sinful we are and hoping that God will eventually bring us to our senses and change Mandy back into a "real man." Still, they did watch Oprah's shows about transsexuals with their teenage sons and encouraged them to ask questions. I'm grateful that they're not turning their backs on us.

Most of our friends have been amazingly supportive. We've lost a few, but not many. Our church (Episcopal) has been supportive in the main, but we've had a few disturbing run-ins with some people. Before they left the church in a huff some kind souls went around to all the families in the church and asked them if they weren't afraid to send their children to a place where people like us were welcome.

One Easter Sunday a local dentist showed up at our church and came forward for communion dressed only in his boxer shorts. He said he thought it was no more inappropriate than my partner showing up (always very tastefully dressed, I might add) in women's clothes. Bless his liberal soul, the visiting bishop didn't bat an eyelid or miss a beat! The vestry reaffirmed in a statement to the whole church the next Sunday that our church has no dress code. The dentist, however, lost several patients.

Integrity, the Episcopal gay/lesbian justice group with which I have done advocacy work at several of the denominational General Conventions, draws a line between gay and transgendered. At the 2000 General Convention, I mentioned to the person coordinating our legislative presence that my partner had hoped to come for at least a few days to see what it was like. He told me, "Well, it's good that he didn't. The church isn't ready for *him* yet." Amazing how even the outcasts are so good at casting out others!

We are both quite hardheaded. There are a lot of decisions that one of us makes that the other just goes along with, but we also talk things out. We argue over how much money Mandy spends on clothes, hormones, and surgery, but it's not a major issue. Mostly, we keep his, hers, and ours checkbooks (hers, hers, and ours?) to avoid money squabbles.

In terms of the transition process, and decisions we will make as we get further into it, we have made a conscious, joint decision to remain open-minded and not to overly prescribe the outcome. We both know that we will be significantly changed as we move through this process. It's best not to try to decide the future at this point.

We have gained a widened perspective of the world and tolerance for diversity. We have discovered people we wouldn't have bothered with at one time, and found that they are beautiful people with much to give. We have realized that some of the people we looked up to and wanted to know weren't worth the effort. We have learned to live with fear and to face oppression without letting it drain more of our energy than it is wise to lose. And we have learned the gift of taking one day at a time.

We are treated with more respect at some times than at others. When we eat out, we take notice when the server continues to respectfully address us as "you ladies," even when we suspect that my partner has been **"read."** We are much more likely to tip generously, which any professional with sense ought to understand. So, we wonder what ours could have been thinking when, one evening at a small, expensive restaurant, the waiter seated me with a flourish: "Madam," then turned to my partner and said derisively, "And you." We found other uses for the nice tip he might have made, and we found other restaurants to enjoy.

Before she developed boobs of her own (a very adequate B cup after just one year on hormones), I was amazed at how much curiosity my partner's breast prosthetics generated. It's amazing how often people have asked to touch them or have just grabbed them without even asking. It seems that when people perceive that it's a man behind the makeup, they don't observe normal rules about physical space and personal privacy. For my part, I didn't mind the look, but I was not so keen on them when I tenderly leaned my head into her breast and it sprang back like bouncing off a superball. It's much better now, except that they are always tender like a nursing mother's. I get to commiserate with the married men we know whose wives also say, "Don't touch!" We're told that this too will pass.

Any thought of ourselves as a typical married couple, or typical *anything*, has gone out the window. We are very much aware that most couples facing this kind of challenge do not make it as far together as we have. So, we have learned to be very good friends and to be supportive of each other even as we wonder whether in time we may choose to separate. I think one thing we have gained is an appreciation for how important friendship is, and how important it is not to be alone in major decisions and difficulties. We are much more appreciative of each other, of the friends who have stayed close, and of the family members who stand by us and support us.

Sandy's initial hurt about Mandy having deceived her was accompanied by the feeling that a lot of their closeness must have been a lie. Sandy wondered how much more of what she believed that they as a couple had together was not real. This is a common reaction. Some partners go further, insisting that their entire relationship has been a lie and worth nothing. Such extreme thinking does not bode well for the survival of a relationship or, if it does endure, for the SO's emotional stability.

Mandy's deception seemed to cause Sandy to question her self-worth. It is not unusual for insecurities to emerge and for partners—taking it personally—to feel shaky about their own identity and whether they are loveable. Sandy expresses a sentiment that we also heard from Melissa, that is, her sense at times that her purpose in life is supposed to be to support the gender-variant spouse, particularly in making "the big decision."

Whereas for some SOs, their partners going full-time is the most difficult part of transition, other wives of transsexuals mention that life is easier for them once that change is behind them. Similar to Sandy, they find it stressful when they are with someone whose presentation alternates between that of a man and that of a woman. This can threaten the SO's emotional equilibrium. It's also difficult to keep up with who has and has not seen the partner in each gender presentation.

Although uncertain about whether she will ever be in relationship with a man, Mandy admits that she is beginning to feel some attraction to men. Despite this, Sandy is still with her. Sandy has the flexibility that's required to support a spouse every step of the way through the transition process, and to meet life on life's terms. She has faced fear and oppression, and held on to her faith and her positive attitude.

Chapter 22

Megan and Patrick/Trish

As did Sandy, Megan is supporting Trish steadfastly. Megan is not attracted to women, so she gave up her sex life in order to be with her "soul mate." After Patrick told her about Trish, Megan for the first time disclosed early wounding to her spouse, thus deepening their relationship.

I spent my childhood living on a Midwestern farm in a large family, with a caring mother and father, and many aunts, uncles, and cousins. I grew up with a very warm, protected feeling. My family and most of our relatives were baptized Catholic and believed that our religion was the one and only true faith. With such a large clan to back us up, no challenge to our beliefs would faze us. I had no idea how many subtle prejudices I harbored.

As a young woman I read romantic novels, dreamed of marrying, having many children, and being a grandparent. Things fell into place pretty well. I married a Catholic, and had three children. My husband and I became involved in church activities, and we had a good social life with family, friends, and my husband's business acquaintances. Patrick came from a family almost as large as mine. We were accepted into each others' families with open arms. Our two families became well acquainted and have enjoyed good times together. Life was going very smoothly.

Then, about ten years and three children into our forty-seven-year marriage I found out what it was like to be part of a minority group. A very nervous Patrick told me that he had transsexual feelings. I was uncomfortable with the thought that my husband wanted to wear women's clothes, and I didn't want anyone else to know. The idea of the clothes was prominent in my mind. I was so ignorant about transsexualism that any concern about its true nature was beyond me.

Head Over Heels: Wives Who Stay with Cross-Dressers and Transsexuals
Published by The Haworth Press, Inc., 2007. All rights reserved.
doi:10.1300/5737_22

What was portrayed about the subject on TV, in movies, and on the news suggested that transsexuals were not well accepted. I felt threatened by society's negative attitude toward the issue. I was fearful that harm might come to my husband and possibly to the children and me.

Due to our family's prejudices I was fairly sure that I wouldn't have family rushing to my aid as they had in the past. I was scared that family and friends would abandon me if they know about Trish (Patrick's female name) or that they would try to control my response to the situation. My spouse is a very special, loving, and caring person. I was determined to stay with him and see what we could work out.

Patrick continued to work and function in the male role for the next twenty years. In the meantime he sought information about transsexualism by reading and attending support groups and workshops. I read most of what he found and attended support groups and workshops with him. I also corresponded with several wives of transsexuals. I found that I liked some transsexuals, their spouses, and friends; others I didn't care for, just the same as with any other group of people.

Gradually, as my spouse gathered information and we met other couples in our situation, I questioned my sexual orientation, wondering if I was lesbian. But I had always felt attracted to men, and the thought of being sexually active with a woman turned me off. Eventually I realized that I hadn't, unbeknownst to myself, been attracted to the woman within my spouse.

All the while I had hopes that Patrick would decide to give it all up and live out his life as a male. When I realized that he was not going to turn back, I had two years of therapy with a very special therapist, at the same time attending a support group. I was urged to stop trying to change my husband and instead determine what I wanted and needed for myself.

I kept my husband's transsexualism from everyone we knew in the beginning. Since he dressed only in the privacy of our home, I felt no urgency to tell others. He worked as a man until he retired and functioned in our sex life as a man for about twenty years after revealing his real identity to me.

Since childhood, my self-esteem had been rather low. I had experienced sexual abuse as a young child, and carried the scars without discussing it with anyone until later in our marriage. Finally, I got up the nerve to tell my husband my history sometime after he told me about his struggle with being transsexual, so maybe his disclosure helped me to open up with him.

It took a lot of grieving for me to give up the beautiful fantasy I had of our marriage and of growing old together as man and wife, walking off hand in hand into the sunset. I love the song that John Denver wrote and dedicated to an old couple who were good friends of his, working to save the wilderness of Alaska. The song describes the couple dancing in the moonlight. The only music is the wind on the tundra, and the rhythm is their heartbeats and the love they had developed over the years. My spouse Trish and I have all the love and respect for each other that the couple in Alaska had, but to outsiders, ours may look like an odd arrangement.

We told our children about their father when the youngest was still in college. The two older children were living on their own by then. They were shocked, having no idea that their father was struggling with being transsexual, and they were afraid of the prejudice they would experience if people outside the family found out.

When my spouse started the serious transition to living as a woman, which included taking hormones, we were in our middle fifties. I always knew that he loved me, but I wanted him to have feelings, and particularly sexual desires toward me as a *man* would. The hormones, however, decreased his libido tremendously. We chose to give up our sex life and stay in our relationship as "soul mates," since we had established a very special, comfortable relationship that neither was willing to give up.

When Trish began to spend more time as a woman we would go out of town for entertainment in order to avoid running into people we knew. The trips we took were fun. We would attend dinner theater and symphonies, visit museums, and go sightseeing. We had always enjoyed each others' company, and going out of town gave us the freedom to do as we pleased. After some initial discomfort about having my spouse dressed as a woman, I gradually let go and just enjoyed our outings . . . for the most part. There were, however, some odd moments.

Sometimes Trish would wear three- or four-inch heels that she had little practice walking in. I remember walking through the mall to window shop. Trish clumped along in her heels like a macho male. I purposely fell behind. When she stopped to wait for me I let her know that she was walking like a "man" and that I was pretending that I didn't know her. Once, at a dinner theater, we had to walk down a number of steps from our table to the buffet line. I held my breath for fear that Trish would stumble over her own feet. I told her that if she fell in those heels, I was going to pretend that I wasn't with her.

One day Trish and I were shopping in a department store. I picked out a couple of dresses to try on. Trish also chose something to try on and came into the dressing room with me. She already had a wardrobe that was overflowing, and I was getting antsy about the possibility that she would buy another item. As she tried on the dress, I said in a not too soft voice, "If you buy one more dress, I'll divorce you!" Trish said that she noticed the woman who was in the dressing room next to us got out of there in a hurry.

I guess I did have some negative feelings. Sometimes when we went out together as two women I felt jealous when people complimented my partner on something and ignored me. I resented Trish for being extravagant—buying so many clothes and accessories—because I thought her spending was beyond our means. I had never spent that kind of money on myself. Even if I had, I didn't have the height to show off an outfit like Trish did. There were lots of other expenses related to the transition, such as the electrolysis (which I resented, but knew was necessary if the transition was to be successful). Now, Trish is much more moderate about spending.

Trish and I have had about a year and a half of therapy, preparing for the time when Trish would let the family know she was living full-time as a female and would no longer put on male clothes for family functions, bringing to an end her pretense of being someone she wasn't. Our chief concern was how this would affect our children. We were prepared for some rough times, but were surprised at how strong some of their reactions were. We informed our children that their dad was going to live full-time as a woman several years ago. They are still in a lot of pain which is often expressed as anger. Our son and his wife come by to visit with Trish, as does one of our daughters. Our married daughter with two young children will only talk with Trish on the phone.

My siblings had been aware of Trish's transsexualism for several years when she went full-time. It's difficult for me, especially with my sisters, who don't try to understand what a transsexual is. Instead, they have their own ideas about how I should react to Trish. They have told me that although I will always be welcome in their homes,

Trish is not. They have said that Trish should accept the fact that God made him male, and that he should not be acting like a woman. All but two of them have let Trish know that they think she has made a "choice" that is wrong.

Other than one, all my siblings are angry with Trish for causing a disruption in my family's relationships. They were cordial as Patrick continued to function in the male role when around my family. Now, they will only relate to Trish as Patrick. Even though I have told them that our relationship is celibate, they let me know that as far as they're concerned, I shouldn't stay in the marriage if Patrick is living as a woman. They have expressed fear that Trish and "her kind" have brainwashed me. They are also afraid that the kind of "group" that Trish and I are part of may be a cult.

Several of Trish's siblings have the same attitude toward Trish as my siblings. They do not want her in their homes as "Trish," but, like my siblings, are civil on the phone. They continue to have contact about once a month. One brother is very supportive of Trish and keeps in close touch. He is interested in knowing about transsexualism and discusses the subject often with Trish. Another of Trish's brothers and his wife are supportive of the two of us, letting us know that they think we have a right to live our lives as we see fit. I realize that the reactions of our children and our siblings are part of their grieving process. I hope everyone reaches a state of acceptance.

At this point, Trish and I are very visible in the community at church, social affairs, and places of entertainment. We are active in social causes, and we educate the psychiatric community, university classes, and various other groups about transgender. Our current circle of friends is primarily composed of people we have met since Trish went full-time. Since then we joined a more liberal and welcoming church. Many of our social friends are from the church, and others are from support groups, such as **PFLAG** (Parents and Friends of Lesbians and Gays). We are still close to our neighbors, even the ones who knew Trish before transition.

Trish, our children, and I are all working hard to come to grips with our situation. There are few, if any, role models for a family like ours. We have been fortunate to have the therapeutic help that we found. There is so much misunderstanding about transsexualism. Even well educated people and the psychiatric community know very little about this phenomenon. Trish and I take every possible opportunity to talk to classes, workshops, etc., in order to help people better understand.

Our relationship has improved, becoming stronger as we have learned to communicate more thoughtfully, each checking out what the other meant and dealing with this most difficult issue. We each learned to appreciate the struggles that the other had to endure to come to terms with the situation. Both of us have sacrificed to accommodate the other. I think the biggest impact on me of dealing with Trish's transsexualism has been an increase in my capacity for compassion toward those who suffer unfair discrimination. I got my bachelors degree at age fifty, and have had a new career, in which I utilize this compassion, for ten years.

I am more willing to try to understand where another person is coming from if we are in disagreement over an issue. I have learned to be more accepting of people who are "different." Our current friends and acquaintances are much more diverse and interesting than those with whom we associated before the transition. I'm willing to let others know when I think differently than they do, and I care less about what they think of me if we disagree. The soul-searching I've engaged in regarding our situation has made it possible for me to gain a more solid sense of self.

Megan mentions that she and Trish each made sacrifices to accommodate each other. However, it is clear that, as in most such relationships, the nontransgendered person is the one who is called upon to make most of the sacrifices. Women of Megan's generation were socialized to believe that part of their role is to attend to and accommodate their husbands' and children's needs more than their own.

Megan was not interested in relating sexually to a woman, but wanted to retain her relationship with her "soul mate." In order to stay with Trish, she willingly relinquished her sex life, as did Angelita This is a path shared by numerous wives of transsexuals. Some women feel genuinely incapable of erotic response to another woman, even if that woman is the person they've been in love with for many years. Others eventually find that they can have some form of sexual relationship with their partners, whether or not they alter their view of their sexual orientation. In the latter case, they may simply focus on the delight of two people who love each other, offering each other pleasure, just as they would if an illness or disability required modification of familiar behaviors.

It can be a real benefit when the gender-variant person's disclosure opens the door to a spouse's revelation of a previously unshared piece of personal history. The relationship may deepen, and the partners can enjoy new understanding of each other as well as the sense of being known at a profound level. This seems to have happened when Megan felt able to share information about her sexual abuse after she learned that Trish was transgendered. In this volume, we have seen a number of examples of increased emotional intimacy subsequent to disclosure.

As a couple, Megan and Trish are courageous in their visibility in their community and their church. They are performing a significant service, educating the local psychiatric and university community. Imagine the ripple effect of their generous consciousness-raising efforts!

Chapter 23

Mary and Jim/Jan

Mary describes her spouse as a male-to-female transsexual. She took the disclosure of gender variance well, but later felt rejected, humiliated, and depressed by her partner's disinterest in physical intimacy. She felt a sense of loss and distance and a yearning to be validated as a woman. Unlike Megan, who had no interest in relating sexually to Trish, Mary would be happy to maintain an erotic life with Jan, despite Jan's gender variance.

My spouse, Jan, who is also known as Jim, is an MtF transsexual. I found out about her gender issues when we had known each other for a bit over a year. We had been good friends. I'm not even sure we even planned to start dating; it just happened. Our feelings for each other were growing at an accelerated rate. At some point, I couldn't help but notice that something was bothering my good friend.

One evening, I went over to visit Jim. I knew we were going to talk, but I had *no* idea what Jim was going to tell me. Actually, I was relieved that he didn't admit to having been a spouse abuser, since that was the reason why I had divorced my former husband. I didn't know what to think about what he *did* tell me. I had never even heard the word *transgender.* I asked Jim a lot of questions. The first was, "Are you gay?"

What Jim told me was fascinating. When I left, many hours later, I thought about how much courage it had taken for him to tell me. He took a risk that made him extremely vulnerable. I'm sure Jim knew that even if I didn't want to go further in the relationship because of this I would keep his secret, and that beyond that, I would still be a good friend.

But I had already fallen in love with Jim. I called early the next morning to reassure him that all was well and that I still loved him. I was unsure about where all this would lead, but when I looked at Jim

Head Over Heels: Wives Who Stay with Cross-Dressers and Transsexuals
Published by The Haworth Press, Inc., 2007. All rights reserved.
doi:10.1300/5737_23

I saw a sensitive, caring person with whom I wanted to share significant parts of my life. I told him that I respected him for having taken the risk to tell me. I believe that if things had progressed further between us before I was told I would have felt betrayed and lied to. For me that would have precluded any future with Jim.

That was six years ago. Since then, I've read all I was able to get a hold of. I started going to support group meetings and even helped to get one started closer to home. I've learned a lot at seminars at the Southern Comfort Conference. I've absorbed an amazing amount of information about this topic since Jim first disclosed to me. I was working on a master's degree in counseling. When it was time to select a topic for my thesis, it made sense to me to research transgender issues.

Certainly there are many ways in which having a spouse who is transsexual has impacted me, but I'm a woman who has no issues with her sexual identity. I don't need others to define me. I like men, always have. Yet when our relationship became sexual I could respond to my partner's femaleness as well as her maleness. At first there was more variation in the way Jim/Jan presented than there is now. I responded differently when she presented as male from when she presented as female. Other aspects of the person I fell in love with are more significant to me than gender identity.

Our only problem is that I'm more sexual than my partner. Disparity in desire is an issue for many couples, but when you throw in transgender, it becomes bigger. Jan is on hormones, and some of our sexual issues are related to their impact on her libido and functioning, but the issues began long before she started HRT. I need to be validated as a woman; I need to know that I'm attractive to my partner. Difficulties with lovemaking or intimacy depress me. I think this is natural. Women want to feel desired. I know that Jan loves me dearly. She tells me and shows her love in myriad ways, which makes the sex issue seem so ridiculous, but when there's a problem in this area it becomes the elephant in the room. You tiptoe around it or bump into it.

At first I wondered how I could make this person desire me. I tried every which way and ended up feeling upset and humiliated by the rejection. I stopped trying. Neither Jim nor Jan was interested. We're never physically intimate now. Our current celibate status is almost better than feeling bad about myself and watching Jan feel pain. The biggest problem is seeing how stressful Jan finds her inability to feel the same need for intimacy that I do. With two women in relationship, there is a different dynamic. Both want and need the affirmation of being desired. If the transgendered partner is not capable of making this transition emotionally, there is a sense of loss, and this can develop into distance between them.

I now know that a disinterest in sex has been a lifelong problem for my spouse. It's the reason why two former wives left. Jim loved, cherished, and wanted each of them as partners, but because sexual intimacy was missing, they sought other lovers.

Intellectually, I can understand where Jan is, but emotionally I cry out for closeness on that deeper level. Jan and I have talked about this for the past three years. She desperately wants to feel sexual desire, but there has been no change. Sometimes I pout and wonder whether things will ever be as they once were. I feel selfish asking Jan why she won't love me the same way she once did. She can't. I had to recognize that it was "can't," rather than "won't." Until recently I believed that it was really "won't," and I was very resentful.

Now we have entered a new phase of our relationship. We can't have the sexual relationship I crave on my terms, so we must redefine the terms. I'm looking at intimacy in a new way. Intimacy is what two people make it. It's an extremely personal and individual thing. I would still like a sexual relationship, but in the current circumstances, I must redefine *sexual* as well as *intimate*.

No one outside the transgender community knows about Jan's transgender status. This community is our extended family. We talk about our elephant in the room. We talk about pain, and trust, and secrecy, and abandonment, and stigma, and health concerns, and moving forward, and surgery. What we discover is that we are coping. We give each other the strength to be in the moment each day. We are living and changing and redefining who we are as a couple.

In this relationship I have gained a better insight into who we are as individuals and as a couple. I have a better understanding of the pain a person must suffer not being able to be oneself. I know the courage it takes to get up each day and carry on. I better understand the meaning of trust and risk taking. In moments of closeness, I have felt Jan's pain, frustration, and fear. It was scary, but it made me much more aware of the internal struggle she has endured. I get up each day and live my life. The world sees my real self. Jan gets up each day and has to be the person the world wants her to be. I couldn't live that way. I admire all TG persons for their perseverance.

I believe that it is possible for spouses and significant others to support their transgendered loved ones—to ignore labels, to embrace and enjoy this aspect of their relationship. I don't know what the future holds; I do know that I want us to be together.

Mary is dealing with the widespread issue of disparity of sexual desire in her relationship due to Jan's low libido. Failed attempts to interest their gender-variant partners in physical intimacy often elicit feelings of rejection and humiliation in SOs. It's not unusual for these feelings to trigger depression. Similar to Mary, SOs often say that they need to feel attractive to their partners and desirable in order to validate themselves as women. Sometimes the loss the person experiences when she doesn't feel desired causes self-esteem issues for her and distance between her and her partner. Although a therapist could encourage Jan to pleasure Mary despite Jan's low libido, Mary seems much less interested in sexual activity itself than in the gratification she receives from a partner's genuine desire for her.

Mary and Jan communicate on an unusually psychologically sophisticated level. They are dealing with deep issues together, such as pain, trust, secrecy, abandonment, and stigma. In part, the profundity of their communication may be related to Mary's being in a program of study to be a counselor.

Mary has an incredible capacity for acceptance. She quickly adjusted to the news about Jan being transgendered. Despite the pain it has caused her, she has accepted the limitations of their physical intimacy, choosing to redefine and adapt to what's possible rather than cleaving to rigid interpretations of how a relationship "should" be.

Chapter 24

Gracie and Jane (formerly James)

Whereas Mary is focused upon issues within her relationship with Jan, Gracie is more concerned about the way she and Jane interface with the world as a couple. A number of the women who shared their stories with us were not interested in maintaining a sex life with a transitioning partner. Gracie has been willing to be creative on that front, and unlike Mary's partner, Jan, Jane has retained some libido.

My story chronicles my life with Jane and our journey through transition. Jane and I were married in 1967 when, of course, Jane was still James. When we had been married for three years and I was pregnant with our daughter, James told me that he had felt all his life that he was really female. He told me that he remembered having dressed in women's clothes since kindergarten, and that he had suffered pain, guilt, shame, and self-exile for as long as he could remember. James begged me to forgive him for having misled me, explaining that when we first met he thought that with me he would be able to do the right thing and "be a man."

All this was confusing and quite disturbing at first, and off and on we've had a very difficult time. I've tried hard to understand. After all, I love James very much. Eventually, I permitted James to cross-dress around the house when our daughter, Nell, wasn't around, and even bought him some women's clothes. We discussed transition, and finally I accepted this eventuality, and my ability to be part of it. We decided to wait until Nell was grown and out of the house for James to live full-time as a woman and have sex reassignment surgery. Nell now knows that James is transgendered, but when she was at home, he was "in the closet," and deeply depressed.

Finally, in 1995, James began the lengthy process of facial electrolysis and we found a doctor who prescribed female hormones.

Head Over Heels: Wives Who Stay with Cross-Dressers and Transsexuals
Published by The Haworth Press, Inc., 2007. All rights reserved.
doi:10.1300/5737_24

There were some problems with the therapist James was using, and eventually we found someone else to work with on an ongoing basis. We moved from our home of many years in one southeastern city where we had many friends to a larger city several hours away. For a while we lived in an apartment while we looked for a house to buy. We experimented with new public behavior. I'll never forget the day I invited Jane to go for a walk in our new neighborhood "dressed." She obviously enjoyed that walk more than I did, but I got through it.

One day in January 2000, Jane and I were out shopping and she wanted to try on some women's clothes. The idea made me very uncomfortable. Previously she had shopped without using women's dressing rooms, at least in my presence. Around the same time, Jane announced that she wanted to go full-time the very next month! Deep down I knew that it was inevitable that this time would come, but the immediate reality was upsetting. Suddenly everything seemed to be moving very fast.

Jane had wanted me to tell significant people about her transition sooner than I was ready to do so. I finally had to be really direct with her to quit pushing me to deal with family and friends on *her* timetable. I decided that this was one thing I would do my way in my own time and that would just have to be okay. All along I had been concerned about telling my sister about Jane's transition. I was afraid of losing her. She seemed to be distancing from us, and I heard through the family grapevine that her boyfriend doesn't "go along" with this "gender stuff."

Jane liked to visit a transgendered people's chat room she found on the Internet. It seemed to give her a sense of community that was important to her. Before long she was spending a great deal of time there. It seemed to me that she was becoming deeply involved in the lives, dilemmas, and dramas of the other participants. There's a special time for partners only to gather in the chat room and Jane wanted me to join that, but I didn't want to be sucked into the transgender community. I just didn't feel a need for that kind of contact. Jane seemed disappointed, but on this I took a stand and honored my own preference.

March 2000 was a big month for us, and the beginning of a very stressful period. Jane's name change became final. I told my best friend about Jane's transition, and, thank God, she was okay with it. Jane wanted to be with me even more than the usual 24/7 and I needed space. She tends to have issues about feeling excluded, so I've tried to handle my need for time apart from her sensitively. I mean the 24/7 quite literally. We own and operate a business together, and other than when Jane is on a business trip, we are together all the time.

At times I've become very frustrated with Jane. She's not the only one for whom this transition has been difficult. It's made me vulnerable too. There have even been times when I've gotten scared that she'd leave me once her transition was complete. She insists that will never happen. I hope that's true; I hope that fear comes only from my own insecurity.

It feels good to me when Jane acknowledges my feelings about what's happening. She finally told me that she recognized that prior to her beginning transition life was harder for her, whereas now that she's in transition it's harder for me. I know that I've done nothing to cause her discomfort, but she's very much aware that her issues are the source of mine. So Jane easily gets defensive.

When we explained to our grandsons that their grandfather was going to become a woman, the six-year-old just said, "That's fine." The ten-year-old said, "That's kind of weird!" During early transition, when our two grandsons would come to stay with us, it was not unusual for conflict to arise between Jane and me. We often disagreed about how to pace transition around them. I remember one point at which I didn't think the boys were ready for Jane to color her nails or dress in the more feminine fashion she preferred.

We took the boys to our therapist who said they seemed to be adjusting well to Jane's transition. She made some suggestions about helping them to decide who to tell and who not to tell. She also urged ongoing monitoring and support, particularly for the older boy. As it is, sometimes he's bullied in the playground and called a girl. This could become more of an issue for him given what's going on in our family.

After Jane went full-time we ran into some difficulty concerning our daughter Nell's wedding. The fact that Jane had begun her year living full-time in her desired gender made it quite difficult when Nell wanted her *father* to walk her down the aisle. Despite the wedding plans, Jane continued on her transitional path. She let her hair grow and had it styled, let her nails grow, and dressed in a more and more feminine fashion. Jane never guessed how tough it would be for her to go backward, masquerading as a man in order not to let Nell down, but she made it through the wedding as the *father* of the bride. It was very painful for Jane not to be invited to the women-only events, such as the bridal shower, instead being expected to participate in those that were just for men, such as the bachelor party. Jane tends to be more emotionally demonstrative than I am. In fact she is, at times, sensitive and expressive in the extreme. This wedding proved to be the most excruciatingly emotionally provocative event during Jane's transition, for both of us.

By August 2000 we had bought and moved into a lovely townhouse in a very nice suburban area. It appeared that we had a number of unencumbered women as neighbors in our little cul-de-sac and we discussed ways to present our relationship as we were getting to know them. Jane had agreed to leave this decision in my hands. She knows that I've been uncomfortable from the beginning with her blithe disclosures to everyone from the mailman to strangers on planes. I felt strongly enough about this to discuss it with our therapist. Some of the options Jane and I had discussed were:

- Jane is a transgendered woman, my (former) husband, and (current) spouse (the truth).
- We are a lesbian couple.
- We are sisters.
- We're sisters-in-law.
- We married the same idiot (thus the same last name) and killed him off! Now we live together (shades of *Diabolique*!). This is Jane's favorite.

In the end, we decided to present to the world as "partners" with the same last name. Anyone who wants more information about our relationship will have to ask. We will figure out how to respond depending on who's asking. We must also anticipate questions such as, whose are our grandchildren and our daughter.

It's become more and more clear to me that although I can live with people seeing us as two women in relationship, I do not want everyone knowing that Jane is a transsexual woman. There is too much ignorance and prejudice about transgender issues. Most people don't know a thing about this condition. I'm afraid that people will treat us like freaks, which I know we are not, but it would hurt me all the same to be treated that way. So I prefer to live in "stealth mode" with our new friends, although obviously that's not a possibility with family and old friends. Every now and then we have a conversation with our new neighborhood women friends that we giggle about afterward. I remember when we were all talking about our symptoms of menopause. Jane joined in and said some things she had heard me say and sounded like "one of the girls."

Finally, I wrote a letter and sent pictures to all family and old friends who didn't yet know about Jane's transition. I dreaded it, I postponed it, but had to be done. It's worked out well. We've experienced very little rejection. We are even accepted at our Catholic church, although I'm not sure what people make of us.

In October 2000, Jane had feminizing facial surgery, which also made her look much younger. The result was excellent. But then, a month later she threw two pulmonary emboli, possibly from the high dose of estrogen she had talked her endocrinologist into prescribing. She landed in the hospital in critical condition. She came out of this okay, thank God, and her estrogen dosage was decreased.

At times it seems as though Jane wants to merge with me, and I feel engulfed. I think she's insecure about developing her own relationships with genetic women without me. If I'm getting together with any women friends or relatives, she wants to be invited to participate "as one of the girls." It's hard for me to have any life of my own. Jane feels hurt and excluded if I want to do anything without her, and if I speak up, I feel like a heel. We haven't quite resolved this. The hormones make her more sensitive, too. She's upset more easily and can be mean to me sometimes.

Jane and I flew to Portland, Oregon, for Jane's genital reconstruction surgery (phase one) in April 2001. We had a great time there and met very interesting people. We returned for phase two three months later. Jane is absolutely thrilled to have completed this last part of the formal transitional process. I was relieved that it was over and that she survived.

I thought the SRS was the end of it, but *no!* When Jane announced that she wanted breast enhancement surgery that was the last straw. She's not satisfied with the development she's gotten from the hormones. I am *not* pleased about the idea of this surgery. I don't want her to have larger breasts than mine! I'm going to dig in my heels on this one.

The first time I tried to make love to Jane after her SRS it was rather uncomfortable for her. Jane was a bit sad. We may have tried too soon, so we decided to wait a while and try again. I have no problems with her new genitals. My primary connection to Jane has been as best friends, but we've always been lovers of a sort too, and we can enjoy our erotic life regardless of just how we work out the details. We figure we can buy a book about lesbian sex and follow the directions. How hard can it be?

Sometimes I'm very much aware that Jane appreciates the support I've offered her over the years, and her gratitude feels good to me. She has said that I have helped her through the most difficult times and provided stability in her life. We enjoy each other and get along better than ever. Life is good!

Gracie shares discomfort with the speed of her partner's transition with many SOs. Gracie is not alone in experiencing Jane going full-time as the most difficult time in transition. Coping with public reactions and telling significant people can be quite uncomfortable. Fears arise about friends and family members turning their backs, about the possibility of losing closeness and support.

Significant others often feel pushed to move more quickly than they would prefer, particularly in terms of telling their families. Transgendered people are understandably in a hurry to move ahead, yet it's essential that the gender-variant spouse take her partner's feelings into consideration in these matters, and that she be respectful of her partner's timing. Gracie stood up for herself, setting limits, making it clear that she would tell her family when *she* was ready and not sooner. She was also firm about her unwillingness to become active in the transgender community.

Another common issue Gracie and Jane faced was how they would present their relationship as two women to new people in their lives. Couples ask themselves if they should be honest about the transition or keep it a secret, i.e., go **stealth.** Couples manifest a great deal of diversity in their choices about how to handle this. Jane had tended to be quite open about being transsexual, but became more discreet in response to Gracie's concerns about society's ignorance and prejudice toward gender-variant people. Given Gracie's fear that they would be treated as freaks by their new neighbors, Jane agreed to cooperate in presenting themselves as "partners" with the same name, not mentioning that Jane was a transsexual.

Gracie seems still to be working on how to have a life of her own, rather than allowing Jane to engulf her. Some MtF transsexuals seem insecure about interacting publicly without their wives. One reason for this is that they have not managed to develop a sufficiently feminine vocal quality, and need their SOs to "be their voices." For instance, they may prefer that their partners order for them in restaurants, or query salespeople. In Gracie's case, however, the issue seems to be more a matter of the necessity for Jane to deal with her own exclusion issues, so that at least at times, Gracie can comfortably interact with people independently retaining an individual identity and social life.

All through their years together Gracie has been empathic about Jane's gender issues. When the time seemed right, she supported Jane in her desire to transition, even though the process was not always comfortable for her. Gracie seems to have called upon her wonderful sense of humor to cope with difficult times. She has been open to maintaining a marriage, albeit an unusual one, and even an erotic life with her spouse. She and Jane have figured out ways of presenting themselves that work for them in various contexts.

Chapter 25

Sarah and Natalie (formerly Nathaniel)

Similar to Gracie, Sarah was sensitive about negative attention from others. As Natalie's breasts began to develop, Sarah became obsessed with concealment from family, friends, and neighbors. The in-between life was not working for Sarah, and she realized that it might be better in the long run for Natalie to transition fully.

I've been with my partner (who was once my husband) for two decades. We have a very young child, and we both have careers from which we derive a great deal of satisfaction. My partner Natalie is a transsexual woman. She has fully transitioned at home and on the job and has had SRS. We remain together, two women raising their child. Those last three sentences say so much in so few words, but that's about the size of it now. At any rate, I'll try to fill in the gaps a bit.

When we had been dating for a few weeks, Nathaniel told me that he liked to wear makeup and female attire. Back then, from my perspective, it was usually, but not always, associated with sex. (Halloween was a time when we could do cross-gender dressing in public, and that certainly wasn't related to eroticism.) I can't really remember the exact details of my initial reaction. I do recall being willing to go along with it, although at times it made me uncomfortable.

I didn't want Nathaniel to cross-dress without me, because I didn't want any secrets between us. I thought that in the long run, if Nathaniel hid aspects of his life from me, it would drive a wedge between us. On some level I realized that this was an integral aspect of Nathaniel's identity, so I didn't ask him to stop.

Our relationship went on like this for many years, through career and family changes. Until a few years ago the outward expression of Nathaniel's transgenderism was occasional cross-dressing. My feel-

Head Over Heels: Wives Who Stay with Cross-Dressers and Transsexuals
Published by The Haworth Press, Inc., 2007. All rights reserved.
doi:10.1300/5737_25

ings about that ran all over the map, from encouraging it to avoiding the thought of it, depending upon a number of factors.

But a few years ago, the cumulative stress of gender conflict began to cause Nathaniel a great deal of pain, turmoil, and sleeplessness. Over time, with the help of therapy, reading, researching transgender issues on the Web, and a lot of introspection, Nathaniel began to realize that his gender conflict involved much more than cross-dressing. He recognized that it always had been more, and he began to feel that he could articulate that to me. I think Nathaniel was trying to tell me something when he started buying breast forms and shaving his legs. At the time I couldn't integrate our family life with transgenderism.

Eventually, Nathaniel started HRT to relieve gender-related stress. For a while we lived in stealth mode—one life within another—but that was just another kind of stress. As Natalie's breasts developed, I became obsessed with concealment: from family, friends, and neighbors. At the same time, in the bedroom, we became closer. I didn't have any internal strife about what it might mean about my own sexual orientation. In bed I was just reacting, and the experience was positive. But each day was different for me. Some were good, some were not so good. It was the proverbial roller coaster. We did talk all the time about our feelings. This was crucial. The doors of communication never closed.

We began to realize that the in-between life we were trying to live as Natalie changed was not working. During one discussion I mentioned that transitioning fully might be better in the long run instead of trying to live as a person/couple that we weren't. I couldn't imagine doing that for the rest of our lives, and I couldn't imagine what the stress of our constantly living an in-between life would be like for our child. We briefly talked about splitting up, but the thought of that was too bleak.

This was quite amazing given that literally only months before, even the discussion of transition wasn't possible for us. Natalie had dreamed of it, but didn't want to push it for fear of losing our child and me. I faced my fears as well: fears of loss, and of our son and me being ostracized.

I've gone through the classic stages of reaction to a loss: denial, anger, grief, depression, and acceptance. Now I'm trying to live a more day-to-day, week-by-week existence, but there are certain facts to which I keep returning when I reflect on what guided me at every turn. We love each other very much. Gender identity disorder is not a condition that is chosen, a person is born with it, and we're in this together, for our sake and our child's. In the end the decision to stay and make our family work, albeit in a new way, was a simple one for me. We were both ultimately seeking peace of mind and good health, and the path we chose was the best way for us as a family.

We hope the biggest changes are behind us now that Natalie's SRS is over. Emotionally and physically SRS itself and the transformation it entails weren't that traumatic for me. Natalie's SRS was not as traumatic for me as some may surmise. By the time SRS rolled around I was at peace with the direction in which we were headed. I was present right before and after the surgery. Other friends helped out at other times during the trip. To be sure, I was concerned. It was, after all, major surgery, with the concomitant risk of infection, complications, etc., but I would have been worried about that with any major surgery, not just one with the social stigma that this procedure carries.

But here's an interesting twist. Before the second coming out as it were, I felt some ennui about life. In a way, dealing with Natalie's transsexuality and what it means to our family's future and my own has led me to take more responsibility for my own happiness. It's helped me not be so caught up in needing approval from outside sources to validate my existence, self-worth, or happiness. This is something I've always wanted to work on, but now it's a coping mechanism. It's kind of a freeing experience. I don't look so far into the future anymore, either.

Remarkably, all this has strengthened our relationship. I always thought there was an inaccessible part of Nathaniel that couldn't be revealed, for whatever reason. Now I think Natalie is letting me see all aspects of herself. We communicate better, although it gets more emotional at times than it used to. We have fun joking about hormonal ups and downs. Natalie has been pretty much up front with me throughout this journey. So, fortunately, the deep level of trust we've developed over the years hasn't eroded.

Sarah is unusual in several ways. For example, unlike some significant others, she wanted to be present whenever Nathaniel dressed en femme. Sarah thought that if Nathaniel kept significant aspects of himself private, it would drive a wedge between them. Their close relationship was important to her and she wanted to avoid secrets. It is more often the case that partners prefer to avoid seeing their husbands cross-dressed.

Sarah is also unusual in that, as Nathaniel entered transition, she took erotic pleasure in the changes in her spouse's body without concern about her sexual orientation. It is much more common for partners of gender-variant people to have issues of varying intensities about their own sexual orientation.

As her spouse progressed with the physical changes brought about by hormonal treatment, Sarah, similar to other partners, was anxious about people noticing that Natalie was changing. She became obsessed with concealment from family, friends, and neighbors, particularly as Natalie's breasts began to develop. This discomfort is one of the reasons that the "in-between life" doesn't work for many partners. Fully transitioning often works better in the long run than going back and forth. Similar to Sandy, Sarah found this to be the case.

Although she is mourning her past life, Sarah is exquisitely self-aware about the pitfalls of living in a state of fear and self-pity. In fact, dealing with Natalie's transition facilitated Sarah's growth, helping her to be more self-validating and less concerned with the opinions of others. She does a magnificent job of maintaining a positive attitude, staying in the here and now, and nurturing her relationship. Sarah and Natalie's relationship seems actually to have improved, with each partner gaining an increased capacity for open, honest, and direct communication since Natalie disclosed her gender issues.

Chapter 26

Bonk and Gwen

Bonk and Gwen are, perhaps, the youngest couple represented in this collection. It may be that the influences of her age, her openmindedness, and Gwen having made the disclosure prior to their marriage enabled Bonk to adjust relatively easily to Gwen's gender variance.

My nickname is Bonk, a derivation of my actual name, Bonnie Kathleen. In the fall of 1998, Gwen and I met in a beginning graphic design class in college. She had a big beard then and went by a different name and gender presentation. She also made me laugh a lot. I was dating someone else at the time, so we just saw each other in class.

The next semester, Gwen and I happened to take the same intermediate graphic design course. We sat side by side and bounced design ideas off each other. Somehow we got around to doing our projects together—a lot! So, dating ensued, we fell in love, and a couple of years passed.

We both went to work full-time, bookstore for me, copy store for her (still with the beard and male identity). We made plans to marry in my church, and went through the obligatory counseling with a pastor. Finally we discovered that we were too poor to get married in my church after all. My parents were not thrilled with my choice, and her parents could not afford to help us because of a recent bankruptcy. So, we made plans to get married (in costume!) at the big Renaissance Faire that we both loved and attended yearly.

Now we get to the nitty-gritty. Gwen had been realizing while we were making our marriage plans that something was not right. Six months before our wedding, she decided to come clean. I had no real idea what she was going to tell me that night in the restaurant. I did know that it was something about her that was pretty important,

Head Over Heels: Wives Who Stay with Cross-Dressers and Transsexuals
Published by The Haworth Press, Inc., 2007. All rights reserved.
doi:10.1300/5737_26

something I would need to know before committing to a marriage. Gwen is a very honorable and decent person. That's one of the countless reasons I decided to plight my troth with her.

Despite my faith in Gwen's decency, I anticipated her telling me something about a crime she had committed. I thought she might tell me that she had been in jail. Instead, she told me that she sometimes liked to wear women's clothes. My immediate response was, "Sounds like fun!" Undoubtedly I was relieved that it wasn't something illegal, and that she wasn't breaking up with me, and that she still wanted to get married, but I still meant it!

After a day or so of further consideration I realized that Gwen had already been doing a bit of this cross-dressing. She had stopped for quite some time when we started dating. She hoped that being *with* a woman would "cure" her of the desire to *be* a woman. My swimsuit had been left at her parents' house for a week, and when I came back to claim it, it was all stretched out. I started encouraging her to cross-dress in my presence. We found a couple of shops in our area, and a support group. She also hung out online with other transgendered folks and made some friends that way.

I mentioned getting married at the RenFaire, which we did in May 1992. We got married in costume, so Gwen could not lose the beard beforehand. She could start growing her hair though! I liked the beard, and all the other body hair as well, but I was more concerned with her mental and emotional well-being. When she told me that she was going to shave her beard off, I was willing to go along with it.

So the beard came off two weeks after the wedding. The body hair started to follow. She started growing her nails a bit, and her hair was past her shoulders. I liked the androgynous Gwen, too. At this point, I started realizing something about myself. I had fallen in lust with this woman at work whom I otherwise couldn't stand. I had to figure out what was going on with me or else go crazy. I talked it through with Gwen and came to the conclusion that I was probably bisexual because there had been other women I was strongly attracted to. This was harder for me to come to terms with than Gwen's cross-dressing or androgyny.

Then we attended a cross-dressing convention and met Melanie Phillips, whom we had already been in touch with online. She had made a videotape voice training program called "Melanie Speaks." She described her transition from male to female with some more videotaped illustrations (she was involved in the entertainment industry as a tech I believe), and I watched a lightbulb come on in Gwen's head. "Uh-oh," I thought. "How do I deal with this?" We sat in our hotel room after our visit with Melanie, and talked for a few more hours. I knew that I would still love Gwen no matter what, but now I had to decide if our marriage was going to work for me.

Gwen and I each did some more work on coming to terms with our own sexuality. I came to realize that I love this person no matter what her gender is, what she looks like, what I look like to other people, and what we as a couple look like to others. I made a commitment, and I mean to stick with it, through good times and bad, in sickness and in health, etc.

Next on the agenda, Gwen had to figure out how to transition at work. She liked her job well enough to want to do this without changing jobs. She had also started dabbling in activism. She knew she had to stay employed, especially if she was going to start therapy, hormones, and possibly opt to have surgery. Cross-dressing was not enough, and androgyny didn't cut it. She was a woman, and had to get her body to agree with her mind to some degree.

We started coming out to friends and eventually to family. My parents were the last of our closest circle to be told. I didn't want to alienate them, especially after the reactions of Gwen's parents, who didn't take the news well. But they had to be told before Gwen transitioned, otherwise I'd have to disappear from their lives with no explanation—not an option.

So transition day came along, in November 1994. Gwen lost contact with her dad entirely and almost with her mom and sister. She went to work as Gwen for the first time, and received excellent support from co-workers. Support from me was absolute at this point. The rest of the world would have to adjust.

We went through some very rough financial and emotional times shortly after this. Gwen lost her job for some stupid reason (someone didn't like her). My family did not want a queer in it (I took over the title of Black Sheep from my mom's sister, who was on welfare at the time), so I no longer attended my family's events either. My parents have been in more contact than Gwen's have. Our mothers' responses are more positive than our fathers in both cases, although each of our dads talks to both of us at this point.

Gwen started the Remembering Our Dead project in 1998. The annual Transgender Day of Remembrance (see http://www.gender.org/remember/day) began the next year, along with a biweekly column in San Francisco's *Bay Area Reporter.* She also started working with then city councilmember Mark Leno on transgender issues and policy around this time. It has taken me a little time to understand why Gwen feels compelled to devote most of her time to a career in activism that does not pay the bills. She is very passionate about anti-transgender violence in particular. She also works hard for the more mundane rights to equal housing, employment, and marriage for transgendered and gender-variant people. I can appreciate her passion, and it seems that others do too.

Finances eventually settled down to a point where Gwen could start saving for her sex reassignment surgery. She had a substantial collection of Hot Wheels cars from childhood, and was able to sell many of them on eBay to pay for the operation. She also earned a grant from an organization because of her activism work. We went to Neenah, Wisconsin, together in July 2000 for this dramatic change.

Gwen created a Web site for friends and interested relatives to keep track of the eleven-day trip. While we were in Neenah, I was posting updates from my hotel room across the river, which included my commentary on each day's events. Anyone who is interested can visit the site at http://www.gwensmith.com/gender/alter. We also put together a scrapbook to show folks.

We do have contact with my family now. My parents travel a lot, and they stop by our neighborhood for a day or two when they're passing through. We also visit with them for the winter holiday. Generally speaking, my mother will use the proper pronoun and almost always the correct name when referring to Gwen. My father does not speak much to Gwen, and recently made what I took to be a very mean comment when Gwen could not go with us to a restaurant. He said, "Now we can go somewhere nice." I haven't decided whether or not I am going to confront this. He was better behaved during the next visit.

My brother has always thought that I was weird. He tends to react to Gwen like my dad does, but has at least tried to have conversations that are not so "guy-oriented" (Gwen's 1964 Rambler is her pride and joy, but it's not the only thing she likes to talk about). When we have phone conversations or write letters to each other, my mother always passes on a greeting to Gwen.

Gwen's parents have been excluding her from family events. She usually finds out about a marriage or new baby from her sister, with whom she has always been very close. Her sister was allowed to visit us the summer between her freshman and sophomore years in high school. This was a big step for the child who had been told that her sibling had a major problem, but was excluded from family discussions about it. Gwen and her sister instant message daily at this point. They have developed a strong friendship to go with their sisterhood.

Gwen's mother finally made good on a promise to tell her own mother about Gwen. Grandma now sends birthday and holiday greetings each year. Gwen got to talk with her grandmother for the first time since she transitioned, and was very surprised that she got this opportunity. Her father had not wanted to acknowledge Gwen's continuing existence until a cousin who lived in San Francisco died. He came up for the memorial, and later spent a small amount of time with us "catching up." He has mentioned possibly visiting again.

Gwen talks with another cousin via e-mail (one who recently remarried, and had invited Gwen to the wedding). She also met with an aunt at the recently deceased cousin's memorial service. I have not been in contact with any family members except my immediate ones (mom, dad, and brother) since Gwen's transition. Gwen's family was always much closer to us than my own.

Gwen's doctor is in Los Angeles, so when Gwen has a checkup, her mother now picks her up from the airport. The last visit to the doc included an extended stay at her parents' house (her sister lives there too) during which she visited with both of her grandmothers, the cousin who recently remarried, and her cousin's new baby.

We have tried to make our marriage as "normal" as possible. We care for each other; we face our challenges and savor our victories together. We agree on most things, but don't let the disagreements get out of hand. We like, love, and lust after each other. I can still see us growing old together, hand in hand. I think I'm still with her because I do care about people getting their various components (body, thoughts, personality, emotions, etc.) to be congruent. I have always striven just to be myself. I was one of the smart outcast types in high school, fortunate to find others like me to hang out with.

We just happen to be a male-to-female transsexual and her non-gender-specific spouse. My own gender has come into question several times, and I simply "go with the flow." I can pass quite well as male, female, who-knows, but when cornered on it, I now confidently answer, "I'm me."

Bonk and Gwen's story is a wonderful illustration of families gradually becoming more accepting. It's not unusual for the families of origin of both transgendered people and their partners to reject them at first, and then slowly begin to acknowledge, tolerate, and accept them. Families often go through stages of grieving, as did Bonk and Gwen's. Couples often work with their psychotherapists on optimizing the success of disclosure to family members and dealing with their reactions.

Bonk was readily and unusually accepting of Gwen's gender variance and of her transition. This is probably due in part to being in her twenties, and also to the disclosure having been made prior to marriage. Much credit, however, goes to Bonk's flexibility and capacity for introspection and honesty with herself.

Despite her initial uncertainty about whether a relationship with a woman would work for her, Bonk quickly realized that it would. She struggled with her sexual orientation and came to terms with being capable of attraction to women.

Although initially experiencing some difficulty understanding Gwen's need to invest so much of herself in her activism, Bonk seems to have accepted this facet of her partner's personality and way of life. She also decided that being with Gwen was more important than any disapproval she would have to endure. Bonk is clear about her identity now, and is fine with just being herself.

Chapter 27

Miriam and Linda (formerly Gregg)

Unlike Bonk, who has come to terms with this aspect of her life, Miriam still struggles at times with others' perception of her sexual orientation, and she found it difficult when she realized that she would be in what was ostensibly a lesbian relationship despite being straight.

My marriage is very 1950s traditional. The husband goes to work every day and sometimes has to go out of town for business. The wife stays at home and cleans, sometimes wearing her pink jumper and pearls. The husband spends most of the evening in the La-Z-Boy while the wife tidies up the dishes after dinner. The husband yells at the kids when the wife complains that they're taking her for granted. But, in *my* marriage, I play the role of the traditional husband, and Linda, my male-to-female transsexual spouse, plays the role of the wife. It's been interesting dealing with the issues I've encountered being the straight spouse of a transsexual.

Back in 1970 Gregg and I met in the school library. We quickly became best friends, although each of us already had a significant other. In 1971 I attended Gregg's wedding, and in 1972, he attended mine. We lost touch when Gregg and his wife joined the navy in 1974.

My first marriage lasted almost fifteen years. My husband was quite content working in the family business. His other interests were racquetball and golf. I quickly became bored with staying at home being a housewife, so I started working. After several years I went back to school at night, and graduated seven years later, with a bachelor's degree in business administration. By the time we divorced (quite amicably, by the way), I was earning almost three times my husband's salary.

While I was moving up the corporate ladder it became clear that I was brighter and more ambitious than many of my male colleagues.

Head Over Heels: Wives Who Stay with Cross-Dressers and Transsexuals
Published by The Haworth Press, Inc., 2007. All rights reserved.
doi:10.1300/5737_27

In 1987, about the same time as my divorce, I was working in technical services for an information technology company. This is where "the rubber meets the road," or the software meets the hardware. Even today, thirteen years later, at a recent managers' conference, the ratio of men to women was about 10 to 1. I found it so refreshing to see a line outside of the men's room instead of the ladies' room for a change.

In the late 1970s I read the book *Conundrum* by Jan Morris (1974) and I found myself wondering, "Am I really a man in a woman's body?" I didn't think so; that interpretation of my dynamics didn't feel right. I'm a girl, and I enjoy being a girl.

Jump to 1993. After a really lousy year I got a letter from my old friend Gregg. He was back in town and wanted to see me. We got together one night for drinks and I found out that he was in the middle of his third divorce! We quickly realized that we belonged together and got married four months later.

Gregg moved in with me right after the first time we made love. Shortly afterward, one night he said, "I have to tell you something." I held my breath. He explained that back in the 1980s he'd seen a psychiatrist who had thought he was a transsexual. I thought, *That's it? You didn't kill somebody? The police aren't after you?* I knew what a transsexual was and, as Gregg says, I didn't run screaming into the night. He said he had it under control now, and was okay as a male. So I was quite aware of Gregg's issues before we got married, but, when we married, it was as man and wife.

It made absolutely no sense for me to quit a high-paying job and become "Suzy Homemaker." Gregg had not worked in his field of computer programming since 1991, when his gender dysphoria began interfering with his work and his marriage. So I continued to work and set Gregg up in his own video production business.

Gregg was a Christian, and he patiently, kindly, and gently led me back to Christ. I'd been raised as a Methodist but had left the church when I was sixteen. My logical, scientific mind couldn't make the leap of faith that was required to believe in a risen Christ. It was easier to think of mindless forces of good and evil, and believe that the Bible was just a book of good fiction, but Gregg answered my questions, prayed with me, and took me to his church. In July of 1993 I accepted Christ.

Then things got complicated. As part of the divorce Gregg's ex-wife got custody of their two children. She began to get in touch with her "inner slut." When we saw the children, they were dirty and hungry. We tried joint custody for a while, with the kids living with us for a week and then with her for a week, but we still felt that the children were at risk. This was especially so when she left her husband of a year, in the middle of the night, during a blizzard, to move in with her boyfriend. Soon we found ourselves with full custody of the children, their mother out of state, and Gregg in a new role as "Soccer Mom."

I'd noticed that Gregg had begun wearing pantyhose under his jeans. He said they kept him warm in cold weather. Then he began wearing a nightgown to bed. He said it was more comfortable. Then, he began wearing concealer to hide his wrinkles and blemishes. During this time he was subconsciously taking small steps on the way to becoming a woman.

Late 1997 was a difficult time. Gregg had serious health problems and was, at one point, close to death. Finally he was well and things settled down with the kids. Nightly, I prayed to God to make me the best possible wife to Gregg that I could be. One day, after making love, I said, "You are such a wonderful man." That's when he said, "I've been meaning to talk with you about that."

Things got complicated again. Gregg said that he wanted to get in touch with his feminine side, to transition to being female. We talked about it, and I said, "Let's try taking baby steps. But when I get uncomfortable, can I say, 'stop,' or 'let's slow down'?" Gregg agreed.

Some male-to-female transsexuals seem to want to go full steam ahead, damn the torpedoes. "This is who I am and who I want to be!" Oddly enough, to me, this seems like a very male attitude. Gregg and I, however, *did* take baby steps. We agreed that the bottom line was that divorce was *not* an option. When we got married, we committed to forever. Actually, I believe that when you make that kind of decision, from there everything else becomes easier. You're more willing to compromise and look for alternatives.

In 1998 Gregg shaved off the mustache that I *so* loved. That hit me very hard. His face was becoming more feminine. He'd been taking phytoestrogens that we'd buy at the local vitamin store every couple of weeks. (I always wondered what the clerk thought, since I was in there buying PMS pills so often.) We also went on our first shopping trip for a bra for Gregg, which was quite an experience. "How does this look? How does this make me look?" After a while, he had nicer underwear than I did, because personally, I hate shopping for underwear. It's incredibly depressing when I find out that I've gone up another panty size.

As Gregg became more feminine, he became more relaxed and less prone to fits of anger. In June 1998, for our fifth anniversary, we renewed our wedding vows in church. This time, it was with full knowledge that Gregg was on his way to becoming a woman.

I think of Gregg's transition as having begun formally in January 1999, when he started therapy to get a referral to begin hormone treatments. At one point we went to the therapist together. She wanted to see and talk to both of us before actually giving him the referral.

Gregg saw an endocrinologist in April 1999 who did put him on hormone therapy. We went to the initial visit together. It was exciting living with someone who, every five minutes kept checking down his shirt to see if "they" were getting bigger. And sure enough, after a little while they did become bigger.

Despite the hormones, Gregg was still fully functional as a male. But after a while, I found myself making love to someone with breasts. I also noticed that his genitalia were shrinking, which were all normal effects of hormone therapy.

While the kids were around, Gregg was still Gregg. Only while they were at school could Gregg become Linda. During that summer, they spent a month with their mother, and for a whole month, Linda got to come out and play every day.

Seeing my husband in a skirt for the first time did make me uncomfortable. I was slammed with the realization that, if I am a woman and my spouse is a woman, then I am a lesbian (or at least I'm in a lesbian relationship). But just looking at Pierce Brosnan gets me hot; Ellen DeGeneres and Portia de Rossi don't do a thing for me. When we make love, it's between Gregg and Miriam in my mind. Unfortunately, I can't think of Linda in that situation.

Linda and I talked a lot during this period. We also attended meetings of TransFamily, a transsexual support group. I was finally given the vocabulary that I needed to express feelings that I'd had for years. Gender identity *is* separate from sexual orientation. Gender identity is not binary, it is not on or off, one or zero, male or female. It is analog, a continuum. Some women are more masculine than some men, some men more feminine than some women. Linda says I think like a man, in a straight line, very logically.

At about that same time I experienced self-doubt. I went to a "Women of Faith" conference and encountered gay bashing there. I heard some interpretations of the Bible that suggested that homosexuality is wrong, and that men shouldn't wear female clothing. That caused me to step back and think, "Wow, am I totally off base here? Is Satan leading me astray?" Then I remembered my prayers to God, asking for help being a good wife to Gregg. I realized that God had answered those prayers in His own way. He was letting *me* be the best spouse to Linda that she could ever have.

On a summer vacation trip to Toronto Linda had a chance to go out on the street as herself in a tolerant atmosphere. We, of course, went through the "How am I passing? How do I look? Do I look like Linda or do I look like Gregg?" After a while, Linda began to be more recognized as a woman.

After having been out in public with Linda, I thought, *If I'm a woman and I'm showing public affection to another woman, then people probably think I'm a lesbian.* I had dealt with my own private issues about my sexual orientation, but this was about other people's perception of me. After a while, I had to decide, "Do I really care anymore?" I still dither about this from time to time. Sometimes, when my energy resources are depleted, when my self-confidence has been eroded, when I'm having a hard time coping, it bothers me, and some days, I couldn't care less.

After a whole month of Linda being Linda, the idea of going back to being "Gregg" when the kids returned was not pleasant for her, so we decided that it was time to tell them. Let me explain that these are not the easiest kids in the world to raise. They both have ADD (attention deficit disorder) like their father. They don't do well in school and are protected by Individualized Education Plans. They also seem to attract trouble like flypaper attracts flies.

We prepared by visiting the therapist again, and strategizing approaches and explanations. We knew that the deadliest thing to do would be to call a family council or sit everybody down formally; those were reserved for when the kids really messed up. We wanted to keep the atmosphere relaxed and bring the subject up in a casual way.

We set up at least three family dinners, and waited for the opportunity to bring up the subject. As many of you with teens know, sometimes it's very hard to get a word in edgewise, let alone bring up a delicate topic. Each time we failed to talk about it was devastating to Linda. It wasn't easy on me either.

Finally, we got our chance. Linda started the conversation by saying that Dad was changing and that we needed to talk about that. Then, by prearrangement, she turned it over to me. We felt that, if the explanation came from me, the kids would understand that I accepted and approved of this and they'd take their cue from me.

I explained that sometimes a girl's brain winds up in a boy's body, and sometimes a boy's brain is in a girl's body. This was a birth difference, like a mole. This wasn't something that was inherited like eye color or hair color. I thought it was important for the kids to understand that they should, in no way, be concerned that this would happen to them.

I told them that Dad had started to become a woman back in April, and I asked them to compare their relationships with Dad now to back then. There were no more fits of rage, and not as much yelling. My stepson, especially, had benefited from Linda's transition, and he immediately did recognize the change.

We explained that, for the time being, when we went out in public, Dad would be "Gregg." If they brought friends home, they had to give us warning so that Linda could become "Gregg," and protect them from uncomfortable situations. After about fifteen minutes of talking about this, we wrapped up the conversation by telling the kids that they could ask us questions about this any time.

Less than two months later, the story of California transsexual high school teacher Dana Rivers was on ABC's *20/20*. My stepson came into the room while we were watching it, and sat down to watch it with us. Afterward, he gave his father a big hug and said, "I understand." That meant the world to Linda.

Linda has been living full-time as a woman for almost three years now. During that time we've dealt with a variety of issues: the kids telling their friends, me telling the people at work, and "coming out" to our families. Some people have been very supportive, and some have not. We were asked several years ago to leave our church. But when God closes a door, He opens a window. We've become members of an open church that accepts and loves us.

Linda is looking forward to her upcoming gender reassignment surgery, which will complete her transition. Although it will make a profound difference in our physical relationship, we will deal with it as we have with the other issues that have arisen: with love, with humor, and together with God. We pray together every night. We thank God for the wonderful, unique relationship that we have. We pray that our example may help others who find themselves in this situation to realize that they are not alone.

Being a "straight spouse" does not automatically mean ending your marriage. It does mean that you have to decide what is important to you, how flexible you can be, how flexible you are willing to become, and how committed you are to each other and to the marriage.

Certain landmarks in transition exist that are difficult for many significant others. For instance, it was difficult for Miriam to see Gregg's face look so much more feminine when he shaved off his moustache. She was also uncomfortable the first time she saw him in a skirt. Such milestones make transition an "in your face" experience for the nontrans partner. It becomes necessary for her to look closely at her life, acknowledge the ways in which it is changing, and take stock of her reactions. The relationship is more likely to thrive if she does not subjugate her needs to those of her gender-variant partner.

Miriam found that their commitment to their wedding vows—no matter what—made flexibility and negotiation a stronger possibility. Similar to most people who stay in relationships with gender-variant partners, Miriam recognized the importance of communication and of honoring her need to stay attuned with and honor her comfort level. She was able to ask Gregg to slow down the transition or even stop for a while when it felt necessary to her maintenance of equilibrium. The transition is likely to be fraught with less discomfort for SOs who have, or develop, the capacity for assertiveness, and who are with gender-variant partners who are willing to see beyond their own needs and consider the needs of their significant others as well.

Miriam was slammed by the realization that her marriage would appear to be a lesbian relationship despite that she is straight. She recognized her compartmentalization of Gregg and Linda, and that making love was only between her and Gregg. Linda wasn't part of her consciousness during erotic moments. Later, she dealt with her feelings about other people's perception of her sexual orientation. She vacillates between feeling at ease at some times and distressed at others when she is seen as a lesbian by others.

When the time came to disclose to the children, Miriam and Linda sought therapeutic assistance. The strategy they settled on seemed to work well for their family. Miriam took the lead, hoping that the children would take their cue from her acceptance of their Dad's transsexuality. She explained the biological origins of gender variance in a simple, age-appropriate manner, while avoiding pathologizing Linda's condition. It was very important that she reassured the children that gender variance is not inherited, so therefore they need not be concerned that it would happen to them. She also emphasized that Dad's transition was already proving to have a positive effect in that an improvement in his mood was noticeable to the children.

Miriam was very loving and accepting of Linda's transition. Even the homophobia and transphobia she encountered among her spiritual "peers" did not deter her from her support of her spouse, despite initially finding herself questioning whether Satan might be leading her astray. She soon recognized that her belief system supported her sense that God's guidance was helping her to be the best spouse she could be.

Chapter 28

Kat and Anna (formerly Dave)

Unlike Miriam and Linda, who have been together for thirteen years, Kat and Anna have been married for well over three decades. Kat ignored Dave's initial disclosure of gender variance. The gender issues seemed to go underground, so Kat was able to use her finely tuned power of denial for many years. Now that Anna's desire to transition is out in the open, Kat is so attuned to Anna's needs that she makes it a priority to adjust to whatever would offer Anna a fulfilling life.

We have been married for thirty-seven years. Anna told me about her gender issues early in our marriage. The problem was that when she did tell me, she did not know much about the whole phenomenon. She didn't say that she was a cross-dresser because she actually was not sure what that meant. I can't remember just what she said, but it was frightening to me. I felt as though my marriage was threatened; I was afraid I was losing my husband. So, I put it out of my mind. That's what I always did when there was something I couldn't deal with. If I didn't think of it, then it didn't exist. I was quite good at this.

So I ignored Anna's initial disclosure, and her gender issues seemed to go underground for many years. Then, she began cross-dressing little by little. At some point, Anna began wearing women's underwear. She would tell me that it was more comfortable than men's. I didn't object, although it did make me somewhat uncomfortable. If I came into a room when she was putting something feminine on she jumped. I pretended not to notice. I figured that when she wanted to talk with me about it she would. You see, I had "forgotten" what she had told me in the past, so this was all new to me.

Anna then progressed to wearing nightgowns. I really had trouble with that, especially when she wore mine. In fact, if she wore a nightgown of mine I wouldn't wear it afterward. I began to feel that I was somehow in a lesbian situation. At that time that was a problem for

Head Over Heels: Wives Who Stay with Cross-Dressers and Transsexuals
Published by The Haworth Press, Inc., 2007. All rights reserved.
doi:10.1300/5737_28

me because I was self-conscious about my size and the way I moved. My sister had always told me that I walked and talked like a guy. My family members were all small compared to me. I took after the Pennsylvania Dutch side of the family. With my friends, too, I was usually the taller one or larger one.

I realize now that back then, even though there were times when I was at an ideal weight, I was always made to feel that I was overweight. My stepdad used to say that I should be a sumo wrestler. I never felt very feminine, so I looked to my husband to make me feel feminine. I guess I always wanted a macho man who could literally sweep me off my feet. What I got instead was a best friend who would take care of me and help me grow into a far better person. God knew what He was doing when He put us together, even though we fought from the onset.

Anna eventually found information. For instance, she found Peggy Rudd's book, *My Husband Wears My Clothes* (1999b) and learned about Tri-Ess and SPICE. The cross-dressing community and SPICE have been the greatest things that ever happened to me. I know that probably sounds funny, but I was a person who had no self-esteem. I thought, "Wow! If these people can accept themselves and one another then surely they can accept me as I am." And it was true. In the community of cross-dressers and their significant others, I could be truly myself.

Then when I went to my first SPICE conference, I found that the conference was not really about cross-dressing. It was about learning to communicate, and it was about gaining insight into myself as an individual. We had been having a lot of problems, many of which, I think, stemmed from low self-esteem on both sides. Poor Anna did not really know who she was.

In the beginning, Anna did not know what being transgendered meant, whether it meant that she was gay, or what. Then she found that there were others out there like her. She found her own answers and recognized that she is a biological male who has a feminine mental gender and she enjoys wearing women's clothes. She enjoys her so-called soft side; it is just part of who she is.

Being in relationship with a transgendered person has taught me that there is a difference between a person's sex and their gender, and that sex and gender don't necessarily match. We all have both genders to different degrees. Anna just happens to have a greater feminine gender than masculine.

In recent years, my feelings toward Anna have actually grown stronger. Anna's acceptance of her feminine side has brought her a sense of peace. This and increased self-esteem for both of us have improved our relationship.

Attending SPICE has helped us a lot in dealing with difficult personal issues, and has brought us much closer together as a couple. We've met new people, made new friends, and found that there are people who really like us. It's been great. I've worked to know my real self and what is important to me. I have my own identity now. I've watched other couples and noticed how they respond to each other.

I've tried to pay attention to Anna's needs. It's been hard, but I think we're actually closer now that everything is out in the open. Anna now knows that I care about her, love her, and am there for her. I was able to come to terms with Anna's gender identity and I've accepted her. We have worked hard on communication, which is so difficult. Now we listen to and believe each other.

It would be a wonderful world if we would stop judging others and just let people be who they really are. I wish we didn't put people in boxes. Why do we want to believe that men should not show feelings? God forbid we see tears from a man! I myself have always felt that if a man can show his tears to me, then he is not afraid to let me know that he is human and has feelings. Yet too often, people, especially men, are taught not to show that side of themselves. How sad!

I must say that I have enjoyed all the wonderful friends we have made in the gender community. I have also enjoyed the special friendship that has developed between Anna and me. It's different. We share so much. It really is like having a best girlfriend. I really enjoy attending the presentations they have on dressing, makeup, and color at transgender events. Some wives would never attend one of those meetings because, after all, they are already women and aren't supposed to need that kind of instruction. The way I see it, just because I'm a woman doesn't mean I am an expert in these areas. I've learned a lot. My life is so much richer now in every way.

Anna and I have done a lot of talking and soul searching. We have agreed that it is okay for her to go ahead and have her name changed. In addition, at some time in the future, we will go to Thailand, where she will have SRS. I just want her to be true to herself, to be who she is in every aspect. The fact that this is okay with me is a huge indicator of how much I have grown and changed. The fears I had in the beginning just are not there now. I actually don't care if people think I'm a lesbian. If they do, that doesn't matter. What matters is that Anna has a fulfilling life. She shouldn't have to try to live two lives, going back and forth between being Dave and Anna. After all, she really is Anna and has been for a long time.

I will have to learn how to deal with what will seem like the death of my husband, and find new ways to relate to others. I've always been proud of how long we've been married, but I won't be able to say that now. I have a lot of uncertainty about how one addresses a relationship like ours in the straight world. We'll learn, though. Things are going great for us. We know each other better and better each day, and I am enjoying our emotional intimacy so much.

Often, particularly years ago, when not much information was available about gender variance, transpeople were not able to understand and articulate their gender issues, even to themselves. It was considerably more difficult for them to be clear when they made initial disclosures to their partners. This seems to have been the case when Anna first tried to tell Kat. It is not uncommon in such situations for the gender issues to go underground for years. It is no wonder that Kat managed to ignore Anna's initial disclosure, remaining in denial. As Kat mentioned, her power of denial was already exquisitely developed.

Kat is truly present for Anna in ways few people are for a spouse. One of her highest priorities is for Anna to have a fulfilling life. If a couple similar to Kat and Anna came into therapy with me I would want to explore whether Kat is as interested in her own fulfillment as she is Anna's. She seems so accepting, loving, and giving that I might be concerned that she is, to an unhealthy extent, putting her own needs on the back burner. This might be the case, given her old issues with self-esteem and insecurity. I would encourage her to make sure that she isn't sacrificing what she feels, wants, and needs to what may be her somewhat exclusive focus on Anna's fulfillment.

Chapter 29

Anne and Diane (formerly Dick)

Despite her issues about her spouse seeming to look at her with envy, and her concerns about her own femininity compared to Diane's, Anne offered Diane generous support and reassurance about the acceptability of his wearing women's clothes. As with Kat, Anne seems determined that her spouse will have a fulfilling life. Anne, similar to some other SOs, found that Diane's sex reassignment surgery had less impact on her life than her coming out as transsexual and beginning to live full-time as a woman.

Our story started out to be fairly ordinary: Midwestern college senior and college freshman meet, fall head-over-heels in love with each other, date, get engaged, and marry. Then, two years into the marriage, I discovered that my very proper husband, Dick, was wearing panties and nylons in bed. Oh my! This was in 1965, long before any talk shows told us what this was all about.

I was confused and stunned that my husband liked to wear women's underclothes, but could not see any reason why such a private matter need concern anyone else nor why it had to be a cause for breaking up a happy marriage. (Dick told me later that he had set up being "caught." He was so embarrassed, ashamed, and fearful of losing me that he could not bring himself to just tell me—a scenario I hear often from other wives.)

Dick had extremely negative feelings about his cross-dressing, which primarily involved women's undergarments. So, he had never told anyone else and he had also avoided talking about it to me. This left me holding a secret for thirty-two years that, respecting his fear of discovery, I shared with no one. In some ways, this was easier than it sounds. It turned out that our family was not typical in other ways. In addition to our two "homemade" sons, we adopted eight school-age children from around the world, many with special needs. Parenting

Head Over Heels: Wives Who Stay with Cross-Dressers and Transsexuals
Published by The Haworth Press, Inc., 2007. All rights reserved.
doi:10.1300/5737_29

our ten children kept both of us too busy to spend much time ruminating about our own personal problems.

Still, my own frustrations and concerns arose from time to time. I never felt omnipotent enough to have caused Dick's cross-dressing, which he told me had started in childhood. Nor did I suffer from "if only" syndrome—if only I were sexier or more feminine or whatever, he would stop this. But feeling that my husband looked at me as I dressed or put on makeup with envy rather than admiration did not exactly bolster my ego. I resented having an unwanted secret and its results, such as not being able to welcome our children to jump into bed with us on a Saturday morning because Daddy was wearing a nighty. (It turns out that we now know families who have successfully been open with their children about the cross-dressing, but back then Dick did not want his children or anyone else to know.) Because Dick fully cross-dressed only a couple of times during all those years, we did not have to deal with issues about going out in public.

In his forties and fifties Dick became increasingly rigid, angry, stressed, and depressed. He covered it up when in the outside world by whistling and staying in control, but at home he was less and less fun to be with. Finally, when he was fifty-six, he purged for a whole year, trying to get rid of this part of him that he felt he could not control. He blamed his increasing stress on work problems, and I believed him. I didn't recognize how seriously depressed he really was, nor identify its real cause.

Finally, I confronted Dick about what was going on. He broke down and confided how he felt and how hard he had tried to rid himself of his desire to cross-dress. I finally was able to convince him that cross-dressing was not so bad. I pointed out that he was a good husband and father and teacher. I told him that if he wanted to wear women's clothes, the only problems with it would be related to the beliefs of society, not morality. Somehow I was able to get through to him. Together we broke down the barriers he had intended for self-protection that had nearly killed him instead.

Dick's self-acceptance emerged as though he had flipped a switch. He started exploring his ability to come out, first with a gay/lesbian group at the college where he taught, then with transgender support groups. With the children grown and gone he was able to fully cross-dress at home. Soon it was out onto our deck, then up the driveway, then out to the store. Then he was coming out to the world, telling colleagues, neighbors, and family that he was a cross-dresser. He told people that he would be appearing as a woman from time to time. His femme self, Diane, became the third partner in our former life as a couple, and she appeared more and more.

It all felt so sudden to me. One of the things that really helped was Dick's willingness to ask if I was okay with each step, and to slow down and let me catch up if I was not. I felt like my life was spinning out of control. What might have seemed like wanting to control him was more a matter of wanting to regain control of my life and myself. I was accustomed to dealing with lots of intense issues because of our children's needs. I was very good at making lemonade out of lemons. So why was I having such emotional trouble accepting this trans coming out that, intellectually, I supported and encouraged.

There were a whole bunch of things going on for me. I was stressed and tired; dealing with such change used up a lot of energy. I am very protective of Diane. In the early days, each time we went out I was prepared for any verbal, and perhaps even physical, attack on her. Also, living with Diane was like living with another person (albeit a much nicer and happier one than Dick), and the constant change in relating to one "person" then the other was tiring. Sometimes I would say, "No, I don't want you to cross-dress today," simply because I did not have the energy to deal with it that day.

I was also sorting out my own role. Was I any less feminine if my husband dressed more femme than I? Where was *my* "space" as my husband moved into what had been mine alone? I, who had never cared much about clothes and resented the "Barbie doll" image of women, had a husband who seemed obsessed with clothes and was helpless while his nail polish was drying. It taxed the latent feminist in me to accept what I later realized was the teenage primping I had never wanted to do.

For the most part, my feelings fell into place when I realized that I was in the grieving process. I was grieving the loss of my husband as Diane became an ever more constant part of our lives. Legs had been shaved for years, but there went the arm hair—I had never thought about it being sexy until it was gone. I helped with clothing selection and makeup, and saw in the results the disappearance of more pieces of the image of the man I had lived with for thirty years. The grief process took the usual turns, starting with numbness and denial. "You can do it, but I don't want to hear about it or see it." (Some wives stay stuck at this stage of grief.)

Next came anger. By this time I understood that Dick had not chosen this trans dilemma nor could he will it away. I realized that his ability to be "her" self as much as needed was the only way for me to have a happy, healthy—and alive—spouse. So I got mad at the fates, who unfairly threw this at us. We were about to enjoy retirement and travel after so many years of taking care of children, parents, and others. (Some wives, I suspect, get stuck in anger at their spouse, either because of their lack of understanding of his need or because of his lack of consideration for their needs. Anger is a terrible place to stay.)

Sadness followed the anger stage, but that was no fun either, so I moved on to acceptance, which was much more comfortable. I had help from others along the way. Dick/Diane was (and still is) so appreciative of my acceptance and help. Contact with wives in the trans group we started helped me know I was not alone in my situation and my acceptance of Diane. Most of our children, young adults by now, showed concern for my welfare and acceptance of Diane.

Our two homemade sons' reaction to their dad telling them he was a cross-dresser was, "Is that all?" and "We thought it was something serious." One son sat up all night talking with me and gave me important insights, sharing with me his feeling that, "Love is great, and sex is fine too, but the core of my relationship with my wife is that we are best friends." He also said that in this case, "bisexuality is loving the person and not being concerned what body they are in." Aha! Best friends—loving the person, more than the body—that fit.

Lest all this sound totally serious, I should point out that throughout the process there has been considerable humor. Breast forms provided several good laughs. There was the popped water balloon one, the birdseed set, and finding the single, orphaned one inexplicably left on our coffee table by someone at our TG potluck. During the first year Diane got **"read"** (or "clocked") in public. She caused some really impressive (but harmless) double-takes. The best one was a double double-take that threatened to swivel the person's head off.

Two years after Dick had started his/her coming out process as a cross-dresser we went to Hawaii for two weeks. Accompanying us were two of our daughters and Diane's mother, who, bless her heart, had greeted the disclosure that Dick sometimes was Diane with, "Welcome!" After returning I heard Diane tell a friend that "Androgynous 'D' was in Hawaii." I asked what was androgynous about wearing long hair, jewelry, women's blouses, shaved legs, and white tennies with pink laces. I told her that I had gotten used to Diane and that it would be fine with me if she cross-dressed for the whole summer.

Diane was ecstatic, although she "toned it down" for me. After two weeks, when we needed to go to a funeral for a colleague of Dick/Diane's, cross-dressing and drawing attention did not seem right, so on went Dick's clothes. After only two weeks of Diane full-time, in my mind, Dick was gone, so what I saw was Diane in male drab. Her face was softened thanks to the end of depression and true joy. Her hand motions were fully feminine, and everything about her was changed. This helped me to understand that Diane was the true self; Dick was a male impersonation.

I could only imagine the stress caused by having to monitor and control every movement, action, and word for every waking moment. Dick had realized at age eight that showing the way he is different would make him unacceptable and unlovable to family, church, and world. So, he developed a mask. No wonder he became depressed.

Many of our trans group members who are forty-five and older tell of no longer having a choice about coming out. Not surprisingly, by the end of that day of trying to be Dick, Diane was again tense and angry and we were arguing. All of this made it easier for me to agree that Dick needed to stay gone. We mentally left him on a beach in Hawaii, because he had tried so hard and didn't deserve to "die."

Whoa! Here we went again with a whole new range of issues and accommodations. Now I was married to a transgenderist. I never considered leaving the marriage—we had too much shared history and still loved each other. Did living with and loving a woman now make me a lesbian? Since I know that there is nothing wrong with being lesbian or gay, it did not matter if the world considered me a lesbian. I defined myself as a "situational lesbian." I am not a religious person, so church beliefs were not a problem.

There was plenty to deal with, though. First of all, when someone lives "full time" there is no longer any "time off" for the partner. I was seen with Diane everywhere we went. I was glad that I had already worked through many of my fears. I was getting more comfortable being out with her. I still wanted her to look as good as possible. Taking pride and pleasure in a spouse's appearance does not stop because they cross-dress.

Now, everyone knew about us, and if they did not, the newspaper article that came out locally and then nationwide two weeks after Diane started teaching, certainly told them. It was a sensitive and kind piece, and much to our surprise, we got absolutely no *direct* negative response from it. It did, however, afford Diane the honor of being trashed by Rush Limbaugh, and having former students call and shut Rush up with, "Best teacher I ever had!"

Continued employment at the college was not in question as long as Diane's transgenderism did not affect her teaching. Well, actually, it did. Students said she was always a very good teacher, but even better and more fun now. As had long been planned, she retired the following year. We still give twenty or more talks about transgender issues to classes each year, so Diane has not really given up teaching. Our children now have friends and co-workers who know about their dad. Their responses have ranged from "No problem," to being okay once they found significant others were accepting, to seeing a therapist for assistance with it (while being supportive of Diane); to refusing to see Diane for two and a half years. Now all of them seem to be fine with her trans status. Many call her Diane in public, but in private she is "Mom," or "Ama" (from the Korean word for mom), or "Dad," which is all right with Diane. I see this as an opportunity for growth for them as well as myself.

Diane and I each have two brothers. They were accepting, as were other extended family and most, but not all, friends. We had some advantage in that having a family with ten children, most adopted with special needs, weeds out friends who might tend to be unaccepting, and prepares the rest for almost anything.

We live in a liberal area near San Francisco, but we have also spent time in Diane's small Midwest hometown, in Great Britain, in Canada, on the East Coast, and camping in Hawaii, all without a single problem. This was true even in the early days, when Diane did not always pass. Now we are seen as a lesbian couple. If, however, her transsexuality comes up in conversation (we do not hide it), people are not hostile—they usually just comment on the fact that we have been married for nearly forty years.

By now I accept that Diane is a woman, regardless of the body she was born into and the gender she was socialized as. Living full-time with another woman has its challenges. There are "turf" issues: sharing not only my clothes and "my" kitchen but even my name and gender. It took me over a year to appreciate what a sweet gesture it was that Diane saw me as her model of a woman and even incorporated my name into hers: Dick + Anne = Diane.

The swing from Dick being "the man of the house" to Diane learning her role as a woman left me feeling like a too-powerful parent. I was tempted to "get even" for some of the hurts that Dick had unknowingly or unwillingly inflicted. That we genuinely loved, cared for, and respected each other helped us toward what seems a fairly good balance, though we are still working on it. I do not know of any really successful couple, trans or not, who do not attend to their relationship throughout their marriage.

As we both adjusted to Diane's increasingly womanly appearance, enhanced by electrolysis and then feminizing hormones, we came to accept that her last male vestige was more like a birth defect, and did not belong on a woman. In 2000 she had sex reassignment surgery (SRS). I wanted to offer her support when she went for surgery, so I accompanied her. Diane's SRS has less of an impact on my life than her coming out and her going full-time. Those were very public; SRS is a private matter between us.

Sex is the subject we (MtF) transsexual (TS) couples sometimes avoid or split up over. If sex had been good before and survived loss of the male image in cross-dressing, then a wife is likely to miss the male body and heterosexual sex. If sex as a man is truly an "act" put on by the buried woman "self," a full and mutually satisfying sexual life may never have developed. The TS couple is dealing with both their sexual interaction and their newfound status as a lesbian couple.

From the people we have met, we have learned of many varying approaches to this. Some live as platonic friends, ignoring sex, cuddling and touching, and relearning sexual pleasure. We have also known couples who seemed to be doing fine who then separated a few years down the road because one or both could not get their sexual needs met. Not surprisingly, this seems to be less of a problem for older couples (a lower libido has its advantages in this situation), and in couples in which the MtF transsexual is attracted to women. Actually, in our case, we are so monogamous that each of us is just attracted to the other, and we have no doubts that we will stay together.

Besides, why would I want to leave now, when the fun is really beginning? We have each other and the enjoyment of retirement, shared activities, and family. We have the satisfaction of being able to give back through talks, peer-counseling, and an ongoing potluck-and-talk support group at our house. Our world has been widened through our trans associations and the wonderful people we have met. We have done the hard work, most of it in the first years of coming out, and now we get to enjoy the benefits.

We are in a unique position to speak on the subject of same-sex marriage since we have a legal marriage of forty-three years yet are now both women. Our marriage cannot be dissolved by any government agency or court—only we can seek divorce—yet we are considered married or not depending on which side of various state lines we stand on. (In Texas, Diane is considered a "man" and could presumably legally go topless.) Life sure gets interesting, doesn't it?

The adrenaline jolt of coming out has ebbed and life is calm, though, knowing our lives, I wonder what new adventures lie ahead. Except for when I am involved in trans support activities, I almost never think about Diane's being a transsexual. She is just my wife and soul mate, and we live a normal, if not typical, life. Years ago when I disliked the secrecy around Dick's cross-dressing, and I had read about someone who openly cross-dressed and was accepted in his community, I thought, *Wouldn't that be ideal? But of course we never could do that.* Well, guess what: we do "that" and more. We live openly and very happily as a transsexual couple, and at this point in my life I would not want it any other way.

When Dick's self-acceptance emerged Anne was overwhelmed by what felt to her like a sudden coming out. Feeling as if her life was spinning out of control, she was concerned that her need to get back in charge of her own life might seem like an effort to control Dick. This reflects the era. Had this happened when TG issues had a social presence in the culture, Anne's story might have unfolded differently, with more attention to her needs.

Anne's attitudes and behavior reflect her socialization in the 1950s and 1960s. It would be interesting to know what the rules in her home were when she was growing up. As Sandra Cole has pointed out (personal communication, April 25, 2004) for many women of this era, "taking care of your man" was a sociocultural rule. Many households were modeled on a very *Women's Day, Father Knows Best* ideal. Early in Anne's story she describes discovering, in 1965, two years into her marriage, that her husband was wearing panties and nylons to bed. Anne, being a product of her times, must have agreed to go along with this unquestioningly, and to be complicit in keeping the secret for thirty-four years.

It seems that Anne's whole life was generously geared to taking care of Dick and the children, and perhaps not so much herself. Keeping the secret from the children isolated her. The situation would have been different if she and Dick had disclosed to the children shortly after Anne's initial discovery. That way, they could have been a family with a secret. A therapist working with a couple in a situation similar to this might help them to look at family communication regarding secrets, silence, and superficiality in general, and particularly in regard to sexuality.

Anne reported having experienced a disturbing feeling that many partners of gender-variant people mention. Women tend to like knowing that their partners find them attractive; they enjoy feeling admired. It can be a blow to the ego for a woman to experience her partner looking at her with what appears to be envy rather than admiration when she is dressing or applying makeup. This can be an important, albeit rarely easy, issue for a significant other to broach. Such a discussion would have to be opened very gently in order not to trigger defensiveness, withdrawal, and denial in most spouses. Discussion of feelings in such situations is usually vital to the well-being of the relationship.

Anne has extraordinary understanding about gender variance. Unlike many wives, she willingly engaged in an unusual kind of role reversal with Dick, reassuring him about how morally benign cross-dressing is. This seemed to comfort Dick, contributing immeasurably to his own self-acceptance. More often it is the transgendered person trying to convince the partner that the only problem with cross-dressing is related to society's beliefs rather than to any intrinsic depravity.

Anne articulated several concerns that a significant number of other SOs share. Some MtF's like to dress in an extremely feminine manner. The SOs may wonder that if their spouse dresses more femme than they do if it makes them any less feminine. And if so, does it matter? If the non-gender-variant spouse is insecure, it may matter a great deal to her. This is another instance in which self-validation is essential.

MtF gender-variant people, as they come into their own, may want to wear their SO's clothes. This, just as a transwoman's increased interest in sharing or taking over household tasks, can give rise to turf issues that have to be worked out. These issues are sometimes more about the partner's sense of self and individual identity than territoriality. Intrusion into the partner's wardrobe, jewelry box, and even her household routine, particularly if combined with an extreme feminine presentation, can feel like a violation of the partner's unique sense of herself. She may feel that her identity is being usurped. As a therapist I often coach the transgendered individual to be sensitive to this issue and respectful of the partner's feelings. If sufficient sensitivity is not exhibited, I suggest that the non-gender-variant partner express her feelings in a gentle but firm manner.

Anne seemed to feel cheated and somewhat betrayed by the turn of events that made their long anticipated retirement years so different from what she had foreseen. She describes feeling angry, then sad, then quickly becoming accepting. I wonder whether she had a choice, given that she is a product of her times, adjusting, accommodating, continuing to "take care of her 'man.'"

Anne helped Diane with makeup and wardrobe selection. In an unusual demonstration of support, it was actually Anne's idea for Diane to cross-dress for a whole summer. She may really have been ready for this, but I wonder if Anne might have taken control in order not to feel assaulted by Diane's transition process. Partners of gender-variant individuals often find ways to regain some measure of control over their lives within the relationship (S. Cole, personal communication, April 25, 2004).

Finally, in order to offer Diane support, Anne accompanied her when she went for SRS. Every step of the way, Anne has shown great love for her partner. In addition, for years Anne and Diane have engaged in community education efforts about gender variance and have hosted a potluck-and-talk transgender support group at their home for other couples similar to themselves. With great generosity of spirit they have reached out and helped many people.

Chapter 30

Judi and Mindy

Judi avoided the experience of deceit and feelings of betrayal because Mindy disclosed her cross-dressing so early in the relationship and, soon after, admitted that she was transsexual. Judi, however, unlike Kat, took the information in, rather than going into denial. Judi and Mindy have dealt well with the evolution of their eroticism, and Judi looks forward to Mindy's sex reassignment surgery. Their children are handling Mindy's transition well.

My name is Judi and my "husband/wife" is transgendered. I met Mindy in 2000 at work. Although I was unhappily married, I had never considered divorce. Yet I found myself very attracted to Mindy. He was about to switch to a different shift and I was concerned that I might never see him again. I knew that I needed him in my life.

It might sound strange, but Mindy was macho with a hint of femininity. Before I found out that he was transgendered he had proven to me that a man could be a man and still be as sensitive as a woman. I had once asked a girlfriend about the possibility that he was gay, and was relieved when she said no. He wore tight jeans, cowboy boots, a long leather coat, long hair styled with gel, and a goatee. He had a wonderful body with well-sculpted muscles. I classified him as a model type, but more macho, and come to find out, he did model.

We talked about places to dine and things we liked to do. I felt jealous when I considered the possibility that he might choose to date someone else. I wanted to be the one with whom he shared all these wonderful things. On his last night there, as we worked third shift together, I couldn't get the phrase from the movie *Dirty Dancing* out of my mind. In one scene, Baby said, "I am afraid of walking out of this room and never feeling the rest of my whole life the way I feel when I'm with you!" That phrase played over and over again in my head. I was just about in tears when it was time to go home. There was some-

Head Over Heels: Wives Who Stay with Cross-Dressers and Transsexuals
Published by The Haworth Press, Inc., 2007. All rights reserved.
doi:10.1300/5737_30

thing so intriguing about Mindy. I didn't want to let him walk out of my life.

Mindy finally suggested that we exchange phone numbers so we could arrange play dates for our kids. I had a seven- and five-year-old; he had a six-year-old. I went home, my husband left for work, and I took my kids to preschool. I sat with the phone in my hand for what seemed like forever. I started to dial and hung up over and over again. Instead of focusing on the possible consequences of reaching out to Mindy, I considered what I could be losing if I didn't place the call.

Finally I dialed his number. Mindy knew that I was unhappy in my marriage and that tender affection was missing, so I asked if I could come over and talk and maybe he could hold me. He said to come on over. Our life together began then and there. I left my husband and jumped into Mindy's arms. Before, I had always done what was expected of me, yet I knew that this time, I needed to think of me first.

After a few dates Mindy told me that in the past he had cross-dressed and at one point questioned whether he was gay. He had even lived with a man for a while. He quickly realized that this was not for him, but still knew that he was different. Since this had occurred in the past and was not going on currently, I accepted it and just chalked it up to experimentation and the fact that Mindy had grown up in the 1960s and 1970s.

About a month later he told me that he still liked to dress in woman's clothing, shaved his whole body, and felt he was a woman trapped in a male body. He had been diagnosed as having gender dysphoria and had spent three years in counseling. He had been on and off female hormones several times, so some changes, like softer skin, had already taken effect.

I was shattered by Mindy's revelation. Here I was with two small children, and in the process of divorcing my husband of ten years. I felt as though the doors to real love that had finally opened were now slamming shut. How could I drag my kids into a life like this? I spent several days crying for what might have been. Mindy and I decided to back off from each other for a week and reevaluate our situation.

Realizing that the relationship with Mindy was not the sure thing I'd thought it was increased my certainty that I was leaving my husband not just for another man, but because it was the right decision. My marriage had been a safety net, but it was predictable and unloving. I felt more secure and self-confident even though I was uncertain about how my life would evolve.

Within just a few days I came to the conclusion that the doors to real love with Mindy had to close only if I closed them. Even though I had only been seeing Mindy for a couple of months, the way I felt about him was a love like no other love I had ever known. How could I just let it go without a fight? Originally I had distanced myself from Mindy because of what others would think. I decided then and there to keep an open mind. I was not going to prejudge anything. I would just let things happen and see how I felt about them.

When Mindy and I got together, we were excited and scared out of our minds about what being together was going to be like. We cried and laughed, uncertain what it was all going to mean. For a while the transgender issue was the most important thing in our lives and we talked constantly about it.

Mindy never dressed around anyone. One day when I knew that he was at home cross-dressed I drove to his house and used my key to get in. It was the only way I could see him dressed. Of course he ran to hide, but I wouldn't let him. I had to know that I could handle this. My reaction surprised even me. Yes, it was strange to see him dressed as a woman, but what a pretty woman he was! I kissed Mindy, makeup and all. She was the same person I had fallen in love with.

Mindy started seeing a counselor again, and we just let things progress from there. I promised Mindy that if I began to have a hard time with anything I would let her know. We were both afraid that one day I would wake up and say, "What am I doing? This is just too strange!" I waited for that day for quite a while, but it never came.

During his first marriage, Mindy kept flip-flopping back and forth from being macho to being more femme, although he always dressed gender neutral in public. I would not allow him/her to binge and purge, because money was always tight. When Mindy would temporarily reject her transgender nature I'd become the recipient of all her clothes, etc., or at least the become keeper of the clothes until, as I knew they would be, they were needed again.

Mindy laughed at me because I actually started encouraging her to be more open—to be herself and not worry so much what others thought. "All that matters is how *we* feel about it," I said. We came out to my family with mixed reactions. I'm not as close to them anymore, but I'm not sure whether it's because of coming out in particular or just finally living my life my way rather than theirs. We came out to my ex-husband. He still doesn't understand and doesn't want to, but he has not made things difficult. Mindy came out to friends and co-workers as well as to her boss.

We have been married for two years now and have a beautiful daughter together. At first she called Mindy "Momadad," but slowly even the older kids dropped the dad and just began calling her Mama, and me Mom. Mindy's son continued to call her Dad for quite a while, but has come a long way toward acceptance. I was pleasantly surprised to see how well eight-, seven-, and six-year-olds were able to accept such a thing. The kids have come out to their friends at their own pace. We discussed what might happen, and left the decisions up to them as to who and when to tell.

Mindy and I are very passionate. I never considered myself to be a lesbian. We joke that for now I'm bisexual. I have the best of both worlds. I loved it when his "equipment" was still operational. I enjoyed *his* penis and *her* breasts! Female hormones and testosterone blockers have rendered *his* equipment nonoperational, though. At this point we can't wait for the operation (although we can't afford it yet). I would much rather she have a vagina that works than a penis that doesn't.

It is nice finally to be out to everyone including friends, family, and neighbors. I have recently come out at my new job with only positive reactions. It has been very nice for Mindy and me. We had braced ourselves for negative reactions from people. Thankfully, we have yet to experience a negative response directly, except that we feel that Mindy was fired from her last job because she told them she was transgendered. For that reason, we currently have a case pending with the Human Rights Commission.

Now that everyone knows, Mindy can progress at her own pace. She has gone from seeing herself as an MtF transgendered person not considering SRS (or at least not considering it until the kids were grown) to discussing the downfalls and the pleasures that would come from having SRS. For financial reasons, full transition is not possible at this time, but Mindy has been on hormones for three years, so her body structure has changed. She has a larger chest than I do. I'm so jealous!

Mindy, who has legally changed her name from Michael to Mindy, now fully expresses her womanhood in public, even wearing subtle makeup. She is just herself now, everywhere she goes. For the most part, we don't worry about passing anymore, because Mindy looks female now. When we are out together, we are always addressed as "ladies." She has not had electrolysis, though, and her voice is very deep. I know that people sometimes wonder, "Is that a man or a woman?" Our favorite song is "Let's Give Them Something to Talk About." Mindy and I just look at each other and laugh. Mindy still gets "sirred" on the phone. She is working on softening her voice.

We have walked through many "walls of fire" and have been singed but not burned. We're always open with each other, constantly communicating about our feelings. I allow myself to experience whatever is going on with me at the time, and sometimes difficult emotions shift with acceptance. There is so much love and support between us that we believe that we can get through anything together. Nothing is off-limits for us—we even wear each other's clothes. It saves money and doubles our wardrobes. We take one day at a time and can't wait to see where life takes us next!

Mindy's disclosure about cross-dressing occurred early in the relationship. Soon after, she admitted that she was transsexual. Thus, Judi had no major issues of deceit, betrayal, or broken trust to deal with. This probably made a difference in her capacity for acceptance.

Their children are adapting well to having a transgendered parent, a testimony to Judi and Mindy's handling of the situation and to the resilience of children. Many members of the general public might assume that having a transgendered parent would guarantee maladjusted children, yet that has not been my experience, nor does the research indicate that that is the case. A number of my clients have brought their children and even their grandchildren in for sessions, to assess their adjustment to transition. As long as their feelings are heard and accepted, and their parents are sensitive to their needs, children of gender-variant parents can be as well adjusted as any other children.

Judi, with her powerful capacity for self-validation, was actually the moving force behind Mindy's quickly paced coming out. She believes that *their own* feelings about their life together far outweigh the importance of the opinions of others. Judi is secure enough to be unconcerned about issues of sexual orientation, a significant issue for many partners of transpeople. She is open to the evolving nature of her erotic relationship with her spouse, and is taking delight in adapting their mutual pleasuring to changes in Mindy's body. She actually looks forward to her spouse's genital reconfiguration. I have heard from Judy about Mindy's successful SRS and the support group they started in their area.

Chapter 31

Conclusion

It is almost universally stressful for a natal woman to find out that her partner is transgendered. The experience can be so intense that, like some of the contributors and some of my clients, she may endure a kind of posttraumatic stress reaction. Given that her faith in her partner's judgment is likely to have been damaged, she may feel as though it is her responsibility to "keep the secret." At least initially, she may very well be quite fearful of others finding out about the gender variance and judging, ostracizing, and otherwise punishing her, her partner, and possibly their children.

Common initial reactions of partners who are not told about gender variance early in the relationship can include shock, disbelief, revulsion, fear, shame, and a sense of betrayal at the deception. Once the initial shock wears off, hurt, rage, fear, anxiety, shame, and a sense of abandonment may prevail. Some women, their self-esteem wounded, will "let themselves go," while others may spend more time on their own appearance inspired by, to keep up with, or to compete with their feminized mates. Some want to be involved, some keep their distance from their partners' activities. There is often a sense of loss of the valued traditional heterosexual marriage. Some SOs reach a place of resignation, tolerance, or even acceptance once they better understand the pain, fear, and shame their partners themselves have lived with, despite this not being what *they* signed on for.

The couple may become involved in power struggles over the boundaries around feminization, such as body shaving, frequency of dressing, feminine expression in an erotic context, and whether/when/where it's acceptable to go out in public cross-dressed. If the gender variance is extreme in its intensity, decisions must be processed about transition and the timing of various steps such as when

Head Over Heels: Wives Who Stay with Cross-Dressers and Transsexuals
Published by The Haworth Press, Inc., 2007. All rights reserved.
doi:10.1300/5737_31

to tell significant others, employment issues, facial hair removal, starting a hormonal regimen, facial feminization, and other ancillary surgeries, beginning to live full-time in female role, and sex reassignment surgery.

Eroticism may be enhanced or eroded by the existence of gender variance in a relationship. The natal female partner's sexual desire may decrease, particularly if her partner manifests interest in feminine expression during sexual intimacy. She may experience libido-impairing repugnance and/or she may have difficulty reaching orgasm. On the other hand she may find the manifestation of gender variance novel, intriguing, even erotically stimulating. A bisexual woman who falls in love with a gender-variant natal male may be excited about her partner being "different" in this way.

The libido of a gender-variant natal male may flourish if the wife welcomes the femme persona in the bedroom. However, if the individual is taking hormones, libido will more likely diminish eventually. Even if hormones are not involved, libido may diminish for other reasons. These might include difficulty becoming aroused by a perceived requirement to play the dominant, initiating, or otherwise traditional "male role," or experiencing the partner's revulsion about the gender variance.

Women who were unaware of their partners' gender variance from the onset of the relationship often have a number of fears and concerns in common:

- Will I lose him because he is going to want to become a woman?
- Will I lose him because he is really gay and wants to be with a man?
- Does my being in love with him mean that I'm a lesbian?
- Will others think I'm a lesbian?
- Is his gender variance because of something lacking in me?
- Will his desire to explore his femininity escalate?
- Will I ever regain trust in him?
- Will I ever get over my jealousy of "the other woman?"
- How can I gain some control in this relationship?
- What else has he deceived me about?
- What about the kids?
- What about our families?
- What about his job?

- What about me? I feel so alone.
- What about the money spent on clothes and beyond?
- Will he ever not experience gender variance as the center of his life?
- Why do I have to do so much of the accommodating in this relationship?

I do not see any common demographic aspects among wives who remain in relationship with their gender-variant partners, either in these participant women or in my clinical work. I have even known fundamentalist, evangelical, religious women who grow beyond ranting and raving about hellfire and damnation into astonishing acceptance. It seems that the commonality among women who stay with their transgendered partners is related more to aspects of their personalities and the nature of the relationship.

Some women who stay do so because of their socialization to attend to the feelings and needs of their loved ones much more so than to their own. I think that in such cases, eventually, resentment may diminish their love for their partners and erode the quality of the relationship.

Women who stay often have the capacity to move from acquiescence, to tolerance, and ultimately into acceptance. Even if they are totally uninformed or misinformed about the topic when they first learn the truth, they are willing to investigate and cultivate open-minded attitudes about gender variance. Given the societal prejudice they face, I find this remarkable. Many of these women battle their own traditional notions of gender. They explore, redefine, and create other ways of looking at relationships.

People who continue in healthy relationships with gender-variant partners often have high levels of ego strength. They have the capacity to self-soothe and self-validate, regardless of the opinions of others. Although empathic, they have good emotional boundaries. They are aware of where they end and others begin emotionally, and are able to identify and express their own feelings and needs. Their unfolding narratives indicate that some of the women whose stories are told here grew tremendously as they coped with, learned about, and lived with their spouses' gender variance.

Women who stay long-term in healthy relationships are connected with their partners at emotional and often spiritual levels. The issues of gender variance, the possible interruption of the couple's erotic life as they have know it, and for some, even the possible reconfiguration of the partner's genitals, can be less important than the deep caring within the relationship. These women often find themselves exploring vulnerable parts of themselves and pushing beyond their comfort zones. In doing so they expand and enhance their own emotional maturity.

The attitudes and behavior of gender-variant spouses make a huge difference. If they respect their partners' limits and boundaries, if they attend to their partners' needs rather than being totally self-absorbed, and if they invest time and energy in showing their devotion, their relationships stand a better chance of survival.

Perhaps the best suggestion I can offer to couples with challenges would be that they practice nonvioloent communication (Rosenberg, 2003). To do so, you would listen deeply and compassionately for the humanness in each other even when one partner isn't coming from the highest and best part of herself or himself, and try to reflect back verbally your guess about the partner's feelings and unmet needs. When a partner does something that you don't like, it would be helpful to pay attention to what is alive in you, expressing the feelings you have about your partner's behavior. Then, rather than suggesting that it is the behavior that is the cause of your feelings, identify a need that isn't being met and let your partner know that the unmet need is the cause of your feelings. Finally, make a clear request for behavior by your partner that would meet your need. This form of communication makes it more likely that people will be invested in contributing to making each others' lives more wonderful.

Many of the relationships described in these pages are based on profound emotional and spiritual values. Transgendered people and their partners color outside culturally acceptable lines, struggling to deal with unusual relational dynamics and to find ways to make their relationships work. Their courage and devotion inspire my respect and awe.

Appendix

Resources

Online Support Groups

CDSO is an online support group for natal female partners of cross-dressers. Some say that the particular focus is people who are having difficulty accepting the cross-dressing.
http://www.tri-ess.org/spice/CDSO/CDSO.htm

CDWSOS is an online support group for wives and girlfriends of cross-dressers.
http://groups.yahoo.com/group/CDWSOS

Helen Boyd's (My Husband Betty) Online Support Group for Couples dealing with TG in their relationships.
http://groups.yahoo.com/group/CDtgOD/

Lacey Leigh's Group for Successful Crossdressers, although more specifically for cross-dressers, is couples-friendly.
http://health.groups.yahoo.com/group/TheSuccessfulCrossdresser/

Ronnie Rho's Group is an online support group for Gen X couples.
http://groups.yahoo.com/group/marriedgenxcrossdressers/

Support for Wives and Significant Others of Crossdressers is an online support group for genetic female partners of heterosexual cross-dressers.
http://groups.yahoo.com/group/sfwasocds/

Transfamily Discussion Lists are e-mail support groups addressing the special needs of transitioning youth, adults, their spouses/life partners, children of transpeople, including adult children, parents, and couples. A separate group exists for each relational category.
http://www.transfamily.org/emailist.htm

Head Over Heels: Wives Who Stay with Cross-Dressers and Transsexuals
Published by The Haworth Press, Inc., 2007. All rights reserved.
doi:10.1300/5737_32

Transfamily Significant Others' Discussion List addresses the special needs of significant others of MtFs, FtMs.
http://groups.yahoo.com/group/tgpartners/

Transfamily's Couples' Group
http://groups.yahoo.com/group/TransfamilyCouples/

TransFamilySpouses is the sister group of TransFamily Couples, and is for partners only.
http://groups.yahoo.com/group/TransFamilySpouses/

Transgender Significant Others is a support group for the natal female significant others of natal male transgender people.
http://groups.yahoo.com/group/tgso1/

Note: Helen Boyd *(My Husband Betty)* screened all of the previous resources except CDSO for positive attitude toward SOs.

Information/Organizations/Publications

Crosssdresser's Secret Garden is a Web site with a section containing stories of significant others of transgender people.
http://cdsecretgarden.femmegetaway.com

Dana's site for SOs is a site at which one can access stories and experiences of genetic female partners of transgender people.
http://www.webdotgal.com/main/html/soforum.html

Gender Education and Advocacy (GEA) is a national gender variance education and advocacy organization formed from the merger of AEGIS and It's Time, America!
GEA
P.O. Box 33724
Decatur, GA 30033-724
http://www.gender.org

Gender Public Advocacy Coalition (GenderPAC) works for gender, affectional, and racial equality.
GenderPAC
1743 Connecticut Avenue NW, 4th floor
Washington, DC 20009
202-462-6610
http://www.gpac.org

Harry Benjamin International Gender Dysphoria Association, Inc. (HBIGDA) is the organization that meets biannually to set down and update guidelines for professionals working with transgender people. This organization is in the process of changing its name to the World Professional Association for Transgender Health (WPATH).
HBIGDA
1300 South 2nd Street, Suite 180
Minneapolis, MN 55454
612-625-1500
http://www.hbigda.org/

International Foundation for Gender Education (IFGE) offers information, referrals, and books. They also publish the quarterly magazine *Transgender Tapestry* and sponsor an annual transgender conference.
IFGE
P.O. Box 229
Waltham, MA 02454-0229
781-899-2212
http://www.ifge.org

Intersex Society of North America (ISNA) provides information and support, primarily for intersexed persons.
ISNA
4500 9th Avenue NE, Suite 300
Seattle, WA 98105
206-633-6049
http://www.isna.org

Parents and Friends of Lesbians and Gays (PFLAG) was originally for loved ones of gay, lesbian, and bisexual people. This organization's Transgender Special Outreach Network (TSON) also offers information and support for both transpersons and their families. They also sponsor the Straight Spouse Network.
PFLAG
1726 'M' Street NW, Suite 400
Washington, DC 20036
202-467-8180
http://www.PFLAG.org

Renaissance Transgender Association, Inc., provides support, education, and social outlets for cross-dressers and others. The organization has chapters and affiliates throughout the United States.

Renaissance
987 Old Eagle School Road, Suite 719
Wayne, PA 19087
610-975-9119
http://www.ren.org

Society for the Second Self (Tri-Ess) is a national educational, support, and social organization for heterosexual cross-dressers and their families, with local chapters offering programs on a regular basis.
Tri-Ess
P.O. Box 194
Tulare, CA 93275
http://www.tri-ess.org

Spouse's and Partner's International Conference for Education (SPICE), sponsored by Tri-Ess, is an annual event for wives and other partners of cross-dressers. Cross-dressers may attend, but they may not dress "en femme."
http://chi-triess.org/spice

Transcend is an organization based in British Columbia whose stated purpose is to address the systematic social, political, and economic conditions that negatively affect trans people, intersex people, and their families by providing peer support, advocacy, workshops, and information.
http://www.transgender.org/transcend/index.htm

Transgender Law and Policy Institute describes itself as a nonprofit organization dedicated to engaging in effective advocacy for transgender people by bringing experts and advocates together to work on law and policy initiatives designed to advance transgender equality.
http://www.transgenderlaw.org

Transgender Tapestry, IFGE's quarterly publication, offers diverse coverage of topics of interest to transgender people, partners, and allied professionals. It also contains support group listings.
subscriptions@ifge.org
781-899-2212
http://www.ifge.org/tgmag//tgmagtop.htm

TRANSGENDERLEGAL.COM was created by Phyllis Randolph Frye, Esq, an "out" transgendered attorney in Houston, Texas. It includes most of the more than two decades of her writings and other items that might assist TG people.
http://www.transgenderlegal.com

Glossary

Other than the briefest mention of female-to-males, the emphasis of these definitions and descriptions, for the purpose of the topic of this book, is upon male-to-female gender variance.

binge: To go on a buying spree for clothing, jewelry, wigs, cosmetics, etc. (often followed at some point by the purge phase of the cycle).

clocked, read: Identified as transgendered when out in public.

closeted: Keeping one's gender-variant status a secret.

come out: To reveal one's gender-variant status.

cross-dresser (CD): A man who at times wears women's clothes and other accouterments and takes on a feminine persona, expressing the feminine side of his personality for relaxation and comfort, and for some because it is experienced as erotic.

en femme: A French term that means in feminine mode, i.e., a male dressed in feminine garb.

en homme/en drab/en bubba: In masculine mode, i.e., a man dressed in ordinary, masculine garb. Tri-Ess monthly meetings will often have sessions, e.g., breakfasts, to which significant others are invited and at which cross-dressers are not welcome to dress. These are sometimes called "Bubba Breakfasts."

FtM or F2M: A female-to-male transgendered person, also called a transgender man.

gaffe: Item of underclothing worn by pre-op or **non-op** transwomen to conceal the shape of male genitals under their clothing.

gender dysphoria: Ranges from mild emotional discomfort to extreme distress at the mismatch between one's mental gender identity and biological sex.

gender identity disorder: Defined in the fourth edition of the American Psychiatric Association's *Diagnostic and Statistical Manual of Mental Dis-*

Head Over Heels: Wives Who Stay with Cross-Dressers and Transsexuals
Published by The Haworth Press, Inc., 2007. All rights reserved.
doi:10.1300/5737_33

orders (American Psychiatric Association, 1994) as strong and persistent cross-gender identification (not merely a desire for any perceived cultural advantages of being the other sex). In adolescents and adults the disturbance is manifested by symptoms such as a stated desire to be the other sex, frequent passing as the other sex, desire to live or be treated as the other sex, or the conviction that he or she has the typical feelings and reactions of the other sex. Persistent discomfort with the birth sex or a sense of inappropriateness in the gender role of that sex also exists. Symptoms may also include preoccupation with getting rid of primary and secondary sex characteristics (e.g., requests for hormones, surgery, or other procedures to physically alter sexual characteristics to simulate the appearance of the other sex), or belief that he or she was born the wrong sex. The disturbance causes clinically significant distress or impairment in social, occupational, or other important areas of functioning. (For information on Gender Identity Disorder of Childhood, a description can be found in the APA diagnostic manual [American Psychiatric Association, 1994].)

gender-variant: An umbrella term that includes anyone who transgresses societal/cultural gender norms.

"go TS": An expression used to indicate that someone who once self-identified as a cross-dresser is now identifying as a transsexual.

going full-time: A dramatic point in transition, when one begins the real-life experience.

HBIGDA: Harry Benjamin International Gender Dysphoria Association, the organization of physicians, psychotherapists, sexologists, social scientists, and attorneys that meets biannually to investigate the phenomena of gender variance and to set down and update professional guidelines for working with transgendered people. The organization is changing its name to **WPATH.**

HRT: Hormone replacement therapy, testosterone for transgender men, estrogens, progesterone, and antiandrogens for transgender women.

MtF or M2F: A male-to-female transgender person, also called a transgendered woman.

natal female/woman: Someone who was assigned as female at birth.

natal male/man: Someone was assigned as male at birth.

non-op: A (nonoperative) transsexual who cannot, or chooses not to, have sex reassignment surgery.

nontrans: Nontransgender.

out: Known as transgendered to one other person, to one's immediate circle, or in the greater community.

pass: To be perceived as one's desired gender. Gwen Smith, a transgender activist, once suggested to me (personal communication, September 28, 2000) that to talk about passing was talking about deception, which is not what being gender-variant is about. She said that she preferred talking about being recognized as a woman or being mistaken for a man. I recommend Jessica Xavier's (2001) and Holly Boswell's (1991, 2001) controversial articles about passing.

PFLAG: Parents and Friends of Lesbians and Gays, a support organization that now also addresses the needs of gender-variant people and their significant others (see the Resource section for access information).

post-op: Post-operative transsexual.

pre-op: Pre-operative transsexual.

purge: To dispose of all of ones cross-gender clothing and accouterments (often followed at some point by the binge phase of the cycle).

real-life experience (RLE): The twelve-month period suggested by the Harry Benjamin International Gender Dysphoria Association's Standards of Care, during which one presents at all times and in all settings in the target gender.

SO: Significant other (used in many contexts other than for gender-variant people).

SOC: Standards of care, the professional guidelines for working with transgender people, focusing particularly on transsexual people going through transition, including surgery (see http://www.hbigda .org).

SPICE: Spouses and Partners International Conference on Education, an annual conference for partners and the cross-dressers in their lives at which the cross-dressers are required to dress en homme.

SRS: Sex reassignment surgery, genital surgery, also sometimes called GRS (genital reconstruction surgery) or GCS (gender confirmation surgery), e.g., vaginoplasty and labiaplasty for male-to-females; metoidioplasty or phalloplasty for female-to-males.

stealth: A way of life in which a transsexual lives in the new gender role without disclosing that he or she is transsexual to the new people in his or her world, including creating a new history.

transgender (TG): An umbrella term that includes anyone who transgresses societal/cultural gender norms.

transition: To change, as much as possible, one's secondary sex characteristics, the sex-role which one presents, and for some people, the configuration of the genitals.

transperson: A gender-variant or transgender person (transman and transwoman are also in use).

transsexual (TS): A person whose mental gender identity is contrary to his or her biological sex.

Tri-Ess (Society for the Second Self): An international organization for heterosexual cross-dressers and their significant others and families. They are comprised of many chapters that hold monthly weekend meetings for support and socialization, and they publish a magazine called *Femme Mirror* (see the Resource section for access information). They also sponsor the SPICE Conference.

underdress: To wear cross-gender underclothing under clothes that conform to natal sex.

WPATH: The World Professional Association for Transgender Health (see HBIGDA).

Bibliography

Allen, M. P. (1989). *Transformations: Crossdressers and those who love them.* New York: E. P. Dutton.

Allen, M. P. (2003). *The gender frontier.* Heidelberg, Germany: Kehrer Verlag.

Allison, R. (1999). Reply to Dr. Ann Lawrence: Autogynephilia. *Transgender Tapestry, 87,* 50-52, 88.

American Psychiatric Association. (1994). *Diagnostic and statistical manual of mental disorders* (4th ed.). Washington, DC: Author.

Bentler, P. M., & Prince, C. (1969). Personality characteristics of male transvestites III. *Journal of Abnormal Psychology, 74* (2), 140-143.

Blanchard, R. (1987). Typology of male-to-female transsexualism. *Archives of Sexual Behavior, 14* (3), 247-261.

Blanchard, R. (1989). The classification and labeling of nonhomosexual gender dysphorias. *Archives of Sexual Behavior, 18* (4), 315-334.

Blanchard, R., Clemmensen, L., & Steiner, B. (1987). Heterosexual and homosexual gender dysphoria. *Archives of Sexual Behavior, 16,* 139-152.

Bloom, A. (2002). *Normal.* New York: Random House.

Bockting, W. O., & Coleman, E. (Eds.). (1992). *Gender dysphoria: Interdisciplinary approaches in clinical management.* Binghamton, NY: The Haworth Press.

Boenke, M. (Ed.). (1999). *Transforming families: Real stories about transgendered loved ones* (2nd ed., expanded). Hardy, VA: Oak Knoll Press.

Bohan, J. S. (1996). *Psychology and sexual orientation: Coming to terms.* New York: Routledge & Kegan Paul.

Bolin, A. (1988). *In search of Eve: Transsexual rites of passage.* New York: Bergin & Garvey.

Bolin, A., & Whelehan, P. (1999). *Perspectives on human sexuality.* Albany, NY: State University of New York Press.

Boswell, H. (1991). The transgender alternative. *Chrysalis Quarterly, 1* (2), 29-31.

Boswell, H. (2001). The transgender revolution. *Transgender Tapestry: The Journal 95,* 1-3.

Boyd, H. (2003). *My husband Betty: Love, sex, and life with a crossdresser.* New York: Thunder's Mouth Press.

Boylan, J. F. (2003). *She's not there: A life in two genders.* New York: Broadway Books.

Head Over Heels: Wives Who Stay with Cross-Dressers and Transsexuals
Published by The Haworth Press, Inc., 2007. All rights reserved.
doi:10.1300/5737_34

Brown, G. R. (1988). Women in the closet: Relationships with transgendered men. In D. Denny (Ed.), *Current concepts in transgender identity* (pp. 353-371). New York: Garland.

Brown, M., & Roundsley, C. (1996). *True selves, understanding transsexualism: For families, friends, coworkers, and helping professionals.* San Francisco: Jossey-Bass.

Bullough, V., & Bullough, B. (1993). *Crossdressing, sex, and gender.* Philadelphia: University of Pennsylvania Press.

Bullough, V., & Weinberg, T. (1988a). Alienation, self-image and the importance of support groups for wives of transvestites. *Journal of Sex Research, 24,* 262-268.

Bullough, V., & Weinberg, T. (1988b). Women married to transvestites: Problems and adjustments. *Journal of Psychology & Human Sexuality, 1,* 83-104.

Chase, C. (Ed.). (1997, Fall/Winter). Special issue on intersexuality. *Chrysalis: The Journal of Transgressive Gender Identities, 2*(5), 1-57.

Cole, S. S. (1998). The female experience of femme: A transgender challenge. In D. Denny (Ed.), *Current concepts in transgender identity* (pp. 353-371). New York: Garland.

Cole, S. S., Denny, D., Eyler, A. E., & Samons, S. L. (2000). Issues of transgender. In L. T. Szuchman & F. Muscarella (Eds.), *Psychological perspectives on human sexuality* (pp. 149-195). New York: John Wiley & Sons.

Crooks, R., & Baur, K. (1996). *Our sexuality* (3rd ed.). Pacific Grove, CA: Brooks/ Cole.

DeFao, J. (2005, March 16). Male or female, always a doctor. *San Francisco Chronicle,* p. B1.

Denny, D., & Green, J. (1996). Gender identity and bisexuality. In B. A. Firestone (Ed.), *Bisexuality: The psychology and politics of an invisible minority* (pp. 84-102). Thousand Oaks, CA: Sage.

Devor, H. (1989). *Gender blending.* Indianapolis: Indiana University Press.

Dixon, J., & Dixon, D. (Eds.). (1991). *Wives, partners and others: Living with crossdressing.* Waltham, MA: Educational Resources.

Docter, R. (1988). *Transvestites and transsexuals: Toward a theory of cross-gender behavior.* New York: Plenum.

Dreger, A. D. (1998a). "Ambiguous sex"—or ambivalent medicine? Ethical issues in the medical treatment of intersexuality and "ambiguous sex." *Hastings Center Report, 28* (3), 24-35.

Dreger, A. D. (1998b). *Hermaphrodites and the medical invention of sex.* Cambridge, MA: Harvard University Press.

Dreger, A. D. (1999). *Intersexuality in the age of ethics.* Frederick, MD: University Publishing Group.

Ekins, R., & King, D. (1996). *Blending genders: Social aspects of cross-dressing and sex-changing.* New York: Routledge.

Ellis, A. L., & Mitchell, R. W. (2000). Sexual orientation. In L. T. Szuchman & F. Muscarella (Eds.), *Psychological perspectives on human sexuality* (pp. 196-231). New York: John Wiley and Sons.

Erhardt, V. (2001). Response to Anne Lawrence and Rebecca Allison on Autogynephilia. *Transgender Tapestry: The Journal 94,* 31-32.

Erhardt, V., & Swenson. E. (1999, February). Coming out to a Partner: Disclosure and beyond. *Transgender Community News, 13* (2), 14, 25, 27.

Ettner, R. I., & White, T. J. H. (2000). Children of a parent undergoing a gender transition: Disclosure, risk, and protective factors. Paper presented at the XVI Harry Benjamin International Gender Dysphoria Association Symposium, August 17-21, 1999, London. *International Journal of Transgenderism, 4* (3). Available at http://www.symposion.com/ijt/greenpresidential/green17.htm.

Feinbloom, D. H. (1977). *Transvestites & transsexuals.* New York: Dell.

Foucault, M. (1980). *The history of sexuality,* (Vol. 1). New York: Vintage.

Garber, M. (1997). *Vested interests: Crossdressing and cultural anxiety.* New York: Routledge.

Gilbert, M. (2002a). Prof. Miqqi goes to work I and II. *Transgender Tapestry, 98,* 12-13.

Gilbert, M. (2002b). Prof. Miqqi goes to work III and IV. *Transgender Tapestry, 99,* 24-26.

Golombok, S.. & Fibush, R. (1994). *Gender development.* New York: Cambridge University Press.

Gooren, L., & Cohen-Kettenis, P. T. (1991). Development of male gender identity/role and a sexual orientation toward women in a 46, XY subject with an incomplete form of the androgen insensitivity syndrome. *Archives of Sexual Behavior, 20* (5), 459-470.

Green, R., & Money, J. (Eds.). (1969). *Transsexualism and sex reassignment.* Baltimore: Johns Hopkins University Press.

Hirschfield, M. (1991). *Transvestites.* Buffalo: Prometheus Books.

Hoenig, J. (1985). The origin of gender identity. In B. W. Steiner (Ed.), *Gender dysphoria: Development, research, management* (pp. 11-32). New York: Plenum.

Howey, N. (2002). *Dress codes: Of three girlhoods—My mother's, my father's, and mine.* New York: Picador.

Howey, N., & Samuel, E. (Eds.). (2000). *Out of the ordinary: Essays on growing up with gay, lesbian, and transgender parents.* New York: St. Martin's Press.

Hunt, S., & Mayne, T. (1997). Sexual orientation confusion among spouses of transvestites and transsexuals following disclosure of the spouse's gender dysphoria. *Journal of Psychology and Human Sexuality, 9* (2), 39-51.

Jung, C. G. (1953). *Collected works.* London: Routledge & Kegan Paul.

Kaye, V., & Kaye, L. (1996). *Life with Vanessa: Straight talk about integrating transgenderism into a loving, caring, and positive relationship.* Oklahoma City: Authors.

Kimmel, M. S. (2000). *The gendered society.* New York: Oxford University Press.

Krafft-Ebing, R. von. (1997). *Psychopathia sexualis.* London: Velvet Publications.

Lawrence, A. (2000). Autogynephylia: Frequently asked questions. *Transgender Tapestry: The Journal 92,* 8-13.

Lev, A. I. (2004). *Transgender emergence: Therapeutic guidelines for working with gender-variant people and their families.* Binghamton, NY: The Haworth Press.

Levine, S. B., Brown, G. B., Coleman, E., Hage, J. J., Cohen-Kettenis, P., Van Maasdam, J., Petersen, M., Pfafflin, F., & Schaefer, L. (1998, April-June). Harry Benjamin International Gender Dysphoria Associations's the standards of care for gender identity disorders [Online]. *International Journal of Transgenderism, 2* (2). Available at http://www.symposion.com.ijt/ijtc0405.htm.

McClosky, D. (1999). *Crossing: A memoir.* Chicago: The University of Chicago Press.

Moir, A., & Jessel, D. (1991). *Brain sex: The real difference between men and women.* New York: Delta.

Money, J.W. (1986). *Lovemaps: Clinical concepts of sexual/erotic health and pathology, paraphilia, and gender transposition in childhood, adolescence, and maturity.* New York: Irvington.

Morris, J. (1974). *Conundrum: From James to Jan—An extraordinary personal narrative of transsexualism.* New York: Harcourt Brace Jovanovich.

Nangeroni, N. R. (2003). Transgenderism. *Transgender Tapestry, 101,* 23-24.

Ochs, R. (1996). Biphobia: It goes more than two ways. In B. A. Firestone (Ed.), *Bisexuality: The psychology and politics of an invisible minority* (pp. 217-239). Thousand Oaks, CA: Sage.

Pauly, I. B. (1990). Gender identity and sexual preference: Dependent versus independent variables. In F. J. Bianco & R. H. Serrano (Eds.), *Sexology: An independent field* (pp. 51-62). Amsterdam: Elsevier.

Pauly, I. B. (1992). Terminology and classification of gender identity disorders. In W. O. Bockting & E. Coleman (Eds.), *Gender dysphoria: Interdisciplinary approaches* (pp. 1-14). Binghamton, NY: The Haworth Press.

Person, E., & Ovesey, L. (1974a). The transsexual syndrome in males: I. Primary transsexualism. *American Journal of Psychotherapy, 28,* 4-20.

Person, E., & Ovesey, L. (1974b). The transsexual syndrome in males: II. Secondary transsexualism. *American Journal of Psychotherapy, 28,* 174-193.

Prince, C. V. (1957). Homosexuality, transvestism and transsexualism: Reflections on their etiology and differentiation. *American Journal of Psychotherapy, 11,* 80-85.

Prince, C. V., & Bentler, P. M. (1972). Survey of 504 cases of transvestism. *Psychological Reports, 31* (3), 903-917.

Prince, V. "C." (1967). *The cross-dresser and his wife.* Capistrano Beach, CA: Sandy Thomas.

Roberts, J. (1995). *Coping with crossdressing: Tools & strategies for partners in committed relationship* (3rd ed.). King of Prussia, PA: Creative Design Services.

Rosenberg, M.B. (2003). *Nonviolent communication: A language of life* (2nd ed.). Encinitas, CA: Puddle Dancer.

Rosenfeld, C., & Emerson, S. (1998). A process of supportive therapy for families of transgender individuals. In D. Denny (Ed.), *Current concepts in transgender identity* (pp. 353-371). New York: Garland.

Rowe, R. J. (1997). *Bert & Lori: The autobiography of a crossdresser.* Amherst: Prometheus.

Rudd, P. (1998). *Who's really from Venus?* Katy, TX: P.M. Publishers.

Rudd, P. (1999a). *Crossdressing with dignity.* Katy, TX: P.M. Publishers.

Rudd, P. (1999b). *My husband wears my clothes.* Katy, TX: P.M. Publishers.

Rudd, P. (2000). *Crossdressers and those who share their lives.* Katy, TX: P.M. Publishers.

Stoller, R. (1967). Transvestites' women. *Psychiatry, 124,* 333-339.

Weinberg, T. S., & Bullough, V. (1988). Alienation, self-image, and the importance of support groups for the wives of transvestites. *Journal of Sex Research, 24,* 262-268.

Woodhouse, A. (1985). Forgotten women: Transvestism and marriage. *Women's Studies International Forum, 8,* 583-592.

Xavier, J. (2001). Passing as privilege. *Transgender Tapestry: The Journal 95,* 24-26.

Xavier, J. (2003). Gender-variance model & guide to using the gender-variance model. *Transgender Tapestry, 101,* 38-40.

Index

Head Over Heels: Wives Who Stay with Cross-Dressers and Transsexuals
Published by The Haworth Press, Inc., 2007. All rights reserved.
doi:10.1300/5737_35

-

25008134R00148

Made in the USA
San Bernardino, CA
14 October 2015